GOOD GAME

GOOD GAME

European & British Game Cookery

Victoria Jardine-Paterson
with
Colin McKelvie

Illustrations by Diana Leadbetter

SWAN·HILL
PRESS

For Judy
and
Michael

Copyright © 1993 by Victoria Jardine-Paterson & Colin McKelvie (Text)
Copyright © 1993 by Diana Leadbetter (Illustrations)

First published in the UK in 1993
by Swan Hill Press
an imprint of Airlife Publishing Ltd

British Library Cataloguing in Publication Data
A catalogue record for this book
is available from the British Library

ISBN 1 85310 377 2

Printed by Livesey Ltd., Shrewsbury.

Swan Hill Press
an imprint of Airlife Publishing Ltd.
101 Longden Road, Shrewsbury SY3 9EB, England

CONTENTS

FOREWORD

by Matthew Fort

You know that haunch of wild boar that's been cluttering up the larder for the last few days? Well, turn to page 127 and your worries are over.

Stumped by the capercaillie that Aunt Wilhelmena was so thoughtful in having delivered to you? Cast aside your un-Christian reflection on your good Aunt. Page 17 has the answer.

And what about dealing with the pike that young William insisted on bringing home? It's all there on page 158.

It may seem a bit invidious to write the foreword to a book in which your own name appears as author of some of the recipes, but I think praise is due in full measure to Vicky Jardine-Paterson and Colin McKelvie. Of course I knew a bit about roasting pheasants, or searing salmon, but really I realise how restricted I was until I plunged into *Good Game*.

We live in a time when most consumers are becoming increasingly removed from the means of production of edible raw materials. There is an increasingly urbanised — and sentimentalised — view of the countryside and the practices in it. The real sadness is that fewer and fewer people grow up with any real knowledge or understanding of the great riches available to us all in terms of raw materials, or of what is needed to keep the countryside that produces them in a fit state to go on doing so.

In spite of this demand for game is growing. Certainly in London we find a fair selection of game available in season — grouse, pheasant, mallard, partridge even and certainly (farmed) venison roosting among the chiller cabinets. After all game does fulfill a good many of the criteria demanded by our increasingly health conscious age. It is virtually fat free. It has not been fed up on the ground-up remains of its fellow creatures. It is not full of growth promoters and hormones, and it has not been subject to some of the more vicious practices of modern farming. And, with few exceptions, it is still relatively plentiful.

And *Good Game* encourages us to make the most of it. The background for each species is scrupulously presented, with a good deal of humour and diverting detail. And the recipes Vicky Jardine-Paterson gives us reflects the extraordinary range that these natural ingredients have given rise to, not only in this country, but all over the world.

We have Vicky's metropolitan sympathies to thank for this, and we should thank her for them. We tend to get rather stuck in our ways when it comes to cooking, to fall back on the tried and tested, and to be fair, the loved too. But here we have *Lepre alla Piemontese* from Italy, *Lososina s Sousoum iz Schavelya i Shpinata* better known as steamed salmon with sorrel and spinach sauce from Russia, *Carcassin a l'Ardennaise* (yes, that's one way of dealing with that leg of wild boar), and *perdikes me syka* or partridges with dried figs as we like to call it.

Good Game is a kind of culinary canter round the continent in the safety of your own kitchen.

Matthew Fort
Guardian Food and Drink Writer

INTRODUCTION

The invitation to write this book came from Colin McKelvie; the genesis for its shape came from Christos Sarakinos. Colin needs no introduction; he is one of our foremost writers on the sporting world, combining his passion for wildlife and the sporting life with a happy turn of phrase, and he has been unfailingly at hand throughout this whole venture. In north east Corfu, Christos needs no introduction either; now Mayor of Kassiopi, from a long line of fishermen who have lived off the fish from the sea and the wildlife from the hills, his charm and broad smile are known and beloved by one and all.

We were having kitchen supper one freezing February night in my brother-in-law's house in Corfu. Huge limbs of olive spattered in the high open fire. "How's the shooting been this winter, Christos?" I asked. "Phant*a*stic," he replied (the way he says it I always imagine it spelt with a ph). "I shoot millions of grouses." "Grouse?" I repeated incredulous. "Yes, grouses," he affirmed. "But Christos, grouse only live in Scotland and northern England." He was totally unfazed. "And here in Kassiopi too," he pronounced. This line of discussion wasn't going to get us very far. "What do your grouse look like, Christos?" "What yours like?" he flings back the question. "Dark brown." "Our grouses dark brown too." (very pleased with himself.) "How do yours fly, Christos?" "How yours?" I made a low-flying movement. Pleased as Punch, he points to himself, beaming. "Ours too." "How big are your grouse, Christos?" I cupped my hands and showed him. "Ours too." (Of course!) "What are your grouse called in Greek, Christos?" "*Ortiki*," he said unequivocally. I suggested it might be a good idea to look it up in the dictionary and turned to *omikrón*. The English translation was quail!

We have since eaten many delicacies with Christos at his house, cooked by his wife, Anthula — *kokoretsia*, cuttle fish, sea urchin, octopus; but not yet quail. But it was Christos's quail that gave me the idea of making little vocabularies throughout this book on game cookery and to cull from all over Europe some of the myriad ways of dealing with all the delicacies from the game larder. The recipes are intended, on the whole, for those of us who enjoy cooking, love food, and are also in a flying hurry trying to fit too many priorities into our timetables. To this end I have had invaluable help from my parents (from my mother who taught me to cook and provided recipes and from my linguist father who helped with research on the dictionaries) and from friends all over the place who have, over the years, contributed recipes or who have helped with the vocabularies, or who have even done both. Amongst these my special thanks go to: Zora Bielitch, Aris Bogdanos, Nick Craze, Antoinette Daridan, Claud Emsens, Peter Fries-Tersch, Kirsten Gordon, Isabelle Harpham, Sylvia Langova-Williams, Giorgio Marsan, Thorold Masefield, Mogens and Agno Mathieson, Agneta Munktell, Tony Page, Mary Ross, Bill Slee, Sprüngli, Alexandra Stancioff, Januez Stechley, Mary Teixeira da Molla, Betty Wilson. Food writer Matthew Fort, longtime friend and cook *extraordinaire*, has given constant inspiration and encouragement, and on top of that agreed to write the Foreword, for which we are delighted and indebted. And, as they say, last but *by no means* least, we thank our other halves Judy and Michael, who have put up with barrages of faxes, endless variations of game, highs and lows, ups and downs, and still remain *aficionados* of game cookery. We could not have done this without them.

Victoria Jardine-Paterson
September 1993

FIELD & MOOR

RED GROUSE, BLACK GROUSE, PTARMIGAN & CAPERCAILLIE

Lagopus lagopus, Tetrao tetrix, Lagopus mutus, Tetrao urogallus

Ptarmigan

Grouse tend to mean one thing to most sportsmen, in Britain at least, and that is the red grouse of heather moorland, especially in northern England and Scotland. And in Britain the numbers of red grouse shot each year average between 500,000 and one million, which is far more than the total annual bag of the other three members of the grouse family put together. Not surprising, therefore, that grouse has largely become synonymous with red grouse.

Once hailed as Britain's unique gamebird, the red grouse is in fact the British subspecies of the Willow Ptarmigan, which is widespread across northern Europe, and occurs also in Asia and North America. But the British race is unique in never turning white on its upper parts, even in the coldest winters, and it can achieve astonishingly high densities where the habitat and climate are favourable. Then it becomes possible to drive the birds forward over a line of standing Guns semi-concealed in butts.

Fast and agile on the wing, driven grouse represent one of the most testing and exciting of all sporting birds, making Britain's northern moors a mecca for game shooters from many other countries from mid August to early November. The Twelfth of August, probably the most celebrated date in the country sports calendar, marks the start of the shooting season, and although grouse remain fair game until 10th December, few grouse moor owners shoot after early November, as winter weather makes it increasingly difficult to organise a successful day.

Red grouse live almost entirely on heather, which makes up over 95 per cent of its diet. Its flesh is dark and has a richly aromatic flavour that is quite distinctive. It can be an acquired taste, but it is well worth acquiring! Opinions vary on how long grouse should be hung before plucking, cleaning and eating, and much also depends on the weather. Two or three days of hanging in warm August weather achieves the same effect as two weeks or more of hanging in the chillier conditions of October.

The ptarmigan is a bird of the mountains of Scotland, its only haunts in Britain, and of many parts of northern and Alpine Europe. It manages to survive in conditions of bleak exposure which might seem unsuitable for any birds. Slightly smaller and lighter than the red grouse, it is a similarly compact and rather rotund gamebird, magnificently camouflaged among the rocks and mosses in its summer plumage of greys and buffs, and its winter plumage of purest snow-white. This is a gamebird for the energetic sportsman, who is prepared to trudge up to the highest tops in hopes of just a few shots.

While the ptarmigan occupies a niche above the red grouse's heathery moorland habitat, the black grouse is chiefly a bird of the lower moorland fringes, close to the tree line. It is a much bigger and more dramatic grouse than its high altitude cousins, and the sexes look quite distinctive. The mature blackcock has a plumage of deepest blueish-black, with prominent red eye wattles, vivid white wing bars when in flight, and a distinctive blueish-black lyre-shaped tail with startlingly white under-tail covert feathers. It weighs up to 3½lbs, over twice the weight of a mature red grouse, and looks much bigger when in flight, which is very fast and with a deceptively leisurely wingbeat.

The female, usually known in Britain as the 'greyhen', is smaller than the male, but still noticeably larger and heavier than a red grouse. She is more subtly camouflaged than the flamboyant male, her plumage a rich mixture of rust-browns and reds. Although they are not legally protected, greyhens are generally not shot in

Britain, although this traditional attempt to conserve black grouse numbers appears to have no practical effect on local stocks.

Black grouse are more catholic in their diet than red grouse, and in addition to heather shoots will eat a wide range of vegetation in the form of buds, berries and shoots, and will readily resort to fields of arable crops such as oats, barley, potatoes and turnips. Birds that have been living and feeding in conifer woodlands may develop a disagreeable resinous tang in their flesh, but this can be overcome by suitable marinading before cooking. In other respects the flesh of black grouse is darkish and rather similar to red grouse. A blind tasting would probably reveal few differences, except among true grouse afficionados, but the size of the bird on a plate or carving dish is quite distinctive.

The capercaillie (gaelic for 'cock of the woods' or 'horse of the woods') is an unmistakeable bird, the largest of the grouse family, and quite the largest true native gamebird to be found in Europe. In Britain it became extinct in the late eighteenth century, but was successfully reintroduced to Scotland in the 1830s. In Europe, capercaillie populations exist in Scandinavia, the Alps and the great woodlands of central Europe, and also in the Pyrenees.

The massive cock bird weighs between 8 and 10lbs and his much smaller mate averages just over 4lbs. The cock is startlingly handsome, with a rounded black head, bright red wattles, a dark and bristling beard, and a powerful horn coloured bill. His upper parts are slatey-black with a white patch on the bend of the wing, and the feathers of the breast are a very dark green. The female is similar in conformation and coloration to a greyhen, but is larger and has a reddish area of feathering on the breast.

RED GROUSE: *Lagopus lagopus*

Habitat:	Heather and moorland
Length:	15ins (38cm)
Weight:	1½lb (750g)
Season:	12 August-10 December
Best time for eating:	August-October

French: *la grouse*
German: *das Moorhahn*
Italian: *il lagopus scoticus*
Spanish: *el lagopado escoces*
Greek: *o agriogalos/i peneagrida*
Portuguese: *o lagopóde*

Serbo-Croat: *tetrïjeb*
Romanian: *cocos de munte*
Bulgarian: *díva kokóshka*
Russian: *díva kokóshka*
Czech: *tetrívek*
Polish: *tardiva*

Dutch: *korheon*
Flemish: *het schatse sneeunhoen*
Norwegian: *en rype*
Danish: *rype*
Swedish: *ripa*
Hungarian: *nyir fajd*

Both on the field and at the table there is a cachet to red grouse unequalled by any other game bird. This is partly because it really *is* exclusive to Scotland and Northern Britain (Yorkshire and Northumberland, mainly), and partly because of its distinctive flavour. You either love it or loathe it; don't risk it on faddy people as a surprise – it's such a waste if they don't like it. I've been caught out wanting to give guests a treat on their visit to Scotland only to discover it's a penance. The other extreme is the mad race amongst restaurants all over Britain to see who can get the first grouse off the moor on the 12th August, delivered and on the table for those diners who *do* love it. This can involve mad chases all over the countryside, aeroplanes, helicopters, motor bikes, anything that will get that first (and usually fearfully expensive) grouse there first!

As with all of the best things in life, good grouse should be eaten simply roasted and served with all the traditional trimmings. The taste is so particular I don't see the need for any fancy tarting up or 'originality'. Pot roasts (again simple) should only be used for old birds which can be incredibly tough.

Roast Grouse

Nothing can beat a young grouse simply roast. I cook it, unconventionally (ten minutes in a hot oven, 15-25 minutes in a cool one), in the same way that I do fillet, and it always manages to come to the table pink, even with delays.

Serves 4

2 brace of grouse
3 tablespoons soft butter
salt and pepper

8 rashers bacon
1 glass (4fl oz./120ml) of red wine, port or sherry

Make sure the birds are clean inside and out, wiping with a damp cloth or kitchen towel if necessary. Do not wash under the tap or you will wash away precious blood which all goes towards the juices in the pan. Place a quarter of one tablespoon (i.e. 1 teaspoon) of butter inside each bird. Smear the bodies all over with the rest (i.e. half a tablespoon to each bird), sprinkle with salt and pepper and cover each bird completely with 2 slices of bacon. Here comes the unconventional bit. Place the birds in a hot oven (230C/450F/Gas Mark 8) for no more than 10 minutes. Turn heat right down to cool (150C/300F/Gas Mark 2) or even better move to a different cool oven (like the simmering oven in the Aga) and leave for a further 20 minutes before eating. They should be pink. It is traditional to cook them on a croûte of toast or fried bread, but I never do this, preferring to keep the juices for the gravy. In any case, with the bread sauce and fried breadcrumbs that are traditionally served with grouse (see pages 173 and 195 for the recipes), I feel a croûte is really rather superfluous. Garnish with a sprig of watercress, and serve with an autumn fruit jelly (crab apple, redcurrant, rowan, elderberry) and warmed potato crisps, or parsnip chips (see page 188).

Devilled Grouse

If ever anyone can suffer from a surfeit of roast grouse – to my mind the best way of eating grouse – then this rings the changes. It is also less daunting to the stomach than a whole – or even half – grouse sitting on a plate before you.

Serves 4

4 grouse
4 slices bacon, cut in half
1 bay leaf
2 shallots
¼pt/150ml dry white wine
1 teaspoon dry English mustard (or more to taste)

1 tablespoon plain flour
1 teaspoon hot paprika
¼pt/150ml double cream
1 tablespoon caster sugar
freshly ground salt and pepper
2 tablespoons butter
watercress, endive or rocket to garnish

Smear the grouse with one tablespoon of the butter, sprinkle with salt and pepper, and cover each breast with bacon. Cook in a medium oven (180C/350F/Gas Mark 4) for about 20 minutes till pink. Remove and carve off each breast and place in a shallow ovenproof dish. Place the carcases in a stockpot, cover with water, add the bayleaf, chopped shallots (or onion) and simmer for about 30 minutes. Strain off the stock, cover the grouse breasts and let them sit in the hot stock for a good five minutes. Drain off the juices and keep the breasts to one side; return the juices back into the stockpot from which you have removed the carcases and onion. Then boil the wine with the remaining stock, bay leaf and mustard for 15 minutes. Make some *beurre manié* with the other tablespoon of butter and flour and add to the stock. Once the *beurre manié* is absorbed add the paprika, cream, sugar, salt and pepper to taste. Boil all together fast for five minutes or so, and then pour over the grouse breasts. Serve with a triangle of fried bread, rice and bitter winter salad (see page 188).

Grouse-moor Keepers' Hotpot

My co-author has a very healthy amount of Irish blood in him; maybe the vital ingredient in this
recipe explains his enthusiasm for this way of dealing with old grouse!

Serves 2

*one brace old grouse (usually available quite
   cheaply off the moor)*
2 cans Guinness
4oz/100g dripping
2 or 3 tomatoes
1 onion

a few peppercorns
2 rashers streaky bacon
4oz/100g mushrooms
4 whole cloves
salt and freshly ground black and white pepper

Allowing one can of Guinness per bird, marinade the old grouse for 24–48 hours in the ale, and then
remove when needed for cooking. Pat dry with kitchen paper, cut in half and fry all over in a heavy frying pan
with enough dripping to lightly brown them all over. Transfer to a heavy casserole, and in the same frying pan
fry the mushrooms, sliced, and the bacon, diced. Add to the casserole with the tomatoes cut in half, the onion,
quartered and stuck with cloves, and all the Guinness from the marinade. Cover tightly with a lid and cook in
a moderate oven (180C/350F/Gas Mark 4) for two hours, or until tender. When nearly ready add some *beurre
manié*, made with 1 tablespoon flour mixed with 1 tablespoon softened butter, stir till well absorbed and bring
to the boil again on the top of the oven to make sure that it is properly cooked and the sauce has thickened.
Serve with potato and celeriac purée (see page 191) and diced beetroot for a touch of sweetness.

Grouse with Cream Sauce

This is a traditional Norwegian recipe which is used for all their main game – blackcock,
moose, roedeer and reindeer. The old method was to cook the bird till tender, but they now
follow the fashion of serving the meat pink.

Serves 4

4 grouse and hearts and liver, necks and gizzards
*freshly ground sea salt and black and white
   peppercorns*
2 tablespoons butter

Sauce
1/2pt/300ml game stock or water
1/2pt/300ml milk

1/4pt/150ml sour cream
5-6 juniper berries
2 teaspoons redcurrant jelly
4oz/100g butter
1 1/2-2 tablespoons plain flour
*Norwegian brown goat cheese - or any other goat
   cheese, failing that!*
1/4pt/150ml cream

Clean the grouse, saving the heart and liver for the gravy, the neck and gizzard for the stock. Truss and
sprinkle the birds with salt and pepper. Brown the birds well in butter in a heavy braising dish, and quickly
sauté the heart and liver which you keep for later. In a roasting tin or heavy cast iron casserole place the birds
breast up. Add the hot stock and milk, crushed juniper berries and cover the breast with the sour cream. Bake
in a moderate oven (180C/350F/Gas Mark 4) for half an hour. Meanwhile in a non-stick pan combine the
flour and butter to make a golden roux, and add some of the pan juices to it. Combine and then pour back into
the roasting tray. Simmer in the oven for another half hour. If the grouse are young they will be ready by now,
if they are older they could need simmering for up to 2 hours. Ten minutes before the end of cooking pour in
the cream. Remove the birds, arrange in a shallow ovenproof dish and keep warm while you make the sauce.
Pour the pan juices into a saucepan, add a few slices of the cheese, the mashed liver and heart, and the jelly.
Simmer for 10 minutes, and season with salt and pepper. Coat the birds in the dish with a little of the sauce
and serve the rest separately in a sauce boat.

Warm Grouse Salad

Perfect for a light lunch or supper, or even as a starter, this can be made with any leftover cold game bird. A family favourite.
Serves 2 as a main meal, 4 as a starter

1 cold cooked grouse
4 rashers smoked bacon
2 thick slices brown stoneground bread
1 clove garlic

2 dessertspoon butter, 2 tablespoons vegetable oil
¾ iceberg lettuce
French dressing (see below)

First take meat off grouse and cut into small neat bits. Place on one side. Cook bacon in 1 dessertspoon butter till done but not brown. Place on one side. Cut bread into largeish croûtons and fry in remaining bacon butter with tablespoon oil till golden. Remove and keep warm in oven. Cut bacon into small pieces and keep warm in oven. Tear lettuce into chunks and scatter over low wide dish. Put second dessertspoon butter and second tablespoon oil into frying pan with the clove of garlic chopped up fine and fry till garlic turns golden. Throw in grouse bits and toss in oil till hot right through but still soft. Remove quickly from pan, scatter over lettuce, then also scatter warm croûtons and bacon bits and sprinkle with French dressing. Serve immediately with warm bread or rolls.

French dressing

1 small teasp Dijon mustard
1 teaspoon wine or cider vinegar
1 teaspoon salt

2 teaspoon caster sugar
twist of black pepper
3 tablespoons/50ml olive oil
¼pt/150ml vegetable oil

Into bottom of small glass jar put the teaspoon of mustard. Mix into it the sugar, salt and pepper and vinegar. Add oils and mix all together.

Black Grouse *Lyrurus tetrix*

Length:	21 ins (53cm)
Weight:	3lb (1.5kg)
Open Season:	20 August-10 December
	Devon Somerset, New Forest,
	1 September-10 December
Best time for eating:	August-Septembert

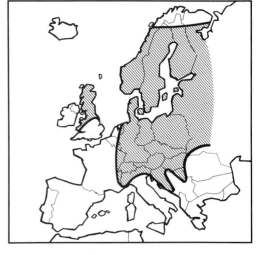

Blackcock (Black Grouse)
French: *le petit coq de bruyére*
    le tétras
German: *der Birkhahn*
Italian: *il fagiano di monte*
Spanish: *el gallo liva*
Greek: *magric papia*
Portuguese: *o galo silvestre*
Serbo-Croat: *tetrieb mali*
Bulgarian: *mázhkiat téterev*
Russian: *mázhkiat tetérev*
Czech: *tetrívek*
Polish: *cretrzew*

Dutch: *korhaan*
Flemish: *het korhoen*
Norwegian: *en årfugl*
Danish: *urfugl*
Swedish: *orre*
Hungarian: *fajdkakas*

Ptarmigan (White Grouse)
French: *le lagopède*
German: *das Alpenschneehuhn*
Italian: *la pernice bianca*
Spanish: *la perdiz bianca*

Portuguese: *o ptarmigão*
Serbo-Croat: *snijeznica*
Romanian: *ierunca, pasare alba*
Bulgarian: *byála yárebitsa*
Russian: *byála yárebitsa*
Czech: *horsky tetrev*
Polish: *tardiva biala*
Dutch: *sneeuwhoen*
Flemish: *het sneeuehoen*
Norwegian: *en fjellrype*
Danish: *fjeld-rype*
Swedish: *snöripa*
Hungarian: *hofajd*

Capercaillie *Tetrao urogallus*
(capercailzie, capercailye)

Length:	34 ins (86cm)
Weight:	9lb (4kg)
Open Season:	1 October-31 January
Best time for eating:	October-November

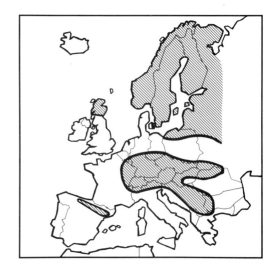

French: *le grand tétras*
German: *der Auerhahn*
Italian: *il gallo cedrone*
Spanish: *el tetras*
Portuguese: *o tetraz grande*
Romanian: *cocos salbatec*

Bulgarian: *golyam glouhár, div petel*
Russian: *golyam glouhár, div petel*
Czech: *tetrev-hlusec*
Dutch: *auerhoen*

Flemish: *het auerhoen*
Norwegian: *storfugl*
Danish: *tjur*
Swedish: *tjäder*

The blackcock, ptarmigan and capercaillie are all cousins of the red grouse, but really hard work to make palatable. Unless you happen on a very young one, they are usually tough as old boots. If you can be sure of their youthfulness, then you can roast them as you can most other game birds; in Scandinavia they roast them with sour cream, cream or cream cheese. Marinating can help, as can hanging, but if it's a canny old bird that has landed before your oven no amount of hanging (up to a month) marinating (up to a week) or slow pot roasting (up to 3-4 hours) will help. It will be tough! The first capercaillie I ever saw was in my teens high in the mountain woods in Styria. It was stunning to look at and like leather to eat. When I arrived in Scotland some fifteen years later, the advice about my first Scottish 'caper' was that the best way to marinate it was to bury it under ground for 4 weeks and then probably forget it. It was said in jest, but there are times when it is apt advice. The other times are an occasion for a culinary challenge. What greater triumph than to produce any of these birds basted in its juices and tender? Older birds can be slowly potroasted or used in pies or pâtés. If they are too 'high' you can try soaking them in milk or basting in milk during cooking.

Casserole of Capercaillie or Black Grouse

The meat of the caper and blackgrouse (also known selectively as blackgame – the male is known as blackcock, the female as greyhen) is very much on the dry side, and the only way of cooking them with any success is either in a casserole, or in a game pie or paté or terrine. The variations are endless as far as casseroles are concerned, but it is worth remembering that the dark meat of both these birds can take quite rich, strong ingredients – a dash of treacle, or cassis, or prunes soaked in Armagnac, horse mushrooms and hot mango chutney etc etc. All these sort of tastes provide a good counterbalance.

Serves 4

1 capercaillie or 2 blackgame, jointed
2oz/50g butter
1 tablespoon oil
6 balls preserved stem ginger, roughly chopped
1 tablespoon stem ginger syrup
4oz/100g smoked bacon, snipped
1 large onion, finely chopped
3 cloves garlic, crushed
8oz/225g horse mushrooms, chopped

2 large leeks, finely chopped
2oz/50g flour
2 tablespoons Soy Sauce
1 pint/600ml game or chicken stock
¼pt/150ml red wine
2-3 tablespoons redcurrant jelly
salt and pepper
fried triangles of bread for garnish

Melt the butter in a heavy bottomed frying pan and fry the snipped bacon. Remove with a slotted spoon and transfer to a casserole. In the same fat quickly brown the jointed pieces of bird and then transfer to the casserole. In the same fat, adding more butter if necessary, soften the onion, crushed garlic, chopped leeks and mushrooms, stir in the flour and then transfer to the casserole. Add all the other ingredients. Mix well together, cover with a tight-fitting lid and cook in a moderate oven (160C/325F/Gas Mark 3) for about 2 hours or until tender. Arrange triangles of fried bread round the edge of the casserole and serve with a mixture of boiled, then sautéed winter root vegetables.

Blackgame Pâté

This will, of course, do for capercaillie as well. The pounding the meat
gets in the food processor should sort out any problems of dryness or toughness if you
are worried about casseroling.

Serves 8

1¼lb/550g blackgame meat
1¼lb/550g belly of pork - half fat, half lean
4 rashers streaky bacon
1 medium onion
6 juniper berries, crushed
2 teaspoons mixed dried herbs
1-2 teaspoons sugar
¼pt/150ml wineglass brandy
1 tablespoon wild fruit jelly
2 teaspoons salt
1 teaspoon freshly ground black pepper

For the game aspic
2 carrots
2 sticks celery
2 leeks
carcase and giblets of the bird(s)
1 bouquet garni
2 egg whites and their shells
⅓oz/10g powdered gelatine

To make the stock for the aspic, chop the vegetables and place in a pan with the blackgame carcases and giblets and the bouquet garni. Cover with 2 pints/1.2 litres water, bring to the boil and simmer for about 3 hours until reduced to about ½pint/300ml. Strain through a sieve. Return to the pan and bring back up to the boil. Meanwhile whisk the egg whites and add, with the shells, to the stock stirring all the time as if making consommé (see page 66). When the stock comes to the boil, the egg white will form a crust, catching all the bits floating around. Allow to simmer, undisturbed, for another half hour, then strain and cool.

Remove the meat from the birds, using a very sharp pointed knife and discarding the skin. Chop the meat very small and cut up the bacon, the onion, and belly of pork very finely. Put all these into one big bowl with all the other ingredients and leave to stand in a cool place for half an hour at least to allow all the flavours to mingle. Transfer the mixture, in smaller amounts, and roughly whizz in the food processor, only enough to break the consistency down from chopped pieces to a slightly more shredded texture. Place the mixture into a 2 pint/1 litre terrine dish, leave to rest for another half hour, then cover and place in a *bain marie* with the water two thirds of the way up the terrine. Cover with foil and cook in a pre-heated oven (170C/325F/Gas Mark 3) for an hour and a half. Remove and allow to cool with the cover off. Once it has cooled make the aspic covering. Dissolve the gelatine in two tablespoons of hot water, sprinkling it on the surface and if necessary heating the bowl in a saucepan of simmering water till it dissolves. Stir to avoid lumps. Add more seasoning to the stock if necessary and stir in the gelatine. Pour this gently over the pâté, having removed any fat that might have risen to the surface. Leave to set and allow the pâté to stand for 24 hours if possible before eating. Serve with toast and pickles.

WINES
GROUSE (incl. ptarmigan, capercaillie & black grouse)

With roast red grouse claret is almost a must, especially for traditionalists, and a stylish Medoc is a perfect accompaniment to it. Excellent alternatives are old red Riojas, Chateauneuf-du-Pape and Crozes Hermitage. Remember also the oaky Cabernet Sauvignons from eastern Europe, especially Bulgaria and Hungary. Ptarmigan is also nicely complemented by any of these.

Black grouse and capercaillie tend to have an even deeper, richer flavour than red grouse, inclining to a slightly resinous quality at times. Really heavy Rhône reds, Hermitage, Côte Rotie and St. Joseph are all suitable, and also the full smoothness of Syrah and Chateauneuf-du-Pape. The richest, oaky reds of Spain and South Africa make good alternatives, and the spicy fullness of the Lebanese Chateau Musar is well worth considering too.

PARTRIDGE

Perdix perdix & Alectoris rufa

Grey partridge *Perdix perdix*

Length:	12ins (30cm)
Weight:	14oz (400g)
Open season:	1 September-1 February
Best time for eating:	October-November

Red-legged partridge *Alectoris rufa*

Length:	13½ins (34cm)
Weight:	15oz (450g)
Open season:	1 September-1 February
Best time for eating:	October-November

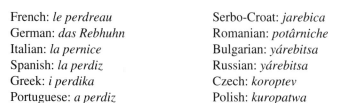

French: *le perdreau*	Serbo-Croat: *jarebica*	Dutch: *partrijs*
German: *das Rebhuhn*	Romanian: *potârniche*	Flemish: *de patrijs*
Italian: *la pernice*	Bulgarian: *yárebitsa*	Norwegian: *en rapphøns*
Spanish: *la perdiz*	Russian: *yárebitsa*	Danish: *agerhøns*
Greek: *i perdika*	Czech: *koroptev*	Swedish: *rapphøns*
Portuguese: *a perdiz*	Polish: *kuropatwa*	Hungarian: *fogoly*

Toujours perdrix! was the lament of the hapless French visitor to English country houses in the Victorian and Edwardian period, who found himself confronted incessantly with roast partridge on the dinner table, and cold or devilled partridge at breakfast. So abundant was the little grey partridge on the farmland of Britain, and such was its popularity as a sporting bird, that its prominence in cookery was assured. The sporting appeal of partridges remains undiminished, although since the 1950s the wild population of native grey partridges in Britain has sadly crashed to a tiny fraction of its former level.

Across Europe, and in North America also, the same story can be told, of a once-abundant gamebird which has succumbed to changes in farming practices, especially the use of insecticide and herbicide sprays, the loss of good nesting habitat, and reduced levels of predation control by traditional gamekeepering.

Among sportsmen in western Europe the decline of the native grey partridge has been paralleled by the increased prominence of the red-legged or 'French' partridge, actually a native of southern European and Mediterranean lands. This alien partridge lends itself more readily to intensive rearing and releasing than its smaller and less vividly coloured relation.

Partridge shooting traditionally began on 1st September, when most broods were expected to be well grown and the fields had been cleared of the last of the cereal harvest, leaving open stubble fields for pointers and setters to range, followed by the Guns. Where thick, well drained hedgerows were present and predatory birds and mammals were kept in check by vigilant gamekeepering, partridges were generally abundant on arable farmland and grasslands across temperate and northern parts of Europe. For Guns in the period up to the mid 1950s the partridge, not the pheasant, was the staple gamebird of European farmland.

In October 1952 the British record bag of partridges was made in Lincolnshire, with a total of 2,069 birds bagged in one highly organised day's shooting, and some 4,000 partridges were bagged on a single day's shooting in Hungary in the last century. Other records from across Europe indicate the extraordinary densities that wild partridges could attain where the conditions were good. It has been estimated that in the 1930s the world population of partridges was around 110 million birds, and by the 1980s this had dropped to less than 25 million, a decline attributable to three related causes - loss of nesting habitat, the excessive use of pesticides, and the decline in active predation control.

The grey partridge is a quietly coloured, self-effacing little bird which fits unobtrusively into the predominant dun colours of the autumn and winter landscapes of western and northern Europe. The redlegged partridge is altogether more flamboyant in appearance and more conspicuous in behaviour, with vivid red-coloured legs and prominent stripes on its flanks, and the mature cock birds frequently perch on fence posts above crops of wheat and roots. The redleg is also a rather larger bird, and can sometimes make a meal for two, while the little grey partridge is definitely one-portion sized.

There is a slight but definite difference in the texture and flavour of the common partridge of northern and western Europe and the larger interloper from more southerly and easterly regions. This is easier for a discerning consumer to recognise than to define. And some people are never satisfied. Take for instance the anonymous composer of this little piece of gamebird doggerel, who seems to have longed for a quite impossible combination of culinary and sporting qualities in his birds:

> *If the partridge had but the woodcock's thigh*
> *'Twould be the best bird that ever did fly:*
> *If the woodcock had but the partridge's breast*
> *Of all game birds 'twould be the best*

There is nothing better than a young succulent little partridge sitting on a plate, just waiting to be eaten. The grey English partridge tends to be more prized than the larger brown French partridge (incidentally the French call partridges *un perdreau* up to six months, and *une perdrix* thereafter, regardless of sex!) Partridge have a very delicate flavour which, it is said, is preserved by being wrapped and cooked in vine leaves. This may explain why it is such a popular and classic recipe from Greece to France and even to Britain.

Partridge are usually hung for about a week and on the whole the young are best cooked very simply - roast, or grilled or spatchcocked. For older birds there is a wonderful traditional French dish which is called a *chartreuse* but it is *very* time consuming to make. A similar classic French preparation of partridge, also suitable for older birds, is the *perdrix aux choux* on page 22. The traditional accompaniments are almost the same as for pheasant (not the bread sauce): game chips or sticks, croûtons or slices of toast, watercress and slices of lemon for garnish, redcurrant, rowan or hedgerow jelly.

Roast, Fanned Partridge Breasts

This is basically partridge roasted traditionally (see below), but instead of being presented in toto the breasts are cut off and then sliced on the diagonal to form a fan (rather like an avocado). These can then be arranged on one large serving dish surrounded by little piles of fried breadcrumbs alternating with little piles of chopped mushrooms fried with bacon and onion, or they can be arranged onto individual plates.

Serves 4

4 young partridge with their livers
4 thin slices streaky bacon, cut in half
salt and freshly ground pepper
4 teaspoons butter
1 chicken liver
1 dessertspoon butter

4 slices bread, crusts removed (preferably not
  pre-sliced!)
2 clove garlic
¹/₂pt/300ml stock (chicken or game)
¹/₄pt/150ml white wine and sherry, mixed

Truss the birds, smear the outside of each with a teaspoon of butter and sprinkle all over with salt and pepper. Pop half a clove of garlic inside each bird (you can also add a wedge of lemon, a chunk of onion, and a sprig or two of parsley, depending on taste). Cover each breast completely with the bacon and arrange in a roasting dish. Surround the birds with the stock and place in a hottish pre-heated oven (220C/425F/Gas Mark 7). Roast for 10 minutes with the bacon on, then remove the bacon and roast for another 8-10 minutes to brown, basting if necessary to help the skin to brown and crisp up. Meanwhile if you want to serve plain roast partridge proceed as follows. Melt the dessertspoon of butter in a small frying pan and lightly sauté the partridge and chicken livers, making sure they stay pink. Remove from the pan and mash into a pulp with a fork. Toast the four slices of bread, spread the liver mixture on each and arrange on a large serving dish. Transfer the birds from the roasting pan onto each slice of toast and keep warm in the oven (160C/300F/Gas Mark 2). Meanwhile scrape the juices in the roasting pan and place over quite a high heat, adding the wine and sherry mixture and seasoning with salt and pepper. Boil rapidly for some 5 minutes to reduce by half, and then pour into a small gravy boat, and serve with the whole partridge. If you just want to serve the fanned breasts, cut them off the carcase at this point, using a very sharp pointed knife. Moving from the pointed end of the breast out to the flatter circular end, making five or six slanting incisions to enable the breast to fan out slightly. Either arrange on a large serving dish as above with various accompaniments, or on individual plates, but *not* on a slice of toast as this spoils the cleanness of the presentation. Garnish with sprigs of watercress.

Perdrix aux Choux

The flavours of partridge and cabbage mingle well, and although the cabbage gets cooked for a long time in this recipe the result is far from the overcooked boiled cabbage of institutional cooking. You can also use this same recipe for pheasant and guinea-fowl, but in France, made with partridge, it is a classic.

Serves 2

2 partridges
1 medium hard cabbage, preferably white
1 smoked sausage or
4oz/100g garlic sausage
4 thick slices rindless bacon, diced
pinch of nutmeg
1 large onion, finely chopped

2 large carrots, sliced
1 bouquet garni
2 whole cloves
1 clove garlic
1½-2pt/900ml-1ltr chicken or game stock
dash of double cream (optional)
2oz/50g butter

Shred the cabbage very finely, having removed the tough outer leaves and stalks. Place in a heavy casserole with the bacon, uncooked sausage, the carrots, spices, herbs and onion. Add enough stock to cover and braise in a medium oven till tender (about 45-60 minutes). Meanwhile smear the partridges with the butter, sprinkle with salt and pepper and brown in a hottish oven (220C/425F/Gas Mark 7) for 10 minutes. Remove and keep to one side. When the cabbage is ready, remove the sausage and bacon and add the partridge, more stock if needed and return to the medium oven for another hour. Check to see if all is tender; if not, continue cooking. If it is, remove the partridge. Add a dash of cream to the cabbage according to taste, stir around, season, then remove and arrange as a bed on a shallow dish. Place the partridge on top, and arrange the sausage and bacon, sliced around the birds on top of the cabbage.

Partridge a Agostino

Agostino cooks in a restaurant in Lisbon; his wife is cook to a private house. Together they have grown up with traditional Portuguese cooking and this is one of Agostino's specials, partridge being the most popular game bird for the table in Portugal.

Serves 8

8 partridges, cleaned and prepared
2 dessertspoons margarine
5 dessertspoons olive oil
4oz/100g diced smoked bacon (toucinho)
4oz/100g diced smoked sausage (chorizo)
4 large onions
4 cloves of garlic

1 small red pepper
2 carrots
1 small bunch fresh coriander
1 or 2 bay leaves
4fl oz/120ml of port wine
salt and pepper to taste

Heat the margarine and olive oil in a flameproof casserole and sauté the partridges until pale gold. Add the chopped bacon and *chorizo*, and fry for another five minutes. Add the chopped vegetables and seasonings. When they are all well cooked and tender, add the port and cook a little longer with the lid tightly fastened. Test the partridges by pricking with a fork and if they are soft and succulent remove from the casserole. Cut each partridge into four pieces and arrange in a large shallow serving dish and keep warm. Remove the bay leaf from the sauce and then put it through a food processor to make a very creamy sauce with which to cover the birds.

Partridge with Lentils

Lentils make a very good accompaniment to any of the game birds. The ordinary orange ones make a good colour contrast, but better by far in flavour and texture are the less common dark green Puy lentils from France (page 188). These needn't be soaked overnight but can be cooked straight from their packet in some light vegetable oil in which you have already softened some crushed garlic, very finely chopped onion and some grated roots of ginger. And even the sludgy brown 'mother earth' lentils work very well in this recipe.

Serves 4

	Lentils
2 partridge	*12oz/350g lentils*
salt and freshly ground black pepper	*1 onion, stuck with 2 cloves*
2 tablespoons butter	*2 cloves garlic*
2 tablespoons olive oil	*1 sprig fresh thyme*
¼lb/100g fat salt pork, diced	*2 sprigs fresh parsley*
1 large onion, finely chopped	*salt and freshly ground black pepper*
2 carrots, peeled and sliced	
¼pt/150ml white wine	
¼pt/150ml game or chicken stock	

Clean and prepare the partridges; sprinkle the cavities with a little salt and pepper and sauté the birds in a flameproof casserole in butter and oil with the diced fat salt pork, sliced onions and carrots. When the birds are golden on all sides, add dry white wine and cook until the wine is reduced by half. Add the chicken stock and season to taste with salt and freshly ground black pepper. Cover the casserole and simmer the partridges over a low heat until tender, about 45 minutes.

To prepare the lentils. Soak the lentils overnight. Drain and cover with water, adding onion, garlic, thyme, parsley and salt and pepper. Bring to the boil, reduce heat and allow to simmer until tender but not mushy. When cooked, drain the lentils and remove onion, garlic and herbs.

To serve. Place the partridges on a hot serving dish and surround with cooked lentils. Skim fat from the pan juices, strain and pour over birds.

Partridge in Port

This is a recipe from a Quinta in the Douro Valley in northern Portugal, a land of grapes, game and old unspoilt estates. White port is used much more (naturally) in Portugal than it is here - we always seem to think of port as red - and this is a wonderfully extravagant use of it. It could only come from people who have it growing at the bottom of their garden!

Serves 4

2oz/50g butter	*4 slices of Parma ham or pancetta (*presunto *in*
4 medium onions	*Portugal)*
4 partridge	*1-2 bottles of white port (don't faint).*
16 grapes, muscatel if possible	

Peel the onions and slice thinly. In a heavy-bottomed pan, large enough to hold four partridges, cook the onions till translucent. Place four grapes inside each bird and wrap each bird in a slice of ham, secured with string. Place on the bed of softened onions and moisten with dry white port. Cover and simmer gently for about 2-3 hours, occasionally adding more port, until the birds are tender and the rich sauce is fairly thick. Serve with plain boiled rice and salad.

Partridge with Savoys

This is another of those good earthy casseroles from east of the Danube.
Serves 5

5 partridge

1½ teaspoon salt

8oz/225g steaky smoked bacon (in Hungary they use Kolozsvár, but that may not be too easy to find here!)

5oz/150g smoked sausage

7oz/200g carrots, sliced

4oz/100g parsnips, sliced

2 onions

4 cloves

freshly ground black and white peppercorns

3lb/1½kg Savoy cabbage

2oz/50g butter

2oz/50g lard

½pt/300ml stock

Clean the partridges, salt the inside, smear with lard over the body, sprinkle with salt and pepper and roast quickly in a hot oven for 5 minutes. Clean the Savoys, quarter, cut out the centre stalk, wash well and blanch in boiling water for 3 minutes, then strain, rinse immediately with cold water and sprinkle with salt and pepper. Butter the inside of an ovenproof dish and lay half the Savoy leaves over the bottom. On those arrange the partridges, bacon and sausages, cover with the sliced carrots and parsnips, add the onions stuck with cloves, then cover the whole with the other half of the Savoys. Add the fat in which the partridges have been roasted, and pour the stock over it all. Cover firmly and cook in a moderate oven for 40-50 minutes, or until cooked through and tender. Remove, lay half the Savoys in the bottom of the serving dish and arrange the partridge on top. Surround with the remaining Savoys and garnish with sliced bacon, sausage, carrots and parsnip.

Serve hot with the juices poured round.

Provençale Partridge

Perdrix à la Provençale

In France partridges under a year old are known as perdreaux, and because they are young and tender are good simply roasted or as a salmis. This recipe is good for the older relatives!
Serves 5

5 partridge

4oz/100g butter

2oz/50g flour

1lb/½kg tomatoes

1 onion, finely chopped

¾pt/450ml white wine

2 cloves garlic

freshly ground salt and pepper

1 bunch parsley

small bunch thyme

1 bay leaf

Halve the partridges, sprinkle with salt and fry in butter in a heavy bottomed pan covered with a lid. When they are tender (after 5-10 minutes), remove and put to one side. In the remaining butter in the pan fry the finely chopped onion till soft then add the flour, crushed garlic, and tomatoes cut into bits, the herbs and finally the wine. Cook till all is well absorbed and transfer to a shallow ovenproof dish. Arrange the partridge halves over the bed of vegetables and heat up in a moderate oven (180C/350F/Gas mark 4) for 10-15 minutes. Serve with rice.

Partridges with Dried Figs

Perdikes me syka

In late August and September you can see figs ripen daily in the warmth of the Greek sun. Picked straight from the tree they make a delicious accompaniment to almost any type of meat, roasted simply, but especially poultry and game. For those of us in cooler climes who don't have such ready access to the fresh fruit, this is a delicious Greek recipe using the dried variety.

Serves 4

2 plump partridge, livers and gizzard reserved (if not available, use chicken's)
2 tablespoons olive oil
¹/₂ teaspoon vinegar
¹/₂ teaspoon ouzo
¹/₂ teaspoon salt
¹/₂ teaspoon dried thyme

Stock
10-12 plump dried figs or 175gr/6oz if not ready plumped
16fl oz/450ml red wine
2 tablespoons ouzo
¹/₂ teaspoon dried thyme

2 bay leaves
2 juniper berries
2¹/₂ shallots/1 small onion
8 cloves garlic
¹/₂ teaspoon vinegar
salt and freshly ground mixed black and white pepper

To finish
1 shallot/¹/₂ small onion, very finely chopped
2 partridge livers or 1 chicken liver
¹/₂ teaspoon olive oil
4 slices wholemeal bread, toasted

Split the partridges in half and remove all the bones except the drumsticks and wing bones. Snip off the wing tips and flatten each partridge half, pressing them with the side of a heavy kitchen knife and then place on a platter. Beat the olive oil with garlic, vinegar, ouzo, salt and dried thyme. Pour this over the flattened birds, making sure you coat both sides, and put to one side to marinate. Next put the birds' bones and trimmings (but not livers) and gizzards with the figs, wine, ouzo, thyme, bay leaves, juniper berries, shallots and garlic and add 8fl oz/250ml water. Bring them to the boil, then cover and simmer very slowly for 1-1¹/₂ hours, until the figs are plump and soft and the stock is reduced and of good flavour. Remove and discard the bones. Remove and reserve all but 2 of the figs. Strain the stock, then mash all the remaining ingredients to a rough purée. Reserve 2 teaspoons of the purée. Stir the rest back into the strained liquid, with the vinegar, and reserve. Grill the partridges, or sauté with some of the marinade in the pan until brown on both sides. Place each half in a saucepan big enough to hold them in one layer. Cover and simmer for 35-40 minutes (15-20 minutes if they were grilled), until the birds are tender and the sauce has reduced. Taste and season with salt and pepper. To serve, chop the shallots and liver together. Mix with ¹/₂ teaspoon olive oil and the reserved fig purée. Spread this mixture on 4 pieces of toast and grill till the mixture bubbles. Place each half partridge on a piece of toast, flank with 2 reserved figs, and pour sauce round them on each plate.

Stewed Partridge

Perdiz estafado

This recipe came from a friend in Madrid who in days gone by used often to travel on shooting parties south of the city to the area around Toledo which abounds in game, particularly wild boar and partridge. The recipe is clean and simple and redolent of Spain.

Serves 4

4 partridge, split in half
4 tablespoons olive oil
1 large onion, finely chopped
6 cloves garlic, peeled and lightly crushed
2 bay leaves

6 peppercorns
1/2pt/300ml dry white wine
1 carrot sliced
8 small pearl onions, peeled
freshly ground sea salt and pepper

Heat the oil in a deep casserole and lightly brown the birds on all sides. Add the onion, garlic and bay leaves and cook till the onion is softened. Add the peppercorns, wine, carrot, pearl onions and salt. Cover tightly and simmer for about an hour or until tender. Parboiled cubed or whole new potatoes can be added for the last 15 minutes.

Bácska Partridge

I love the peasantiness of dishes from Eastern Europe where all the vegetables get thrown in and braised along with the meat. This is just such a one from Hungary where they use caraway in their cooking as much as we don't!

Serves 3

3 partridge
8oz/225g lean bacon, diced
2 onions, finely chopped
1/2 teaspoon paprika
2 cloves garlic
a little caraway seed
1lb/450g potatoes, peeled and chopped

5 green peppers
1/2lb/225g tomatoes, peeled and chopped
1/2lb/225g rice, washed
1 tablespoon butter
freshly ground sea salt and white and black
  peppercorns

Clean and wash the partridges, then cut in half. In a flameproof casserole, melt the butter and fry the diced bacon with the finely chopped onions, minced garlic, paprika, and caraway seed till it is all golden. Lay the partridges over this mixture, sprinkle with freshly ground sea salt and pepper, and cover firmly with a lid and simmer for about 10 minutes until the partridge begins to soften. At this point add the cubed potatoes, green peppers sliced, tomatoes, cabbage and rice. Add the stock, bring to the boil and then transfer to a moderate oven (180C/350F/Gas Mark 4) for about 40 minutes until ready. Sprinkle with finely chopped parsley and serve from the casserole.

Partridges in Wine
Perthikes krasates

A classic Greek dish and made with sweet Mediterranean tomatoes even the toughest old
partridge seems to melt.
Serves 4

4 young partridge
salt and pepper
4oz/100g butter
¹/₂pt/300ml dry white wine

4 medium sized ripe tomatoes, peeled and
chopped
1oz/25g green olives

Clean and sear the birds. Sprinkle with salt and pepper, place in a casserole and roast in the butter until
golden brown. Add the wine and when it has almost evaporated add the tomatoes. Cover and cook over a very
low heat until the birds are tender and the sauce is thick. Serve with pasta, rice, or fried potatoes. This recipe
can also be used for pigeon (see page 103). Follow this method as above but boil one cup of green olives for 5
minutes. Add to the pigeons 15 minutes before they are done.

Partridge in Chocolate Sauce
Perdiz con chocolate

When they discovered the New World, the Spaniards also discovered a great penchant for the
chocolate they found out there. Originally used for seasoning and as a drink, it was only later
that it became used in Europe for sweet things. This recipe harks back to the earliest uses of
chocolate - and you will find that it merely flavours without sweetening. It also makes for quite
a good guessing game with friends. It also goes with any other game.
Serves 4

4 partridge cut in half
3 tablespoons olive oil
2 cloves garlic, crushed
1 onion, finely chopped
1 tablespoon flour
2 tablespoons vinegar
¹/₄pt/150ml dry white wine

¹/₄pt/150ml stock
2 bay leaves
8 cloves
3 teaspoons grated bitter chocolate
freshly ground sea salt and mixed black and
white peppercorns

Split each partridge in half and sprinkle on both sides with salt and pepper. Heat the oil in a casserole and
brown the birds well. Add the garlic and onion and continue cooking until the onion is softened. Stir in the
flour. Add the vinegar, wine, stock, salt, pepper, bay leaves and cloves. Cover and simmer for 45 minutes or
until tender, skin side down. Remove the birds to a warm dish. Add the chocolate to the sauce and stir until
dissolved. Return the birds to the casserole and cook, covered, another 10 minutes.

Roast Partridge with Red Cabbage

Red cabbage is a favourite accompaniment with game throughout Eastern Europe
from Poland down into the Balkans. In the south of Poland, where vineyards flourish in the
warmer climes, partridges are often cooked wrapped in vine leaves. But for the rest
of Poland the version with red cabbage is more common and called *Kuropatwa z czerwona
kapusta*. In Czechoslovakia it is just as unpronounceable and is called *Koptve pecene na
cervanem zeli*. The following is a Czech recipe!

2 partridge
4oz/100g bacon
6oz/175g butter
half a small red cabbage, finely shredded
4oz/100g onion, finely chopped
1oz/25g flour

1-2 dessertspoon sugar according to taste
*juice of ½ lemon or 1 tablespoon vinegar (use
  according to taste)*
a pinch of caraway seed
1pt/600ml stock

Rub salt into the partridges, lard with bacon strips. Place in an ovenproof dish, with ¼pt/150ml stock and
half the butter and roast for 20 minutes. Meanwhile simmer the red cabbage in salted water for about 10
minutes. Melt the remaining butter in a heavy bottomed pan and fry the chopped onion till translucent. Add
the strained cabbage and simmer for a further 10 minutes. Then dust with the flour, add the sugar, lemon juice
or vinegar to taste and a pinch of caraway seed. Add the rest of the stock and simmer for another half hour or
so. Red cabbage doesn't harm from extra cooking so don't worry about leaving it to simmer further. Remove,
arrange on a plate to form a bed, place the partridge on top, and serve with boiled potatoes sprinkled with
chopped parsley.

WINES

PARTRIDGE AND QUAIL

For all practical purposes, wines that go well with the native British and northern European grey partridge
will be just as suitable with the more exotic redlegged partridge, even though the latter tends to have a slightly
darker and more intensely flavoured flesh.

Claret is traditional and excellent with partridge, and probably the very best choices will be from among the
stylish wines of St. Julien and Pauillac. Beaujolais is also a good option, as are the lighter Burgundies and
Crozes Hermitage. There are many excellent Cabernet Sauvignons from eastern Europe, and also from
California and Chile, and it is a matter of personal preference whether or not you opt for one of their oaky
styles. Young red Rioja should also be considered, and there are many delicious red country wines from the
Languedoc and the eastern Pyrenees.

If a white wine is preferred, something with a fairly assertive body and flavour will be best, perhaps a nutty,
spicy Alsace Gewürztraminer or a full Riesling. A rich white Rioja is a good choice, and there are
innumerable fully flavoured Sauvignons and Cabernets from Australia and New Zealand.

QUAIL

Coturnix coturnix

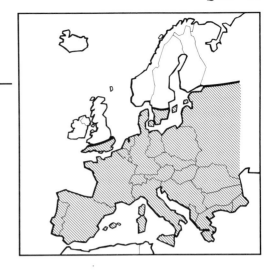

Length:	7 ins (17.5cm)
Weight:	5oz (150g)
Availability:	all year
Best time for eating:	all year

French: *la quaille*
German: *die Wachtel*
Italian: *la quaglia*
Spanish: *la cordoniz*
Greek: *to ortikia*
Portuguese: *o cordorniz*

Serbo-Croat: *prepelica*
Romanian: *prepeliţă*
Bulgarian: *padpadák*
Russian: *padpadák*
Czech: *krepelka*
Polish: *przepiorka*

Dutch: *kwartel*
Flemish: *de kwartel*
Norwegian: *en vaktel*
Danish: *vagtel*
Swedish: *vaktel*
Hungarian: *furj*

The tiny migratory quail of Europe must be distinguished from the innumerable species of East Asian and North American quails that are so decorative and deservedly popular in the private collections of aviculturists, just as the mixed-up hybrid wild pheasant and the product of the game farms should not be confused with the pure-bred ornamental species that are also favoured by collectors.

The truly wild quail of Europe and the Mediterranean lands is a small, rotund little galliform gamebird, looking rather like a miniature partridge. It occurs widely across Europe, but is very uncommon and therefore enjoys total protection in Britain and Ireland, with an estimated annual breeding population of not more than fifty pairs, and this species is seldom found in Europe anywhere north of the lands bordering the southern shores of the Baltic.

Warm, sunny climates suit it best, and it tends to lead a shy and reclusive life in the concealment of cereal crops, long grasses, olive groves and vineyards, where its small size and cryptic plumage of browns, creams and buffs gives it great concealment and camouflage. Its presence is most likely to be betrayed by the cock bird's repeated calling, like three syllables in quick succession – hence its name *co-tur-nix* – and this call is usually rendered in English as *wet-my-lips, wet-my-lips*. Like the grey partridge, it tends to squat and sit tight when alarmed – could this be the origin of the expression 'to quail'? – and this characteristic makes it a popular quarry with those who like to hunt for their game with pointers and setters. Most quail in Europe are shot in this traditional way over bird-dogs by small parties of keen sportsmen.

Quail are resident and sedentary in many parts of southern Europe, but can also be very migratory in their ways, moving long distances by night in large flocks in 'quail years' when their numbers are high.

The biblical account of the miraculous *manna* that was providentially found in the morning in the desert has often been accounted for by a sudden 'fall' of exhausted migrant quail. Commercial quail netting takes place in some Mediterranean countries, and a rich harvest can be taken when the netsmen manage to intercept a large number of quails on migration.

Quail are extremely popular in Greece, and since it was a hilltop discussion about them one wintery February night in Corfu that led to this collection of British and European game recipes, I have rather a soft spot for quail. They are light and delicately flavoured and are, therefore, immensely adaptable – the variations are endless. Probably the most traditional way of cooking quail, as many of the other small game birds, is wrapped in vine leaves, but, like chicken and turkey, they are also a marvellous vehicle for interesting stuffings – especially if they have been boned. Quail fly across the Mediterranean from Africa in the spring (well, February!), landing on islands and promontories like Corfu *en route* to rest from their exhausting flight. This is when they get snared and fattened for export

The word quail is said to come from the old Flemish word *quakele* and sounds very similar in English, French, Italian, Provençal and many other dialects – possibly a reflection of the cry that it makes. The ancient Greeks and Romans used them for fighting, like cocks, since they are very aggressive and hot-tempered. Wild quail have become so scarce in Britain that they are now protected, but there are many quail farms around the country from whom you can get fresh quail, and they are also available, frozen and oven-ready, in most of the larger supermarkets. These are a perfectly acceptable substitute for the real thing in the wild. Quail is white-fleshed and usually very tender (unlike our friend the pigeon) and shouldn't be allowed to get too high. They can dry out very easily during cooking and it is essential to protect them to keep them moist. In France and other Mediterranean countries this comes in the shape of a vine leaf – but bacon and pork fat bards will do just as well, if you want to simply grill or roast them. Most partridge recipes can be used for quail as they look and taste quite similar, but don't overpower their delicate flavour with anything too strong. Allow two birds for a main course, one for a starter.

Spatchcock Quail

Good for a light supper or barbecue.
Serves 2.

4 quail	**Marinade**
salt and pepper	*1 bay leaf*
bunch of parsley	*2 tablespoons oil*
2 tablespoons melted butter	*4 tablespoons lemon juice*
1 cup white breadcrumbs	*1 onion, finely chopped*
2 tablespoons chopped parsley	
4 tablespoons melted butter	
pinch of cayenne	

To spatchcock the quail, split them down the back, open right out and flatten. Sprinkle with salt and pepper all over, and then lay in a large flat dish to marinade for at least four hours. Remove from the marinade, drain, coat each side with melted butter and then dip in breadcrumbs mixed with chopped parsley. Roast, grill or barbecue the quail for 15 minutes basting with the rest of the melted butter and turning half way through.

Quail with Raisins
Quailles aux Raisins
Another French variation on the vine leaf theme!
Serves 1

2 quail
2 vine leaves
2 tablespoons brandy
a handful of raisins
2 tablespoons marsala or madeira or sweet sherry
2 slices back pork fat
2 tablespoons butter
salt and pepper

Stuffing
quails livers
rasher bacon
salt and pepper
1 tablespoon brandy
¹/₂ slice brown bread

First soak the vine leaves in the brandy, and the raisins in the wine/sherry for an hour. Meanwhile make the stuffing by combining all the ingredients in a food processor till finely blended. Then stuff each bird with this mixture, wrap it in a vine leaf and cover with pork fat. Heat the butter in a heavy casserole, brown the quail rapidly and then reduce the heat. Add the raisins and marsala, season, close the lid and simmer gently for 10-12 minutes. Serve with croûtons of fried bread.

Quail in Vine Leaves
Ortikia sta klimatofylla
This is a Greek variation with vine leaves.
Serves 2

4 quails
1 teaspoon Greek honey (it is not as sweet as
*   ours)*
grated zest of 1 lemon
1 teaspoon lemon juice

1 tablespoon thyme
2-3 tablespoons olive oil
4 tablespoons brandy
8-12 vine leaves (fresh or preserved)
salt and pepper

Mix the honey, lemon, thyme, oil, salt and pepper together in a bowl, and then rub this mixture into the skin of each bird. Leave to marinate in a cool place for 2-3 hours, or overnight in the fridge. Heat one tablespoon brandy in a ladle over a small flame. Light and pour over one bird, repeating for each of the others. Wrap each quail in vine leaves, fastening them with a toothpick or string. Bake for 30 minutes at 180C/350F/Gas Mark 4, or a bit longer if necessary.

Baked Quail

This recipe came from a Bulgarian friend. I don't know if it's so representative of Bulgaria –
more of the Balkans in general where tomato purée, mushroom and wine seem to pop up with
just about everything!

Serves 6

12 quail
1lb/½kg onions, finely chopped
4oz/100g mushrooms, sliced
3oz/75g bacon
4fl oz/120ml white wine

3oz/75g butter
2 tablespoons tomato purée
paprika
salt and black pepper

Pluck and clean the quail and soak in water for 15 minutes. Salt birds inside and out, wrap in broad slices of
bacon and fry lightly. Cook onions and mushrooms separately in butter and place in a baking dish, add
flavourings and tomato purée. Arrange the quail on top of them. Pour wine over the birds and bake in a
moderate oven for 20-30 minutes according to preference.

Banana Stuffed Quails

This recipe dates back to the 1930s and no wonder it has lasted so long!

Serves 2

4 quail
½ teaspoon salt
1 teaspoon freshly ground black pepper
2 ripe bananas, peeled

2 slices wholemeal bread
2 teaspoons finely chopped tarragon
1 tablespoon finely chopped onion
¼pt/150ml white wine

Lightly salt the quail inside and out. Mix the pepper into the bananas, mashing them until smooth. Cut the
crusts from the bread and crumble into the banana mixture. Mix in the tarragon and onion. Spoon the mixture
into the quails. Put them on a rack on a roasting tin and roast for 45 minutes at 190C/375F/Gas Mark 5.
Remove from the oven and keep warm while you make the gravy. Skim the fat from the pan, pour in the
white wine, set on top of the heat and bring to the boil scraping any caramelised bits and pieces stuck on the
sides. Add 2-3 tablespoons water, and cook for 5 minutes till it has reduced to half and is ready to serve.

Quails Bianco

A great Swedish friend introduced me to this recipe which seems far more Italian than
Scandinavian from its ingredients!

Serves 4

4oz/100g butter
8 quails
pepper
4 slices parma ham or smoked ham, cut across

10 fresh or preserved vine leaves, parboiled
3 fresh figs, cut into quarters
4 tablespoons pink wine (rosé)
4fl oz/120ml Vermouth Bianco

Rub half the butter into the birds, and sprinkle with pepper to taste. Wrap half a slice of ham around the
breast of each bird, fastening the slice underneath with a toothpick. Place each bird on a vine leaf. Chop the
remaining two leaves. Grease a shallow ovenproof dish and place the quails on their vine leaves in it, placing
in the middle the figs and chopped vine leaves. Pour over the wine and vermouth. Put into a medium oven
(180C/350F/Gas Mark 4) and leave for 40-45 minutes, basting every now and then. Serve with buttered
juliennes of celery and carrot.

Marinated Quail
Codorniches escabechadas

Before the days of fridges, *escabeche* was a common means of preserving meats, especially during the game season when too many partridge, quail and pheasant were caught for immediate consumption. Today *escabeche* still remains popular for its piquant and refreshing taste, and dishes such as this quail make ideal summer meals. Almost any game birds can be prepared this way and *escabeche* dishes will keep in the fridge for at least 2 weeks.

Serves 6

12 quail
6 tablespoons olive oil
2 medium onions, coarsely chopped
1 head garlic, separated and peeled
2 tablespoons diced shallots
4 carrots, scraped and sliced thinly
1 potato, parboiled, peeled and cut in quarters
  (optional)
5 bay leaves
3 sprigs parsley
2 teaspoons thyme

salt to taste
20 peppercorns
½ celery stalk with leaves
pinch saffron
8fl oz/250ml red wine vinegar
1½pts/900ml dry white wine
8fl oz/250ml chicken stock, all fat removed
1 lemon, sliced
2 tablespoons chopped parsley
watercress

First truss the quail, heat the oil in a small saucepan with a piece of lemon peel until the peel turns black. Discard peel. Turn off the flame and add a peeled raw potato to cool the oil. When the oil is at room temperature, discard the potato. Transfer the oil to a large, shallow casserole and sauté the quail slowly until they are well browned on all sides (add a slice of onion to prevent spattering). Transfer the birds to a warm platter. In the same casserole, sauté the onion, garlic, shallots, carrots, and potato until the onions have softened. Add the bay leaves, parsley, thyme, salt, peppercorns, celery and saffron. Stir in the vinegar, wine and stock. Return the quail to the casserole. Cover and simmer 45 minutes. Remove the birds to a round, shallow serving casserole, preferably earthenware, and arrange attractively. Reduce the cooking liquid by boiling for 5 minutes and then pour over the birds. The liquid should cover them, but if it doesn't, the birds should occasionally be turned while marinating. Cover and refrigerate 3-4 days. To serve, bring the quail to room temperature and garnish with lemon slices, chopped parsley and watercress.

Quail á la Duchesse
Quaille á la Duchesse

This is a French variation with vine leaves.
Serves 2

4 quail
4 thin rashers bacon
4 vine leaves (fresh or preserved)
1½oz/40g butter

¼pt/150ml game stock
2 tablespoons brandy
salt and pepper

Truss the birds. Rub with salt and pepper. Wrap each bird in a vine leaf, then in a rasher of bacon. Place in a buttered roasting pan and cook approx 30mins in a hot oven (425F/220C/Gas Mark 7). Baste frequently. Remove from oven and arrange on a platter in nests of duchesse potatoes. Make a gravy with the pan juices, and serve with green vegetables or salad.

Quail with Beans
Cordoniches con pochas

For me this dish encapsulates Spain – the differing flavours of the beans, the smoky *chorizos* (many supermarkets will have something similar) and the quail – rather like all those sublimely different flavours in a *paella:* peasanty and yet sophisticated. This needs to be started a day ahead, but it is worth every minute spent on it.

Serves 4

1lb/450g large dried lima beans
5 tablespoons olive oil
coarse sea salt
8 quail, trussed
1 medium onion, finely chopped
2 cloves garlic, finely chopped

1 medium tomato, finely chopped
freshly ground pepper
1 bay leaf
4 cubes (about 1 inch square) slab bacon
2 chorizo sausages, 2oz/50g each, cut in 4 pieces each

Soak the beans overnight in cold water to cover. Drain. Place the beans the following day in 8 cups water, bring to the boil, cover and simmer 1½ hours. Meanwhile, heat the oil in a large saucepan. Salt the quail and sauté in the oil until they are golden on all sides. Remove to a warm dish. Add the onion and the garlic to the pan and sauté until the onion is transparent. Stir in the tomato and cook 3 minutes. Add this to the beans, along with salt, pepper, bay leaf, bacon chorizo and the quail. Cover and continue cooking 30 minutes more or until the beans are tender (the quail should not cook longer than 30 minutes).

Serve the beans and quail in chunky soup bowls with good crusty bread and a mixed salad.

Quail in Green Peppers
Codornices en zurron

The colourful name of this dish, literally 'Quail in a Knapsack', refers to the shoulder bag, or *zurron*, carried by shepherds in the fields to store their food and belongings. In this recipe the quail are wrapped in cured ham placed inside green peppers and baked with tomato and pearl onions. The result is a dish as pretty as it is good.

Serves 4

8 quail, trussed
2fl oz/75ml brandy (preferably Spanish!)
coarse sea salt
freshly ground pepper
tablespoon olive oil
8 thin slices cured ham
8 peppers, each big enough to hold a quail

8 pearl onions, peeled and parboiled
2 carrots, scraped and sliced
2 cloves garlic, crushed
8 large cherry tomatoes
1½ teaspoons flour
¼pt/150ml chicken stock
2fl oz/75ml white wine

Fill the cavity of each quail with about 1½ teaspoons brandy. Sprinkle the outside with salt and pepper. Heat the oil in a frying pan and sauté the quail until they are brown on all sides. Remove the quail and reserve the oil. Wrap each quail in a slice of ham. Remove the stem and make a lengthwise slit in each green pepper. Remove the seeds and place a quail in each pepper. Arrange in a casserole, preferably earthenware, slit side down. Add the onions, carrots, garlic, tomatoes and the reserved oil. Bake uncovered at 350F/180C/Gas Mark 5 for 30 minutes. Remove from the oven. Sprinkle the flour in the casserole, stir, then add the stock and the wine. Sprinkle with salt and pepper. Continue cooking on top of the stove over low heat for 20 minutes more. Flash briefly under the grill to brown the peppers.

WINES
QUAIL

Quail have a rich yet delicate flavour which goes well with the fuller white wines, especially Burgundy and the oaky Sauvignons of California, Australia and New Zealand. White Rioja and Dão are also good, and it is worth considering some of the delicious white country wines of south-west France and northern Italy.

A good rosé like Tavel is fine with quail, as also are some of the light reds of the upper Loire and Beaujolais, and a light youngish claret is also a good choice.

Quails Bianco

RABBIT

Oryctolagus cuniculus

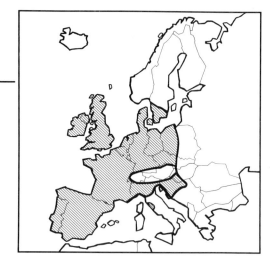

Hutch rabbit *Oryctolagus cuniculus*
Length: 12 ins (30cm)
Weight: 3½lb (1.75kg)
Availability: all year round
Best time for eating: September - November

Wild rabbit *Oryctolagus cuniculus*
Length: 16 ins (40cm)
Weight: 3lb (1.5kg)
Open season   all year round
Best time for eating: September - November

Habitat: open field and woodland
Length: 16 ins (40cm)
Weight: 3lb (1.5kg)
Open season: all year
Best time for eating: September - November

French: *le lapin*
German: *das Kaninchen*
Italian: *il coniglio*
Spanish: *el conejo*
Greek: *to kounéli*
Portuguese: *o coelho*
Serbo-Croat: *kunic*

Romanian: *repure de casa*
Bulgarian: *zemeróvan (pítomen)*
  záek
Russian: *zemeróvan (pítomen)*
  záek
Czeck: *králík*
Polish: *królik*

Dutch: *konijn*
Flemish: *het konijn*
Norwegian: *en kanin*
Danish: *kanin*
Swedish: *kanin*
Hungarian: *kis nyul*

   The familiar little coney is not a true European, but an introduction from western Asia in classical times, originally kept in confinement and reared for its meat. Its colonisation of mainland Europe and the British Isles was to be swift and complete, and was greatly assisted by the mediaeval practice of keeping rabbits on a free range basis, in warrens. Most gardeners have good reason to know how easily rabbits can defeat all attempts to contain or exclude them with fencing or netting, and it proved impossible to prevent the establishment of large wild populations of rabbits over most of Europe's farmland.

   Up to the early 1950s rabbits were present in their tens of millions, and wrought havoc with farmers' crops, consuming a vast amount of arable crops and grass each year, and constituting Europe's number one agricultural pest. Then came myxomatosis. This deadly and unsightly viral disease was introduced to rabbits on a private estate near Paris in 1952 and soon spread like wildfire through the rabbit populations of western Europe. It came to Britain and Ireland in the mid-1950s and killed an estimated 99% of all rabbits.

   Since then, the European rabbit population has recovered significantly, although occasional milder outbreaks of myxomatosis still occur to keep numbers at a much lower level than in the 1940s and before.

   The rabbit has always been accounted good sport and excellent eating, though with a less exalted sporting and culinary reputation than its distant relative the hare. Whether netted, or caught by trained hawks, or coursed with terriers, or shot when bolted from burrows and thick cover, the rabbit has tended to be the ordinary sportsman's simple quarry, lacking all the mystery and the sporting and culinary ritual of the hare.

Rabbit and hare belong to the same family, but their flesh is so different that they have to be treated completely differently when it comes to cooking. Rabbit has been described as poor man's chicken and you can indeed cook it in as many different ways. Farmed rabbit is much favoured for Chinese cooking, and wild rabbit is available in many supermarkets now. Since myxomatosis hit the wild rabbit population, however, many people have become squeamish about eating rabbit unless heavily disguised (I cannot think of the opening chapters of Molly Keane's *Good Behaviour* without retching at the thought of rabbit *quenelles*). But rabbit has been popular since the Romans (who particularly relished baby rabbit) and from the Middle Ages on rabbit appeared on the table in a wide variety of pies and casseroles. For many it was the only available form of fresh meat during the winter.

Wild rabbit is paunched (gutted) as soon as it is killed and then is hung, with its skin on, in a cool well-ventilated place for some 4-5 days. After skinning it should be carefully washed and left to soak in salted tepid water for half an hour. This will make the flesh whiter and should remove any traces of blood, gall etc not completely cleaned away. If you prefer the flesh even whiter still, you can marinate the joints for 12 hours in water with a teaspoon of vinegar added to each pint. This should also break down the fibres a bit if there is a tendency to toughness. Rabbit, if young, is excellent roasted (allow 30-40 minutes) or grilled (20 minutes). It can also be devilled or sautéed in egg and breadcrumbs. Recipes for veal or pork will usually adapt well for young rabbit. Older rabbit does better in pâtés, pies and terrines.

Terrine of Rabbit

Ideal for picnics or salady lunches, this can also be made with any of the other
white-meated game birds.
Serves 6-8

6 rashers streaky bacon
1½lb/675g cooked rabbit
1½lb/675g fat pork, finely minced
2 tablespoons brandy
2 garlic cloves, crushed

1 teaspoon dried thyme/2 teaspoons fresh thyme
leaves, chopped
freshly ground sea salt and mixed black and
white peppercorns

Using the flat of a knife blade, stretch the bacon rashers to make them thin, and then line a 1lb/500g tin or earthenware terrine. Take all the rabbit meat off the bone and mince finely in a mincer or ask your butcher to mince it in his machine. Do *not* use a metal blade of a food processor, as the texture will be all wrong. Put the meat in a large bowl, add the minced pork, brandy, garlic, thyme, salt and pepper and mix them all well together. Spoon the mixture into the container and fold over any overhanging pieces of bacon over the surface. Smooth down. Cover with foil, place in a *bain-marie*, and cook in a medium oven (350F/180C/Gas Mark 4) for 1½ hours. Remove from the oven, allow to cool for half an hour, and then cover with weights until cold, and set firm. Decorate with parsley or sprigs of thyme and serve either straight from the terrine, or turn out and slice.

Potted Rabbit

This is a wonderful standby to keep in the larder or fridge for those panic occasions when someone drops in at the last minute for lunch, or kitchen supper. It keeps for months, is very easy to make and is good country fare. I serve it with a pulse salad (like the one for woodcock on page 112) and hot crusty warm brown bread. You don't need very much as it is quite rich.

Serves 8-10

2lb/1kg rabbit joints (without liver or heart)
1½lb/675g pork belly, diced
12oz/350g hard pork back fat, diced (you may
*   have to get a friendly butcher to cut if off a*
*   joint specially for you)*
1 dessertspoon dried thyme

1 teaspoon ground mace
1 teaspoon ground coriander
freshly ground sea salt and mixed black and
*   white peppercorns*
1 more dessertspoon dried thyme
4oz/100g melted butter

Place the rabbit joints, pork belly and pork fat into a heavy bottomed flameproof casserole with one dessertspoon thyme and a wineglass of water. Bring to the boil and then simmer in the oven (150C/300F/Gas Mark 2) for about 4 hours or until the meat is disintegrating and falling off the bones. Strain through a heavy sieve and then comb through the strained meat removing all bones (watch out especially for those tiny rabbit bones that can look like threads of meat). Take two forks and pull the meat into shreds; do *not* use a food processor as this gives the wrong texture. Mush the meat all up together with the forks and then season well, adding the second dessertspoon of thyme. Add the strained juice, but not necessarily all of it as it congeals very solidly as it cools. The mixture should be sloppy without being runny. Bring the mixture up to boiling point again, add any more seasoning to taste, and then bottle in *rillettes* jars (glass jars with spring top and rubber seal) or put into earthenware pots and seal each with melted butter. If you are going to keep them for any length of time, add cling-wrap seal as well. Keep in a cool larder or fridge.

Limburg Rabbit

This recipe comes from Limburg, in the south of the Netherlands and is very typically Dutch.
Serves 4

one rabbit cut into pieces
butter or margarine
5 large onions, sliced
10 bay leaves
10 cloves
2 thick slices Dutch gingercake ('ontbijtkoek')

3 tablespoons black treacle
a little sugar
vinegar
pepper and salt
prunes (optional) and parsley to garnish

Thoroughly dry the rabbit pieces and rub with salt and pepper. Melt the butter in a flameproof casserole and fry the rabbit pieces till golden. Remove and then fry the sliced onions in the saucepan till translucent. Add one cup water and one cup vinegar, or enough to cover the rabbit pieces when they are back in the casserole. Add the treacle, gingerbread and spices. Stir well and when properly mixed add the rabbit pieces. Leave to marinate for two days in a cool place. Then simmer for two hours, until tender. Remove the rabbit pieces and keep warm in a shallow ovenproof dish. Strain the sauce and if necessary thicken with a little cornflour. If you want to add prunes to this recipe, add them to the casserole for the last 15 minutes, then remove and set to one side while you strain the sauce (as above). When sauce is ready pour over rabbit pieces and garnish with prunes and chopped parsley.

Rabbit with Alioli
Conejo Alioli

This is one of the two most popular ways of eating rabbit in Spain – grilled with seasoned oil,
then baked in white wine and dressed with pungent garlic sauce (the more garlic the better).
Serves 4

¹/₄pt/150ml olive oil
1 bay leaf, crumbled
¹/₄ teaspoon thyme
Alioli Sauce (see page 167)
2¹/₄-3lb/1.1-1.3kg rabbit, cut in pieces

juice of one lemon
salt
Freshly ground pepper
¹/₄pt/150ml white wine

Several hours before cooking the rabbit, mix the oil with the bay leaf and thyme to let the flavours blend.
Also prepare the Alioli Sauce and let it sit at room temperature: for Alioli Sauce, see *Salsa all'aglio* (page 183).
You can now buy rabbit prepared in pieces, but if yours is fresh from outside the easiest way to dissect it is as
follows. Separate the front legs at the shoulder and the hind legs at the hips. Then separate each hind leg into
two parts. Cut the rest of the rabbit crosswise into 4-6 pieces depending on the size of the rabbit.Sprinkle the
rabbit pieces with lemon juice, then brush with the oil mixture. Sprinkle with salt and pepper. Grease the tray
and then grill the rabbit 10 minutes on each side, basting with the oil mixture. Transfer to a roasting pan and
place in an oven at 230C/450F/Gas Mark 8. Add the juices from the grill pan and the wine, and cook for 15
minutes, basting regularly. Serve the Alioli Sauce separately.

Braised Rabbit, Prague style

This is a very homely, unpretentious style of cooking, the sort of thing you might
find in a Prague tavern.
Serves 4-6

meat of 1 rabbit, taken off the bone
4 bay leaves
4oz/100g smoked bacon, diced
1 onion, finely chopped
salt and paprika
2 tablespoons tomato paste
1 small celeriac, diced

8oz/225g peas, frozen or fresh
2 green peppers, chopped
1 dessertspoon flour
¹/₄pt/150ml double cream
parsley
2 tablespoons butter

Make a stock with the rabbit head, bones and bay leaves. Melt the oil in flameproof casserole and in it fry
the diced bacon and onion. Remove and put to one side. Sprinkle the rabbit meat with salt and paprika and fry
in the remaining butter till golden. Return the bacon and onions, add the tomato paste and ³/₄pt/450ml of the
stock, cover with a lid and simmer for 45 minutes. When tender add the celeriac, peas and peppers and cook
for a further 10 minutes. Thicken, Hungarian style, by mixing 2 teaspoons flour with the cream to make a
paste and diluting with stock from the pan before combining all. Bring just up to the boil and simmer for
another 5 minutes. Garnish with chopped parsley and serve with dumplings (see page 192).

Rabbit with Blackcurrants

This recipe needs no advance preparation. It derives from Eastern Europe and is an unusual combination of game and fruit.

Serves 4

1 whole rabbit
freshly ground salt and pepper
paprika
¼pt/150ml single cream
butter

Compôte

1lb/450g blackcurrants, trimmed
6oz/175g granulated sugar
12fl oz/350ml water

Rub the rabbit all over with salt, pepper and paprika. Melt some butter in a frying pan and turn the rabbit in it till golden all over. Place in a baking tray with the butter in a medium oven and roast for ½ hour basting frequently. Pour the single cream all over and roast for a further 10 minutes basting with the cream. Serve with sliced, fried pears, a compôte of blackcurrants, and pommes lyonnaises.

To make the compôte, put the sugar and water in a pan that is large enough to hold the fruit in a single layer, if possible. Bring slowly to simmering point and keep on the simmer until the sugar has dissolved, stirring occasionally. Once the syrup has reached boiling point and the sugar has all dissolved, add the fruit, let the mixture come up to the simmer again and very gently cook the fruit until it is tender, making sure that the skins don't burst. Test with a knife for tenderness and when ready remove from the heat and allow to cool. Serve either warm, or slightly chilled.

Curried Rabbit

Rabbit is just about as versatile as chicken; its light flavour lends itself well to an infinite variety of combinations. Here is one from Germany.

Serves 4

1 rabbit cut into sections (2 legs, and each breast
into 2)
1 tablespoon flour
2 tablespoons vegetable oil
1 large onion, finely chopped
freshly ground salt and pepper

½pt/300ml dry white wine
½pt/300ml chicken or veal stock
1 large tart apple, peeled and sliced
2 teaspoons curry powder
¼pt/450ml double cream
2 teaspoons lemon juice

Toss the rabbit pieces in flour, and put to one side. Heat the oil in a heavy flameproof casserole and fry the onions till translucent. Remove and then fry the rabbit pieces till golden all over. Add onions, sprinkle all over with salt and pepper, and pour the white wine over it all. Add the stock, bring to the boil and then turn down the heat. Add the apple, curry powder and cream, cover firmly and simmer for 1 hour. Then remove the rabbit to a shallow ovenproof dish and put to one side to keep warm. Bring the sauce to the boil, add the lemon juice and cook rapidly for 5 minutes. Taste and adjust seasoning, pour over the rabbit. Serve with rice.

Rabbit in Cream
Lapin á la crème

Another delicious cream variation on rabbit.
Serves 4

1 rabbit (or hare)
¼lb/100g lean bacon, thinly sliced
¼lb/100g fat salt pork, thinly sliced
fresh herbs
2 tablespoons butter

7 tablespoons brandy
freshly ground sea salt and mixed white and
*   black peppercorns*
¾pt/450ml double cream
¼pt/150ml stock or dry white wine

Cut the rabbit or hare into serving pieces. Line flameproof casserole just large enough to hold the rabbit with alternating thin strips of lean bacon and fat salt pork. Cover this with fresh aromatic herbs (tarragon, rosemary, thyme, marjoram). Sauté the rabbit pieces in butter till just golden, place on top of the herbs and then pour over the brandy. Season to taste with salt and pepper. Put the casserole over a very low heat and cook for about 30 minutes, then add the cream and a little stock or dry white wine, cover firmly with a tight fitting lid and simmer for about 3 hours. When it is ready, remove from the heat, sprinkle all over with parsley and serve from the casserole.

Rabbit in two Mustards
Lapin aux deux moutardes

If more people knew how delicious this is we would all be having it as often as we do shepherds pie or lasagne! If you think people might be a bit squeamish about rabbit, just use chicken or pheasant instead – flexibility's the name of the game!
Serves 4

1 plump rabbit
2 tablespoons flour
freshly ground sea salt and mixed white and
*   black peppercorns*
2 tablespoons olive oil
2 tablespoons butter
4oz/100g fat bacon, diced and blanched

4 shallots, finely chopped
1 bouquet garni
¼pt/150ml dry white wine
¼pt/150ml chicken stock
1 teaspoon Dijon mustard
1 teaspoon English mustard, freshly made
½pt/300ml double cream

Cut the rabbit into serving pieces, roll these in seasoned flour and sauté in the olive oil and butter with the diced, blanched bacon in a flameproof casserole till golden . Add the shallots and bouquet garni, moisten with white wine and stock and cook gently, covered, until the rabbit is tender. Drain the rabbit pieces and place in a shallow ovenproof dish to keep warm. Skim the fat from the sauce, whisk the two mustards thoroughly with the cream and add to the sauce in the pan, stirring till it is all properly amalgamated. Taste, and add more mustard if desired, plus salt and pepper. Pour over the rabbit pieces, warm through in a moderate oven for another 10 minutes or so and serve.

WINES

RABBIT

Cooks tend to use the pale flesh of the rabbit as a rather bland basis from which to create many different dishes, a culinary *carte blanche* on which marinades and sauces can be put to work to produce a great variety of results, delicate and fully flavoured, mild or spicy. Wines must be chosen accordingly, and the range is therefore great.

With the milder rabbit recipes, especially those involving creamy sauces, choices can be made from a number of white wines. White Chardonnay and Sauvignon from France, and the New World's oaky wines from the same grapes, are excellent, as is tangy Gewurztraminer from Alsace and (much cheaper) from Hungary and Jugoslavia. The white Riojas are also attractive.

With the more fully flavoured rabbit dishes for which a red wine is preferable, there are attractive light red wines from the Loire and Germany, in addition to Beaujolais, Italian Barolo, and the Riojas and Dãos of Spain and Portugal. Many excellent light red wines come from Provence and the Languedoc, too.

HARE

Lepus europaeus; Lepus timidus;
Lepus hibernicus

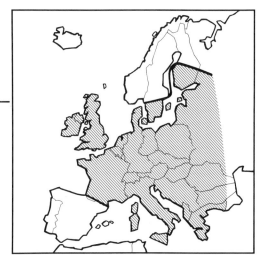

Brown hare *Lepus europaeus*

Habitat:	woodland and open fieldland
Length:	16-28ins (40-70cm)
Weight:	about 7lb (3kg)
Open season:	all year except Sunday and Christmas Day, must not be sold March-July
Best time for eating:	October-January

French: *le lièvre*
German: *der Hase*
Italian: *le lepre*
Spanish: *le liebre*
Greek: *o lagós*
Portuguese: *a lebre*

Serbo-Croat: *zec*
Romanian: *repure*
Bulgarian: *div záek*
Russian: *div záek*
Czech: *zajic*
Dutch: *haas*

Flemish: *de haas*
Norwegian: *en hare*
Danish: *hare*
Swedish: *hare*
Hungarian: *nyúl*
Polish: *zajac*

The leaping hare embodies a richer wealth of folklore, hunting and shooting traditions than any other single sporting animal. Silent and elusive, active by night, fleet of foot, occasionally gregarious and pugnacious - hares are attractive and mysterious objects of admiration, and sometimes of awe.

The hare has always been regarded as the supreme test of the agility and speed of a coursing 'sight hound', while its clever doublings and weavings present a sporting challenge for the huntsman with scenting hounds such as beagles and harriers. Hare hunting with scenting dogs can be traced back to classical antiquity, and has been widely depicted in sporting art of all periods.

The brown hare of low-lying farmland and pastures is much larger than its cousins, the Irish hare and the mountain hares of Scotland and mountainous areas of Europe. A mature brown hare can weigh 8-9lbs and has long ears which, when pulled forward, reach well beyond its snout. The Irish and mountain hares typically weight 4-6lbs and have a much shorter, rabbit-like ear.

Hares are common over much of Europe, and the mountain hare can reach very high local numbers where the habitat is suitable. Huge numbers occur on the drier heathery moorland of the north and west of Scotland, where large annual culls are taken. Many sportsmen from Italy, Spain and France travel to Scotland for organised hare shoots, especially in late autumn and winter. But brown hare numbers have declined seriously in many agricultural areas, owing to toxic pesticides and changes in farming practices.

The flesh of the hare is especially dark and rich in flavour, almost totally devoid of fat, and full of nourishment. Mediaeval writers believed that overindulgence in this dark, rich flesh could also induce melancholy. A tender young hare makes an excellent roast dish, while an older animal may require careful hanging, marinading and slow cooking to produce its best.

For centuries in Britain hare has been known as the 'poor man's meat' and was very widely eaten. For this reason during the Middle Ages, anyway, it was eschewed by anybody who considered themselves well born. After several acts of Parliament were passed, however, to prevent the poor animal from being wiped out completely, the Black Act of 1723, making poaching a capital offence if the poacher was armed or masked, resulted in making the hare not only acceptable, but respectable, fodder and the great recipes for hare, like Jugged Hare, date back to those times. The Romans believed that hares had the power to beautify those who ate them for a week or so after the meal, but both the Jewish and Islamic religions forbid the eating of hare, classing it as a beast that ruminates but has no horns. Despite this, the hare has survived and though unlikely to be found in supermarkets yet, is available from good game dealers. The meat is as dark as venison and many venison recipes will do just as well for hare. Saddle of hare is probably the prime cut and is delicious; otherwise it tends to be cooked in hot pots, or is added to pâtés, terrines and pies.

The two main types of hare in Britain are the Scottish blue and the English brown. The Scottish blue, a scraggier creature than its English relation, weighs about 5-6lb (2½-3kg) and will feed about 6-8 people. It is probably best stewed or casseroled. The English brown hare is a much larger chap, weighing about 7lb or more and able to feed 9-10. Hare can be eaten as soon as it is killed, but it is more usual to hang it, head down, unpaunched and unskinned, for anything between one and two weeks, depending on the weather. Once it has hung, it is skinned and paunched but it is important to catch all the blood if you are to make a rich jugged hare. The blood mostly collects beneath a membrane under the ribs and can be quite easily caught in a bowl. Add a drop of vinegar to stop it coagulating. You can also save the heart, lung and liver to crush and add to a sauce. Wipe the rest of the creature clean with a damp cloth. Marinating can help tenderise the meat. A young hare needs only a few hours, in maybe some oil and brandy and herbs. An older one can be left for several days in an oil and wine marinade. Hare does well with rich additions to the cooking – cream, brandy, wine, juniper berries, fruit jelly, all the traditional ingredients for cooking game. If you are having plain saddle it is important to remove the membrane and then bard it well. Saddle is often eaten slightly pink, but on the whole hare is usually well cooked rather than under-cooked.

Vintner's Stew of Rabbit or Hare

Dark, rich, delicious; an easy substitute for jugged hare.
Serves 4-6

1 hare or 2 rabbits

Marinade
1 large onion, sliced
2 carrots, peeled and sliced
2 cloves garlic
½pt/300ml red wine
4 sprigs parsley
1 sprig thyme
salt and freshly ground black pepper
4 tablespoons olive oil

For cooking
4 tablespoons olive oil
2 tablespoons flour
salt and freshly ground black pepper
½pt/300ml game or beef stock
1pt/550ml red wine

For garnish
12 button mushrooms
12 glazed onions
¼lb/100g fat salt pork, diced
croûtons
2 tablespoons chopped parsley

Skin and clean the rabbit or hare, cut into serving pieces and marinate in the marinade for two days, turning the pieces as you pass so they will be evenly marinated. Remove the pieces from the marinade, dry off with kitchen towel and dip into seasoned flour. Sauté the pieces in hot olive oil in a flameproof casserole until golden, skim fat, and add the marinade, stock and enough red wine to make sure the meat is covered. Bring to the boil, skim and allow to simmer slowly for about 1½ hours by which time the meat should almost be done. Remove the meat to any shallow ovenproof dish and keep warm. Strain the sauce into a clean casserole, skim the fat and adjust the seasoning. Add the rabbit/hare pieces, button mushrooms, glazed onions and sautéed diced fat salt pork to the sauce and cook for another ½ hour or more until the pieces are tender. Serve with croûtons and finely chopped parsley.

Traditional Danish Roast Hare

The Scandinavians use a lot of cream with their game, but this recipe, using a *Béchamel* sauce for basting, ensures that the hare doesn't dry out and also makes for a delicious accompanying sauce at the end.

Serves 6

*1 hare, skinned and jointed into saddle, shoulder
    and legs*
2 tablespoons butter
2 tablespoons plain flour
salt and pepper
1pt/600ml milk
1 small onion
1 small carrot, chopped

*3 apples, halved, peeled and poached in
    1½pt/900ml water*
squeeze of lemon juice
2 tablespoons single cream, or more to taste
1 dessertspoon redcurrant jelly, or more to taste
1 bay leaf
1 bouquet garni

Put the onion, carrot, bay leaf and bouquet garni in a saucepan with the milk, bring just to boiling point and set to one side to infuse for half an hour. In another saucepan, melt the butter, add the flour and stir till the butter is absorbed but not browned. Through a sieve, gradually add the milk bit by bit stirring all the while until you have a fairly liquid *Béchamel* sauce. In a greased roasting pan, place the saddle of hare in the middle, with the legs and shoulders at the side. Pour the *Béchamel* over all and roast in a medium oven (280C/300F/Gas Mark 5) for 40 minutes, basting often. When it is cooked, remove the meat, scraping the sauce from the surface and retaining in the pan. Carve the saddle by taking the fillets off whole, then slicing and arranging back on the bone. Place on a warmed serving dish. Slice the meat off the other joints, arrange around the saddle and cover with foil to keep warm in the oven without drying out. Meanwhile sieve all the pan juices into a saucepan and whisk in a little single cream, redcurrant jelly to taste and a squeeze of lemon juice. Season and add colouring if desired. Surround the meat on the serving dish with half a poached apple per person, each filled with redcurrant jelly in the centre. Serve the sauce separately.

Beginner's Hare

This recipe was concocted in a fever of excitement the night my son shot his first hare. He wanted it done with cream and mushrooms. The following was the results of the contents of the fridge – rich and delicious!

Serves 6

2 fillets and all 4 legs
8oz/225g smoked bacon
8oz/225g mushrooms, sliced
1 onion, finely chopped
1 heaped tablespoon butter
¼pt/150ml Greek yoghurt
¼pt/150ml double cream

¼pt/150ml single cream
1 dessertspoon lemon juice
4 tablespoons brandy (optional)
pinch mixed dried herbs
salt and freshly ground black and white pepper
1 packet noodles

First remove all membrane from the flesh, using a very sharp thin knife. Grease an ovenproof casserole, place all the meat in it and sprinkle all over with herbs. Cover with the bacon, seal with lid and cook in a medium oven (180C/375F/Gas Mark 5) for 1 hour. Meanwhile melt the butter in frying pan, cook the chopped onion till it softens, add sliced mushrooms and cook all together till soft. Put to one side. After 1 hour, remove the casserole from oven, place bacon, fillets and joints on a dish, and reserve juices in the bottom of the casserole. Slice fillets and meat off legs into thin, neat medallions and place in bottom of a clean casserole. Place the first casserole over a medium heat on top of the cooker and into the juices add the onions, mushrooms, yoghurt, cream and brandy. Simmer over a gentle heat for 10 minutes or so till well amalgamated and slightly reduced. Add seasoning and pour over medallions in second casserole. Keep warm in oven while cooking the noodles in salted water for 10 minutes. Serve noodles and hare from separate dishes – with green salad.

Terrine de Lievre

I personally don't like terrines made with sausage meat as I think it tends to dominate the
flavour of the supposed main constituent, and also makes for a very dense texture. A
combination of pork and/or veal, however, complements the flavour as in this simple French
recipe for hare terrine.

Serves 10

1 hare
1lb/450g pork belly and fillet, mixed
1lb/450g lean veal

salt, pepper, mixed spice
4fl oz/120ml brandy (more according to taste!)
12-16 rashers thinly sliced streaky bacon

Take all the meat off the hare carcase (use the carcase for consommé, see page 66) and chop into smallish
cubes. Whizz the meat very roughly in the food processor, together with the liver and place in a bowl. Repeat
with the pork and the veal, making sure that the meat is only very roughly chopped. Season to taste and add
the brandy. Mix all well together and leave to one side. Line a terrine dish with the bacon rashers, making
sure they just overlap so that none of the mixture oozes out between the strips. Fill with the meat mixture and
cover with strips of bacon laid lengthwise. Cover with a lid and place in a *bain-marie* in a moderate oven for
two hours. Remove and leave to cool with weights. Serve either in the terrine or turned out onto a large plate
garnished with strips of salad. Serve with Catalan Sauce (page 178) or Cumberland Sauce (page 172-173) or
Apple and Madeira Sauce (page 179).

Lepre alla Piedmontese

An Italian version of jugged hare, dark and rich and simple to make.
Serves 6-8

1 hare jointed, membrane removed
bay leaf
1 stick celery, chopped
2 onions, sliced
8 peppercorns
1 bottle red wine

1-2 tablespoons butter
1 slice bacon, chopped
1 teaspoon grated plain chocolate
1 pinch caster sugar
4fl oz/120ml brandy

Place the jointed hare in a large crockery or glass bowl with the bay leaf, celery and one sliced onion. Cover
with the wine then cover with a lid, and leave to marinate for two days turning from time to time. If, during
the process of jointing, you can catch some of the blood, pour it into a small bowl, with a drop of wine or
vinegar to stop it congealing, and keep in a cool place. Take a flameproof heavy casserole and melt the butter
over a gentle heat. Fry the other onion, finely sliced and chopped with the bacon till they are both golden.
Remove the hare joints from the marinade, wipe them dry with some kitchen paper and toss in the casserole
till browned all over. Add the marinade and the blood and simmer over a very low heat, with the lid firmly in
place, for 2-3 hours. Test the meat every so often and once it is cooked but tender remove from the pan with a
slotted spoon and arrange decoratively on a shallow ovenproof platter. Reserve and keep warm. Strain the
sauce from the casserole into a saucepan and stir in the chocolate and sugar. Once they are completely
dissolved reheat with the brandy and then pour over the hare and serve with noodles and fresh green salad.

Braised Hare with Onions
Laghos Stifatho

Another good Mediterranean casserole. Stifatho appears on most Greek menus made with beef
or veal, but strictly it should be made with game.
Serves 6-8

1 hare (about 2kg/4lb)
½ pt/150ml vinegar
2 tablespoons olive oil
2 tablespoons butter
3 tablespoons tomato paste
1 teaspoon sugar
salt
1kg/2lb small onions

Marinade
1 onion, chopped
2 garlic cloves, chopped
1 carrot, diced
1 leafy celery top
freshly ground black pepper
1 bay leaf
2 sprigs parsley
1 whole cloves
2 cups red wine

Optional
Small stick cinnamon
pinch cumin
sprig rosemary

Mix marinade ingredients in a bowl, tying herbs in a bunch. Joint the hare, put into bowl and cover with
cold water. Add vinegar and leave for 30 minutes. Drain, dry and add marinade. Cover and leave to marinate
for 1-2 days in the fridge, turning meat occasionally. Lift out of marinade and dry with paper towels. Drain
marinade, reserving liquid and vegetables separately. Add herbs and cloves to the liquid. Brown the hare in a
pan with the heated oil and butter, then transfer to a casserole dish. Add the marinade liquid, tomato paste and
sugar and salt to taste. Add the marinade vegetables and bring the whole lot to the boil making sure the hare is
covered. Then cover tightly with lid and cook in a moderate oven for 1 hour. While the meat cooks, prepare
the small onions. Remove the top and roots and place in a bowl. Cross-out the root ends to prevent the centres
popping out during cooking. Add to casserole. Cook for a further 1½-2 hours until hare is tender. Remove the
bunch of herbs, garnish with chopped parsley. Rabbit may also be prepared in the same way.

Hare with Black Sauce

Zajeci predek macerno

The staples of Central European cooking – *sauerkraut,* pickled cucumbers, cranberries, bacon, sour cream, gingerbread, prunes, apples – cannot but fit well with game. Polish gingerbread, *piernik,* comes into its own as a means of thickening and spicing, all in one go, sauces for venison and hare. The combination bears out the common view of a robust, strong-flavoured, meaty cuisine. But the use of gingerbread is also very typical of Dutch cuisine and the recipe for rabbit with gingerbread and treacle (page 38) is a really authentic recipe from Limburg in Holland. This is its Eastern counterpart – and for hare.

Serves 4

meat off the saddle and front half of the hare;
    liver and heart
salt
4oz/100g root vegetables
4oz/100g onion, finely chopped
4oz/100g butter
3oz/75g diced bacon
3 peppercorns
2 allspice
1 small bay leaf

3-4 strips lemon peel
3oz/75g flour
3oz/75g gingerbread
3oz/75g sugar
3oz/75g rose-hip or plum jam or jelly
1 tablespoon tomato purée
lemon or vinegar to taste
2oz/50g stewed cranberries or plums
3oz/75g flaked almonds

Cut the trimmed meat, liver and heart into pieces, add salt. Fry the onions and vegetables in butter and sliced bacon in a flameproof casserole, and place the meat on them. Add ³/₄-1pt water, spices and lemon peel and braise till the meat is tender. Remove the meat and keep to one side. Dust the gravy with flour, allow it to brown, dilute with a bit more water if necessary, beat and simmer well. Strain the sauce, add grated gingerbread, sugar, plum jam, tomato purée, and lemon juice or vinegar to taste. Finally add stewed cranberries or diced plums and flaked almonds. Serve with dumplings (see page 192).

WINES

HARE

The depth and richness of hare meat calls for something bold and assertive to drink with it. If possible, serve a really fine, full Rhône, Hermitage, Côte Rotie or St. Joseph, or a massive old Burgundy. Among clarets, the wines of Saint Emilion and Pomerol are ideal, and also in a style that hints at claret but with a unique spicy richness there is Château Musar from the Lebanon, which complements fully flavoured hare meat perfectly.

For simpler occasions and tighter budgets, consider the red wines of Bergerac and Cahors, of Côte du Rhône, and also the fruity reds of Languedoc and the eastern Pyrenees. Well worth choosing are the oaky Cabernet Sauvignons of Bulgaria, Hungary and Chile.

MARSH & WATER

DUCK

Anas

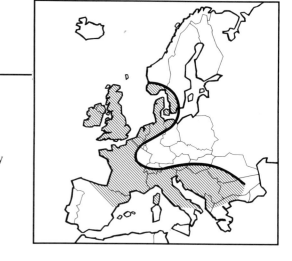

Mallard *Anas platyrhynchos*

Length:	23 ins (57.5cm)
Weight:	2¹/₂lb (1.25kg)
Open season:	*inland*, 1 September-31 January
	foreshore, 1 September-20 February
Best time for eating:	November-December

Wigeon *Anas penelope*

Length:	18 ins (45cm)
Weight:	1³/₄lb (750g)
Open season:	*inland*, 1 September-31 January
	foreshore, 1 September-20 February
Best time for eating:	October-November

Teal *Anas crecca*

Length:	14 ins (3.5cm)
Weight:	14oz (400g)
Open season:	*inland*, 1 September-31 January
	foreshore, 1 September-20 February
Best time for eating:	October-November

Golden Plover *Pluvialis apricarius*

Length:	11 ins (28cm)
Weight:	250g (8oz)
Open season:	1 September-31 January
Best time for eating:	all season

French: *le caneton sauvage*
German: *die Wildente*
Italian: *la anatra selvatica*
Spanish: *el pato*
Greek: *i agriopapia*
Portuguese: *o pato bravo*

Serbo-Croat: *divlja patka*
Romanian: *rata salbatica*
Bulgarian: *diva pátitsa*
Russian: *diva pátitsa*
Czech: *diucka kaekne*
Polish: *dzika kaezka*

Dutch: *wilde seede*
Flemish: *de wild serde*
Norwegian: *en villand*
Danish: *wildeand*
Swedish: *and*
Hungarian: *vadkacsa*

There was a time when the term 'wild duck' was taken to refer only to mallard, probably the commonest and most popular of all sporting and culinary wildfowl in the British Isles and Europe. Other species of wild ducks tended to be known by specific names, such as teal, wigeon and so on. Modern usage is more logical, and all the traditional sporting duck quarry species are now collectively known as wild duck, with individual species' names used to distinguish them.

Wild duck have a long tradition as a specially desirable quarry for the sportsman, from the medieval days of fowling with a net, or hawking with a trained falcon, to modern times. Like the pursuit of wild geese, shooting wild duck can be a hardy and testing sport, at its best in the foulest of wind and weather, and in some of the wildest and most exposed areas of inland marshes, lakes and the sea shore.

Wildfowling, at least from the point of view of the purist, is a tough and usually solitary pursuit of elusive, fast-flying quarry, and will always remain the special favourite of shooters who like to pit their skills of fieldcraft, physical endurance and marksmanship against difficult species in demanding circumstances. But one species of wild duck – mallard – lend themselves readily to a fairly intensive form of rearing, release and management, to provide sport for an organised team of Guns on a more or less formal shooting day, perhaps as a prelude to a day's driven pheasant or partridge shooting. This can be highly successful, and makes very testing sport, when it is well managed; when it is not, semi-tame and over-fed mallard may simply swim about quacking and reluctant to take wing, or flap off in leaden flight in a travesty of real sport.

Just as goose shooters divide geese into the two categories of grey geese and black geese, duck shooters have two broad categories, the dabbling ducks and the diving ducks. The dabbling species include mallard, teal and wigeon, all of which feed on vegetation in shallow water, ducking for it at distances of up to 10-15 inches, while the diving duck will dive deep and swim underwater to feed, sometimes at considerable depths. By general agreement the dabbling ducks are deemed to be by far the most delicate and deliciously flavoured, and these three species are the most likely to be of interest to the game cook.

By contrast, the diving ducks have a coarser and more oily flavour, probably derived from the greater proportion of animal matter in their diet, and from their greater fondness for feeding on fish, and along the sea shore, which can result in an unpleasantly salt, fishy taint to the flesh. Mallard, teal and wigeon will all resort to the seashore to feed at times, especially in very hard weather when their freshwater haunts are frozen, but all are at their best when the birds have been feeding inland on salt-free vegetable matter. Therefore try to find duck that have been living inland, to provide the very best results at the dinner table.

Teal are quite the smallest duck on the European wildfowler's quarry list, and fly with incredible speed and agility, especially in a high wind. They are not only one of the most attractively coloured of all duck, especially the handsome little cock bird; they are also one of the most delicious to eat. But their small size dictates one per person, while a mallard will comfortably feed at least two diners. Wigeon fall somewhere in between, providing either two smallish portions or one sizeable helping for someone with a robust appetite.

All three species of duck are readily available from good game dealers in season, which runs from 1st September to 31st January, but most are at their very best in the period up to the end of December. In particular, mallard that have been feeding on the stubbles of cereal fields after harvest are superb eating, plump and full of fine flavour. Beware, however, of mallard that have been reared and released, and may have been grossly over-fed on flight ponds and lakes. Duck are greedy birds, which will scoff vast quantities of food if it is made available ad lib, which results in their laying down excessive amounts of fat instead of the juicy muscle tissue that makes such good eating. Duck are all slightly oily in texture compared with most other gamebirds, and this further fat is undesirable.

PLOVER
Pluvialis apricaria

The Golden Plover is now the only wading bird that remains on the British sportsman's quarry list, apart of course from snipe and woodcock, which have a curious semi-gamebird status because a Game Licence is required by anyone shooting them. In every aspect – its behaviour, its wild call, its speed on the wing, and not least its delicious flesh – the golden plover is a delightful little bird.

Plover breed on the heather moorlands and upland sheep-walks of the British Isles, and move to lower ground as autumn arrives. They are especially fond of large, flat grassy fields and fresh plough close to lakes and the sea. Across western Europe their winter numbers are swelled by the arrival of vast numbers of migrants, chiefly from Iceland and Scandinavia, forced to move to frost-free wintering grounds by the cruel northern winter weather.

Plover are much more gregarious than the reclusive woodcock and common snipe in their small wisps. They are usually encountered in medium to large flocks, and will feed and preen and rest on the ground, all facing into the wind. On the ground, a 'stand' of plover is like a motionless scattering of muted fragments of old gold against the green of the grass or the duns of a ploughed field, except when a flash of white appears briefly as one of the birds does a characteristic wing-stretch and displays the bright white of its under-wing feathering.

On the wing, plover wheel and soar and dive in unison, as if one mind controlled all those scores of wings. Their collective manoeuvrings seem like that of a single organism, and in Ireland an aerial flock of plover is known as a 'wing'. Oddly, they always tend to dive together and swoop close to the ground when a shot is fired, and it is an old fowler's trick to fire a quick shot to bring a wing of plover down and within range. Skilled fowlers can also call a flock within range and keep it circling by careful imitations of the golden plovers' fluting and melodious calls.

When served whole at the table, it is traditional for the golden plover's dark coloured lower legs and feet to be left intact, and even before your hostess announces that these are golden plover, a perceptive eye will have deduced as much from their distinctive feet. Each has three main toes and no hind toe, not even the fleshly little vestigial hind toe of the woodcock and the snipe.

Slightly smaller than the average woodcock, the golden plover shares many of its physical characteristics, including plump thighs and massive breast muscles. These give it great pace on the wing – the sportsman will fire at no speedier bird than a plover coming downwind in a gale – and of course provide the bulk of the meat. But one striking difference is the plover's much shorter bill, barely an inch long and very different from the woodcock's prominent skewer-like bill. This proclaims a bird that feeds on and only just below the surface of the ground, unlike the deep delvings of woodcock and snipe.

The plover's food consists mainly of insect larvae, worms and other invertebrates, and this gives its flesh a pale delicacy and fine texture which is not dissimilar to snipe and woodcock. But there is no hint of the slightly fishy quality of snipe, unless severe weather has forced the plover to feed on the foreshore, and the great distinguishing quality of plover is its moist and almost sweet flavour – difficult to describe but unforgettably enjoyable.

Of all the various species of waterfowl, the most commonly eaten are the wild duck and the most popular of these is probably the mallard which has a delicious flavour. Teal and widgeon are also eaten, but the pintail and gadwell and shell-duck less so, and their flesh can be fishy in taste. This can be overcome by blanching in salted water to which you can add an onion, or you can remove the skin completely. Many people think that the best eating of all comes in the shape of the plover which also live in the brackish ponds and marshes by the sea.

Wild duck are best hung for 2-3 days. Their flesh is quite oily and can turn sour if it is kept too long. They can be tricky to cook and you have to watch they don't get tough. As a rough guide, you can allow 40-50 minutes roasting time for mallard, 25-30 minutes for teal, and 20-30 minutes for pintail and widgeon. Otherwise you can just take the breasts off any of them (reserving the carcases for game stock), and quickly sear over a high heat or under the grill or over the barbecue. Most of the recipes for all of these are interchangeable, but on the whole all go very well with a tartish sauce or combined with oranges. An orange and chicory or watercress salad always makes a good accompaniment (page 190), and I prefer to serve lentils (the dark green Puy lentils are especially good and do not need prior soaking, page 188) instead of potatoes.

Plovers are treated in the same way as grouse, and should be cooked with their livers inside them. Allow about 20 minutes for roasting and baste frequently. A dash of port or burgundy helps the gravy, and you can serve them on fried bread in the same way as grouse – perhaps with some slices of pink grapefruit as garnish.

Duck in Orange Sauce.

Matthew's Mallard Breasts with Bay Leaves

This is my favourite recipe for duck – and does as well for Jemima Puddle Duck as her wild relations. It is clean and simple and looks good on a plate.

Serves 8

8 mallard breasts with the skin on
32 fresh bay leaves
honey

crushed spices (coriander, cloves, ginger, rose baies, peppercorns, cinnamon, star anise etc)
salt and freshly ground black pepper

Using a sharp knife, gently cut the skin away from each breast leaving it attached along the long, top side. Put four bay leaves side by side on each breast and cover with the skin, then paint the skin lightly with honey. Grind the spices roughly so they remain gritty with a mortar and pestle and sprinkle all over the skin of each breast. Season all over with salt and pepper. Place the breasts on a lightly oiled baking tray and put into a very low oven (150C/300F/Gas 2) for about an hour. Check after 45 minutes to see if the skin is beginning to crisp up and the fat is dripping out. If not move it to a hotter oven (5-10 minutes) or flash under the grill until this happens – but not for too long. Move the breasts back to a cooler oven for 20 minutes before serving so they can relax and unwind. Remove the bay leaves and slice diagonally four or six times into each breast with a very sharp knife. Arrange decoratively on the plate and serve. It is a dish that can work with or without a sauce, but chicken stock reduced and enriched with a little veal stock and cassis makes an excellent sauce that is both deep and dark. Serve with green Puy lentils (see page 188).

Duck with Okra
Papia me Bamies

A lovely, gooey recipe with distinct wafts of the Middle East but be careful not to let the okra go slimy.

Serves 4

2 wild duck
4oz/100g butter
1 medium sized onion, finely chopped
1lb/450g ripe tomatoes, peeled and chopped

4fl oz/120ml white wine
2 teaspoons salt
1/2 teaspoon pepper
1lb/450g small okra

Cut each duck into two, keeping each breast on the bone. Lightly fry each in the butter. Remove to a saucepan. Sauté the onion in the same butter till soft. Add the tomatoes, wine, salt and pepper. Bring to the boil and pour over the duck. Cover and cook over a low heat until the duck is tender and the sauce is thick. Trim the cone-shaped tops from the okra, wash, drain and place in a dish. Sprinkle with salt and vinegar and set aside for 1/2 hour. Wash again, drain and sauté in butter for a few minutes. Remove the duck pieces from the sauce to a serving dish and keep hot. Add the okra to the sauce with 1/4pt/150ml hot water, cover and cook over a very low heat for about 30 minutes. Spoon the okra round the duck and serve hot.

Duck in Orange Sauce

Pato a la Naranja

The French are bound to dispute such claims, but it seems quite likely that this famous and popular dish should have originated in Valencia, which supplies oranges to all of Europe and breeds thousands of duck in its Albufeira marshlands.

Serves 4

2 wild duck (with neck and giblets)	**Duck stock**
salt	*1 tablespoon olive oil*
freshly ground pepper	*1 onion, coarsely chopped*
1 onion	*1 clove garlic, crushed*
3 cloves garlic, peeled	*1 carrot, scraped and sliced*
1 carrot, scraped, in thick slices	*³/₄pt/450ml chicken stock*
3 oranges	*1 sprig parsley*
¹/₄pt/150ml semisweet (aloroso) sherry	*salt*
peel of ¹/₂ lemon	*freshly ground pepper*

Wash the ducks inside and out, sprinkle with salt inside and out, and then place two slices of the onion and 1 clove of garlic inside each. Put the duck in a roasting pan with the remainder of the onion, in one piece, the remaining 2 cloves of garlic and the carrot slices are scattered around the pan. Roast at 350F/180C/Gas 4 for 1 hour, more depending on the size. While the duck is roasting, prepare the stock. Heat the oil in a saucepan and brown the neck and giblets well. Add the onion, garlic, carrot slices and sauté until onion is soft. Add the chicken stock, parsley, salt and pepper. Cover and simmer for 1 hour. Strain. To prepare the oranges, remove the rind – orange part only – from 2 of the oranges and cut the rind into fine *julienne* strips. Place in a pan with water to cover. Bring to the boil and cook 5 minutes. Run under cold water, drain and reserve. Remove and discard the pith of the 2 skinned oranges and separate the fruit into sections. Reserve. Squeeze the remaining orange and keep the juice. When the duck is done, remove it to a warm dish. Discard the onion, garlic and carrot. Skim off as much fat as possible from the pan and then add the sherry. Stir to loosen the particles. Bring to a boil and reduce the liquid by half. Add the lemon peel, orange *julienne* strips, duck stock, and the reserved orange juice. Cook for 2 minutes, remove the lemon peel and add the reserved orange sections. Cook until they heat through. Pour sauce over duck halves.

Mallard Mercedes

Despite the Spanish sounding name, this recipe came from Sweden –
such is the European Community!

Serves 4-6

2 mallard	*juice and finely grated rind of one orange*
salt and pepper	*2 tablespoons marmalade*
1 finely chopped spring onion or a small yellow onion	*6 tablespoons port*

Season the birds inside and out with salt and pepper, and place the onion inside. Rub the orange rind onto the birds and place the birds in a small flameproof casserole in a hot oven (200C/400F/Gas Mark 6). Bake for 20 minutes, basting twice. Heat the marmalade and port in a small pan until the marmalade has melted. Remove half the fat from the casserole and pour the port mixture over the birds. Bake for another 20-25 minutes, basting every now and then. Place the birds on a warmed serving dish and keep warm. Remove as much fat as possible from the casserole, add the orange juice and heat on the top of the oven, stirring, until the sauce becomes smooth. Pour the sauce over the birds and garnish with orange slices, fried croûtons and watercress.

Duck with Olives in Sherry Sauce
Pato a la Sevillana

This is a delicious and unusual way of cooking duck from Seville, home of sherry and the most Andalucian of Spanish cities. It incorporates the typical products of southern Spain – green olives from the groves all over, sherry made only in Andalucia, and duck from the nearby marshlands of the Quadalquivir river.

Serves 4

2 duck (about 4½lbs) with neck
2 slices onion
2 cloves garlic
¼pt/125ml white wine
4oz/100g green olives, coarsely chopped or
 sliced
2 tablespoons olive oil
1 medium onion, chopped
2 cloves garlic, crushed

¼pt/125ml dry (fino) sherry
¼pt/125ml chicken stock
2 carrots, scraped and thinly sliced
1 sprig parsley
½ teaspoon thyme
1 bay leaf
4 peppercorns
salt

Clean inside of duck and place the onion slices and 2 whole, peeled cloves of garlic inside. Roast in roasting pan, along with neck if available at 350F/180C/Gas Mark 4 for 1 hour. Remove duck, cut into halves without the base of the carcase and place on a platter. Drain fat from the pan and deglaze the pan with half the wine. Reserve the pan juices and discard the neck.

Put olives in a small saucepan with the remaining wine. Boil for 5 minutes. Drain. Heat the oil in a shallow ovenproof casserole, and add the chopped onion, crushed garlic and sauté until onion has softened. Add the sherry, stock, carrots, parsley, thyme, bay leaf, peppercorns, salt and deglazed pan juices. Simmer 5 minutes. Add the duck halves, spooning sauce over them, cover and return to the oven for 45 minutes. Remove duck to warm serving dish. Strain the sauce into a saucepan, pressing with the back of the spoon to extract as much of the liquid as possible. Deglaze the casserole with some water or stock and add these juices to the sauce. Stir in the drained olives, heat and pour over the duck.

Duck Breasts with Green Peppercorns and Apple

This is a variation on the classic duck with green peppercorns. The addition of apple softens the flavour.

Serves 4

2 wild duck
1 onion
1 carrot
1 bouquet garni
1 Bramley apple, peeled and chopped

1 dessertspoon green peppercorns in brine, bruised
2 tablespoons Armagnac
3 tablespoons reduced game stock (preferably duck)
3 tablespoons double cream
2 knobs of butter

Cut the breasts away from the carcass, wrap in clingfilm and reserve in fridge. Place the duck carcases in a large pan, add the onion, carrot and bouquet garni, cover with water and bring to the boil. Simmer for 1-2 hours, remove the carcases and vegetables and bouquet garni with a slotted spoon and leave to simmer slowly till reduced to a quarter. Set to one side. Take out the duck breasts and seal, with a knob of butter, in a preheated heavy bottomed frying pan or griddle pan, turning. Leave long enough to seal but not shrivel (a matter of 1-2 minutes). Remove to an ovenproof dish and leave in a warm oven (150C/300F/Gas Mark 2) for 10 minutes to settle. Add another knob of butter to the pan and soften the chopped apple in it. Sprinkle with peppercorns and cook for another couple of minutes till they are almost jumping in the heat. *Flambé* the mixture with two tablespoons Armagnac. When the flames have died down add three tablespoons of the reduced game stock, and three tablespoons cream. Stir all together over a gentle heat. Slice diagonally into the duck breasts and pour the sauce over.

Wild Duck with Olives and Anchovies
Anatra selvatica con olive e acciughe

The combination of anchovies and olives (sometimes interchanged with anchovies and capers) with wild duck is found in various different guises in Italy and France. This is just one example.

Serves 2

1 wild duck	*bouquet garni*
2 tablespoons butter	*peel of a lemon*
2 shallots	*handful of pitted green olives*
1 tablespoon flour	*2 anchovy fillets*
2fl oz/60ml dry white wine	*1 tablespoon chopped chives*
4fl oz/120ml stock	*2 tablespoons lemon juice*

Cut the duck into four, reserving the back to make stock. Brown the pieces in butter. Add the finely chopped shallots, sprinkle with flour, stir well and turn the duck over. Add the wine and let it reduce by half. Add the peel and the bouquet garni to the stock, together with a good pinch of salt, and simmer with the lid on for ³/₄ hour. Add seasoning. Remove the bouquet and cook a little longer if the sauce is not thick enough. Meanwhile stuff the olives with anchovy fillets and add, together with the chives and lemon juice, when the sauce is ready.

Wild Duck with Olives and Anchovies.

Salmi of Wild Duck
(Agriopapia salmi)

This is the Greek version of this very popular way of cooking duck; it works very well.

Serves 4

2 wild duck	*1 medium sized onion finely chopped*
¹/₂ apple, peeled and chopped	*1 clove garlic, crushed*
1 small celeriac, peeled and chopped	*¹/₂pt/300ml white wine*
2 heaped tablespoon butter	*5fl oz/150ml stock*
4fl oz/100ml olive oil	*juice of 1 orange*
salt and pepper	

Clean the birds, rinse well with water and vinegar and then, Greek-style, sear the inside with a glowing piece of charcoal or lighted taper to eliminate the fishy taste (wild duck feed mainly on fish). If this seems a bit too much like *The Good Life*, try a lighted candle, or just sprinkling the inside with salt! Heat the butter and oil in a saucepan and add the birds. Cook until golden brown; add salt, pepper and a few tablespoons water or stock. Then add all the other ingredients and cover and cook over a low heat until the meat is tender and the sauce thick.

Anatra Selvatica Palladio

I prefer just having to cope with the breasts of duck, already boned, at a meal rather than
worrying about the whole joint shooting over the table as I stick my knife and fork in. For lazy
eaters like me this is the answer!

Serves 2

1 wild duck (preferably mallard)
¼pt/150ml fresh orange juice, strained
4fl oz/120ml brandy
1 dessertspoon redcurrant, crab apple or rowan
  jelly

1 medium onion, sliced
1 teaspoon Soy sauce
salt and freshly ground mixed black and white
  peppercorns

Carefully cut away the breasts from the carcase. In a dry frying pan, over a medium heat, put the duck
breasts skin down and brown gently. Turn and cook the other side and continue turning till the breasts are
cooked through but still pink. Drain off the fat and then pour the brandy over the duck breasts, light with a
match and *flambé* till the flames die down. When they do remove the breasts to a shallow dish and keep warm
in the oven. *Deglaze* the pan with the orange juice, jelly and onions. Reduce the liquid to about 4-6
tablespoons, stirring to make sure the jelly is completely dissolved. Add the Soy sauce and seasoning to taste.
Using a very sharp knife cut the breasts across in thin slices but keeping them intact at one side. Arrange on a
plate with a slice of orange and pour the sauce over each.

Wild Duck Terrine with Ginger Wine

There are no half measures with terrines; you either love them or loathe them. I love
them, so when a young South African brought me the first ducks he had ever shot, I made this
up for him and them.

Serves 8-10

the breasts and legs of 2 wild duck
4oz/100g bacon and/or ham, cut into strips
5fl oz/120ml ginger wine
¾lb/350g diced lean pork
1½lb/675g diced pork belly, without the skin

pinch mace
1 dessertspoon mixed herbs
generous amount salt and pepper
10 slices back bacon

Cut the duck breasts into strips and marinate in the ginger wine in a bowl with duck legs and wings, the
bacon and/or ham and ginger wine for 4 hours. Make sure the breasts have no skin on them. When they have
finished marinating, drain them through a sieve to catch all the marinade juices. Take the meat off the duck
legs and wings. Put in a food processor and very roughly and quickly whizz with the lean pork and pork belly,
the marinade juices, mace, and salt and pepper. Make sure the mixture is only roughly chopped to give texture
to the terrine. Transfer to the bowl, stir in the mixed herbs, and more salt and pepper if needed. Line a terrine
dish with the bacon, so that it stretches up the sides and overhangs. Put half the pork mixture into the dish.
Add the strips of duck breast and bacon and/or ham. Cover with the rest of the pork mixture and fold the
overhanging strips of bacon over the whole mixture. Cover the mixture with foil, place in a *bain marie* and
bake in a medium oven (180C/350F/Gas Mark 4) for 1½ hours. Remove from the *bain marie*, cover with
weights and allow to cook in the tin. A lovely pinkish jelly will ooze out, the juices of the duck and ginger
wine, and set once it is cooled like aspic. Use this for decoration when you turn the terrine out. Serve with
salad and hot French bread.

Ducks with Lentils
Caneton sauvage aux lentilles

This is French country cooking at its best. The lentils are cooked with the bird, rather than served separately.

Serves 2

1 mallard	*1 carrot*
salt and pepper	*bouquet garni*
a quarter of lemon	*sprig of parsley*
1 clove of garlic	*4fl oz/120ml white wine*
1 tablespoon oil	*½lb/225g lentils*
4oz/100g bacon	*2fl oz/60ml stock*
1 onions	

First soak the lentils in tepid water for at least 2 hours, drain them and in a saucepan of fresh water bring them to the boil with an onion, a carrot and a bouquet garni. Allow 40 minutes. Do not boil fast or the lentils will harden in the early stages of cooking. Simmer very gently for an hour till they are par-boiled and ready to add to the duck.

Meanwhile rub the inside of the duck with lemon and half a clove of garlic, crushed, season all over with salt and pepper and roast in a hot oven (425F/220C/Gas Mark 7) for about 10 minutes or until brown. Remove. In a flameproof casserole, heat the oil, add the bacon, onion, and other half clove of garlic, all roughly chopped, and toss quickly till softened. Place the duck in the casserole, add the bouquet garni, pour over the wine and cook gently over the heat until the liquid is reduced by half. Add the lentils and stock and simmer for another 40-45 minutes with the lid tightly closed. Check every so often, and add more stock if necessary. Serve from the casserole or remove the bird, joint it, transfer lentils onto a large platter, lay joints on top and sprinkle with chopped parsley to serve.

Rich Duck Pâté

Use any of the wild duck – or a mixture of them – for this. If you're not sure about their tenderness, this will guarantee it!

Serves 8-10, depending on whether it is first course or main course

breasts of 6 duck	*12 juniper berries, crushed*
1 largeish onion, finely chopped	*1 dessertspoon redcurrant (or other wild fruit)*
2oz/50g smoked bacon, finely snipped	*jelly*
5oz/75g lard	*2 teaspoons hot English mustard with enough*
6oz/75g butter	*water to make a paste*
¼pt/150ml brandy	*freshly ground sea salt and mixed black and*
2 teaspoons mixed herbs	*white peppercorns*
2 cloves garlic	*melted butter*

Skin the duck breasts and dice into small cubes. Melt the butter and lard in a heavy-bottomed pan and lightly fry the bacon and onion till they are golden. Remove from the pan and reserve in a bowl. Sauté the diced breasts in the remaining fat till they are lightly cooked, making sure that they are still pink inside. Remove from the fat with a slotted spoon and add to the onion and bacon. Add the herbs, garlic, juniper berries, redcurrant, mustard and brandy to the pan juices and bubble rapidly for 3-5 minutes. Pour half the duck mixture with half the juices into a food processor and whizz until finely ground. Repeat with the other half of the mixture. Add salt and pepper to taste, mixing both halves of the pâté together well. Pour into one large earthenware terrine or individual ramekins, cover with melted butter and leave to set. Cover with clingfilm and leave in the fridge, preferably for 2-3 days before eating to allow the flavour to mature. Eat at room temperature with brown toast.

Juliennes of Duck Breasts with Fresh Cranberries and Oranges

This is such a light way of cooking that it is almost impossible to convert the duck breasts into rubber as sometimes happens. Since the breasts don't need the skin for this way of cooking, it also makes for wonderfully lazy preparation if your duck haven't already been plucked. Just take a sharp knife and cut down the length of the duck's back. Peel the skin away, feathers and all, cut out the breasts and discard the rest of the carcase. Fresh cranberries are now available in many supermarkets.

Serves 4

4 skinned duck breasts
2 oranges
4oz/100g fresh cranberries
1 knob of butter
1oz/30g butter
1oz/30g flour

¼pt/150ml stock (preferably duck, but chicken or
  game will do)
¼pt/150ml red wine
1 dessertspoon redcurrant jelly
generous screw of black pepper
salt to taste

Using a very sharp knife, remove the skin as thinly as possible from the oranges and then cut into long fine *juliennes*. Next, remove all the pith from the fruit and discard. Blanch for a minute in a small pan of boiling water. Drain and leave to dry. Again, using a very sharp knife, cut diagonally into each duck breast to make slim strips or *juliennes* about ¼inch/½cm wide. Keep to one side while you make the sauce. Melt the ounce of butter in a small non-stick saucepan, stir in the flour, and add first the stock, bit by bit stirring all the time to avoid lumps forming. Then add the wine, and finally stir in the redcurrant jelly and season to taste. Heat a heavy bottomed frying pan or gridle pan till it is quite hot, and then toss the strips of duck breasts with the knob of butter and toss deftly till they are just sealed. Make sure you turn then constantly. Remove from the heat and place in a shallow ovenproof dish to keep warm. Reheat the sauce, add the cranberries and oranges gently into it and pour over the duck breasts. Garnish with the *juliennes* or orange skin. Serve with 'Apple potatoes' (see page 192), celeriac sticks and winter salad.

Terrine de Canard Sauvage

This is a lovely rich terrine and worth making at least 24 hours before it's needed to allow the flavours to develop. The great secret of making this an unqualified success is to reduce the stock to a rich concentrate.

Serves 6

4³/₄lb/2.25 kilos wild duck meat - any
  combination of any of the varieties will do
all the livers from the duck
6 rashers rindless streaky bacon
2 sprigs fresh thyme
8 ready to eat dried apricots
1 small orange
4-8 tablespoons brandy, depending on taste
2oz/50g pistachio nuts
1lb/450g minced pork (¹/₂ fillet and ¹/₂ belly
  makes a good balance)
2oz/60g fresh white breadcrumbs (preferably not
  from an 'instant' loaf)

1 teaspoon oregano
1 clove garlic, crushed
1 teaspoon salt
freshly ground mixed white and black
  peppercorns

For the stock
  the duck carcase
  1 stick celery, roughly chopped
  1 onion, quartered and with the skin left on
  1 large carrot, roughly chopped
  1pt/600ml water

Take all the meat off the bone and place the carcases in a large stockpot, having roughly cut them up into small sections. Add the vegetables and the water (leaving the skin on the onion adds a wonderful mahogany hue to the stock). Cover and cook in a medium oven (180C/350F/Gas Mark 4) for 1-1¹/₂ hours. Remove and strain the stock into a saucepan and bring to the boil over a high heat and then let it bubble till it is reduced to about 3 tablespoons. Set to one side.

Meanwhile butter a loaf tin or terrine and arrange the sprigs of thyme on the bottom. Lay the rashers of bacon in strips across the tin, stretching them up the sides as far as possible. Chop all the duck meat (with fat removed) roughly and put into a large mixing bowl with the chopped livers. Grate the zest from the orange, chop the apricots and add these, together with the brandy, to marinate for at least three hours. Subsequently, when you are ready, into this mixture add the minced pork, the breadcrumbs, oregano, crushed garlic and seasoning to taste. Spoon off any fat from the cooled stock and stir the concentrate into the terrine mixture. Finally stir in the shelled pistachios and press the meat mixture into the tin. Cover with tin foil and cook in a *bain-marie* (allow enough water to come about two thirds of the way up the tin) in a pre-heated oven at 170C/325F/Gas Mark 3 for about 2¹/₄ hours. Remove to one side, cover with heavy weights and allow to cool completely before refrigerating.

Terrine de Canard Sauvage.

Stuffed Plovers with Olives
Serves 4

4 plovers plus livers	1 tablespoon fresh white breadcrumbs
10 slices bacon	1 egg yolks
3-4 chicken livers, finely chopped	3 tablespoons butter
6oz/175g sausage meat	4fl oz/100ml dry white wine
1 tablespoon chopped fresh herbs	2 handfuls pitted green olives
1 glass madeira	

Chop two slices of bacon very very finely and simmer in butter with the chicken livers and sausage meat. Add the breadcrumbs, herbs, madeira and seasoning, mix well and cool. Add the two egg yolks to the mixture, kneading all well together. Divide the mixture into four and stuff each bird. Bard each bird with two slices of bacon and then brown in butter in a flameproof casserole. Add the wine, cover and simmer gently for 10 minutes. Blanch olives in boiling water, drain and add to the casserole. Cook for another 10 minutes and serve on croûtons of fried bread with the juice from the pan and surrounded by olives.

WINES

DUCKS & GEESE

Duck and goose are often described as naturally greasy meats, although this is sometimes exaggerated. Good cooking offsets this tendency, and in any case wild ducks and geese have little of the excess fattiness of their pampered and aldermanic farmyard cousins. But it still pays to choose a wine with an effective cutting edge to counteract any traces of oiliness in the taste or texture of the flesh.

Despite their darkish meat, wildfowl go well with some white wines. The deliciously flavoured and spicily astringent wines of Alsace suit perfectly, as do some of the oaky and flowery New World Chardonnays from California, New Zealand and Australia. A richly fruity Riesling is also highly suitable.

But red wine will be most people's first choice with wildfowl, and among French wines my choice would be taken from Burgundy, southern Rhone or the more full bodied clarets such as Saint Emilion and Pomerol. The eastern European Cabernet Sauvignons have a woody richness which goes nicely with duck, as does good red Rioja, Bairrada and Dão.

GOLDEN PLOVER

Much the same principles apply as for woodcock and snipe, since the golden plover's flesh is white and delicately flavoured. But it is also worth remembering that hint of sweetness in plovers' flesh which makes it so specially delicious.

For white wines, try one of the finer Alsace ausleses, or a light and not too dry white Bordeaux such as an Entre-Deux-Mers, gently chilled but not too cold.

Among reds, a light claret is fine, as also is a Beaujolais or a Chianti.

SNIPE

The delicately flavoured and smoothly textured white flesh of snipe can too easily be overwhelmed by too powerful a wine. Red wines should be chosen with care, and whites are often the best choice. The slight hint of sweetness in snipe flavour goes nicely with good quality Rieslings, *spätleses* and *ausleses* for preference, and a smooth Vouvray is also a good choice. White Rioja and Macon are also excellent, but avoid the over-flowery whites of Australia and New Zealand with this delicate meat. A Tavel rosé can be a splendid accompaniment, and if red is preferred, opt for a Beaujolais or one of the lighter clarets.

WILD GOOSE

Habitat:	estuaries and marshland
Length:	Canada goose, 36-40 ins (91-101cm)
Weight:	Canada goose, 10lb (4.5kg)
Open season:	1 September-31 January (and up to 20 February at the seashore)
Best time for eating:	September-Christmas

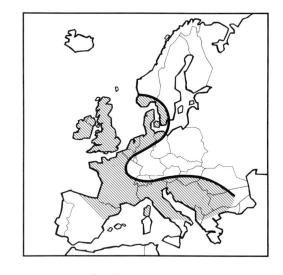

French: *l'oie sauvage*   Serbo-Croat: *guska*   Dutch: *gans*
German: *die Gans*   Romanian: *gâsca*   Flemish: *de gans*
Italian: *la oca*   Bulgarian: *gáska*   Norwegian: *en gas*
Spanish: *el ansar*   Russian: *gáska*   Danish: *gaas*
Greek: *i china*   Czech: *husa*   Swedish: *gas*
Portuguese: *o gauso*   Polish: *ges*

Wild geese are some of the most exciting of all British and European sporting birds, and have always held a special magic for the dedicated Gun who is willing to endure the wild and stormy conditions that prevail on winter foreshores and inland marshes, and to exercise the fieldcraft that is usually required to get within range of these wary and elusive birds. Added to these challenges are the special delights of spectacular dawns and dusks as geese and other wildfowl flight against the wild skies of some of the most scenic parts of Britain, at times when most people are either still in bed or sitting warmly by their firesides.

The wild geese that come south from their breeding grounds in the Arctic to spend the winter in the milder latitudes of the British Isles and Europe are usually considered in two broad groups, the grey geese and the black geese. This is a crude but useful way of distinguishing between the birds that generally make the best eating, and which happen to have predominantly greyish plumages, and the generally darker and smaller species of geese, which are not so highly esteemed to eat. Since most sportsmen only shoot what they can eat, the grey geese are the fowlers' main quarry. In Britain this means two principal species, the Greylag goose and the Pink-footed goose.

Both of these breed in high northern latitudes and come south ahead of the Arctic winter, arriving in Britain and western Europe from September onwards. Their over-wintering numbers usually peak in late November, and the most favoured goose areas will then be occupied by tens of thousands of birds. Greylags and Pinkfeet both feed by grazing, usually flighting in the early morning from their night-time roosting places on lakes and sea inlets to their feeding grounds on arable fields and pastures. Fields of potatoes and many kinds of winter vegetables are especially attractive to them, and the unfortunate farmer who finds himself playing host to daily flocks of geese may suffer very major losses. The old rule of thumb is that three wild geese will eat as much as a sheep, and when a thousand or more geese descend on a few fields their depredations can be serious. Apart from what they eat, geese destroy a lot of growth by paddling it with their large webbed feet and by fouling it with their droppings, so it is hardly surprising that farmers have mixed feelings about them.

Shooting wild geese, like any truly wild quarry, is a legitimate way of taking a modest harvest from a self-sustaining resource, and the grey geese that winter in Britain are not threatened by shooting pressure at current levels. In many parts of northern and eastern Britain their numbers have increased significantly in recent years. But when selecting a wild goose for the table, it is as well to remember that geese are long-lived birds, and some of the fowlers' bag will comprise birds aged ten and more years, that have flown many thousands of miles to and from their Arctic nesting grounds. These may still be perfectly edible, but they constitute something of a challenge to the cook's skills with marinades, slow cooking and other tenderising techniques. A roast wild goose is a delicious dish, but only if it is a young one.

In Britain it is illegal to sell wild geese, and this is a perfectly sensible conservation measure to prevent unscrupulous and unsporting shooters from taking advantage of their large numbers and shooting vast quantities for sale. It is therefore not possible to buy a wild goose from a game dealer or a poulterer, but there are other perfectly legitimate ways of procuring good birds for the kitchen. If there is a wildfowler in the family all you have to do is keep setting his alarm clock and packing him off before dawn until he comes back with what you want. If not, cultivate the acquaintance of someone who does go fowling, or else a farmer or gamekeeper or landowner in an area frequented by geese in autumn and winter. Someone will be sure to shoot one or two for you, and will no doubt be pleased to receive a bottle of something from you in return. A goose shooter will also be able to distinguish between old and young birds, so you should get what is required for the meal you are planning. And if you are offered some nice young geese, remember they freeze very well, either in the feather or oven-ready, to be kept for a future occasion.

The so-called black geese – Brent and Barnacle and White-fronted geese – are all either protected by law, or generally of low gastronomic appeal, so need not concern the practical sportsman or game cook. However, the Canada goose is something of an exception to the general rule that black geese are not table geese. Canada geese, as their name suggests, originate from North America, and do not visit Europe in their natural wild wanderings. They are an introduced species, which have flourished in many parts of Britain and western Europe, and have established large wild populations. They have proved themselves to be highly adaptable, and occur widely on suburban ponds, on rivers and lakes of many kinds, and often colonise flooded gravel pits and similar sites. They are large geese, with large appetites, and in many areas their numbers have to be controlled by shooting, to limit their effects on crops and pastures. All Canada geese are edible, given the right preparation and cooking, but once again the best are always the youngest.

———————————

Wild goose always sounds so romantic and special; maybe it's just all a romantic legacy left in the mind by childhood stories. In fact, since it is illegal to sell wild goose in shops, you can only get them if you shoot them yourself or can get them through other people who do. To watch them flighting is indeed a romantic sight, but when it comes to eating them you have to beware any that are beginning to age. They can be really tough! In fact, with very old geese it's not really worth trying to cook them – not even for stock, as the flesh is likely to be slightly sour. The best eating is probably the Canada goose which is twice as big as the 'grey' geese (greylag, pink-foot and white-fronted), but these can be delicious too. Their rich flavour is a very good addition to pâtés and game pies; if you roast them you have to make sure that they are basted continually as the flesh is quite dry. One trick is to braise them with plenty of liquid – wine, stock, cider or whatever – or to bard them with plenty of pork fat or bacon.

You can hang geese for anything from a week to three weeks, depending on your taste. The Canada goose is about twice the size of the greys, and the Greylag is bigger (about 9lb/4kg) than the Pink-footed (about 7lb/3kg), so you have to adapt cooking times accordingly. A Canada goose will serve about 6-8 people, a Greylag about 4. The easiest way to recognise a young bird is that its underbill will be softer and its legs more brightly coloured. If you have a smokery anywhere near you, or better still, a smoking kit at home, it is worth getting a goose smoked. It is excellent. In fact, smoked goose goes back way into history in a Jewish dish – a form of cassoulet – that is still eaten in Hungary today (see page 66). The traditional Christmas goose, eaten for centuries in Northern and Eastern Europe, was of course domestic.

Roast Goose with Prune, Apple and Celery Stuffing

As goose can dry out easily it's worth making a stuffing to keep it moist. Any sort of stuffing
that does for the Christmas turkey will also do for goose, but I think a very fruity one
compliments the bird well.
Serves 6

1 wild goose
strong cider
8oz/225g ready to eat prunes
2 medium onions
4oz/100g chopped celery
3 pears
3 cooking apples
3 cups brown breadcrumbs
pinch of caraway seed
1 teaspoon lemon juice

1 bay leaf
pinch ground nutmeg
pinch of dried tarragon
1 tablespoon finely chopped fresh parsley
4oz/100g chopped bacon
pinch of ginger
4oz/100g butter
1 tablespoons redcurrant jelly
³/₄pt/450ml stock made from the giblets

Make the stock with the giblets and any spare root vegetables. Wipe the bird inside and out with the cider
and then sprinkle all over with salt and pepper. If you are using dried prunes soak them overnight in cider, and
then keep the liquid for the gravy. If you are using ready-to-eat prunes, chop them roughly with the apples,
pears, celery and onions and soften in a saucepan of melted butter. Add the lemon juice and all the spices
except the ginger. Remove into a bowl and sauté the chopped bacon. Add the bacon and breadcrumbs to the
bowl of fruit, stir all well together and if necessary add a bit of cider to make it all stick together. Spoon the
mixture into the bird. Paint the outside of the bird with a little melted butter and sprinkle with the ground
ginger. Stand the bird in a roasting tin with about ¹/₂pt/300ml stock and cook in a moderate oven
(180C/350F/Gas Mark 4) for about 1¹/₂ hours or until cooked through, basting every now and then. Remove
to a serving dish when it is ready which depends on the size of the bird and keep warm. Remove any excess
fat from the roasting pan, add the ginger and redcurrant jelly and more cider. Heat on top until the jelly is
dissolved, boil rapidly for 5-10 minutes to reduce a bit and adjust seasoning. Serve in a sauceboat,
accompanied by red cabbage (page 191) and potato and celeriac purée (page 191).

Wild Goose Breasts in Brandy

This is a dish for a cook in a hurry – light and pretty on the plate. It also works well with duck.
Serves 8

the breasts of 2 wild geese
¹/₂pt/300ml brandy
4 shallots, finely chopped
1 dessertspoon soy sauce
6 cloves garlic, crushed

1 dessertspoon redcurrant jelly
2oz/50g butter
freshly ground sea salt and pepper
2-3 tablespoons vegetable oil

Marinade the goose breasts overnight in the brandy and oil mixed with the shallots and garlic. Reserve the
carcases for stock or soup (see Wild Goose Consommé page 66). Slice each breast into eight thin slivers. Melt
the butter in a pan and quickly seal the slices of goose in this – a matter of seconds rather than minutes. Add
enough of the marinade to cover the breasts and just simmer till the breasts are cooked but still pink. Remove
the breasts with a slotted spoon and keep warm. Add the redcurrant jelly to the pan juices, stir till dissolved
and then boil rapidly for 5-10 minutes until it is reduced. Arrange breasts on each plate, pour the sauce over,
and garnish with watercress.

Ganseleber Törtchen

These are hot little mousses of goose liver, turned out from their moulds onto a neat little circle of cold tomato sauce. The contrasts between the hot and cold, the creamy richness of the liver with the tart freshness of the tomato work brilliantly. You can, of course, use any game livers for this, or a combination of any, or any combined with chicken liver, or even just chicken liver on its own! It is excellent as a first course, or as a main course for lunch, served with French bread and green salad.

Serves 5 (makes up into 5 ramekins)

1 small onion, finely chopped
1oz/25g butter
1 teaspoon chopped parsley
1 clove garlic, crushed
1lb/450g wild goose (or other game) livers, rinsed and cleaned
2 slices white bread
3 eggs
8oz/200g bacon fat, finely diced and then minced

6oz/150g crème fraîche and 1 dessertspoonful of crème fraîche
pinch of nutmeg
salt and freshly ground pepper
oil or butter to grease the ramekins with
2 large tomatoes (sweet, beef if possible)
10 large basil leaves
pinch sugar

If you aren't sure of the age of the livers, soak them first for 2-3 hours in a bowl of milk to get rid of any possible taint or taste of bitterness.

Melt the butter in a small frying pan and gently cook the onion and garlic till they are softened and translucent. Soak the white bread in water and then squeeze the liquid out. Put the bread, the onion and garlic, the freshly chopped parsley, the liver, eggs, bacon fat and 6oz/150g *crème fraîche* into a food processor and whizz until it forms a very smooth fine purée. Season with salt, pepper and nutmeg and quickly whizz again to mix in properly. Grease 5 ramekins, fill with the mixture, cover each with tin foil and cook in a *bain marie* for half an hour at a temperature of 160C/325F/Gas Mark 3. Meanwhile make the tomato sauce. Skin and deseed the tomatoes and liquidise the flesh with the dessertspoon of *crème fraîche*, a pinch of sugar, salt and pepper and five basil leaves. Arrange smooth even circles of the tomato sauce on individual plates and when the goose liver mousses are ready, turn them out onto the middle of each tomato circle. Garnish each little mousse with a single basil leaf and serve immediately.

Salted Goose

This recipe does equally well for duck, pigeon and turkey as it does for goose. In fact, in Denmark where this originates you hardly ever find roast turkey as we know it – it is nearly always salted, or 'blown up' as the Danes describe it. You can have it hot (as below) or cold when it keeps very well for several days.

Serves 6

12 litres cold water
2lb/1kg coarse salt

1lb/½kg soft light brown sugar
¼lb/100g saltpeter (available from the chemist)

Bring the water to the boil, add the salt and sugar and make sure they are completely dissolved. Leave to cool and when cold stir in the saltpeter. Then immerse the gutted and plucked bird for 1 week (if you are doing pigeons leave them for 24-36 hours, depending on their age; duck will need 4-5 days; turkey, like goose, 1 week). Leave in a cool place with plenty of air. Remove. Take a fresh pan of water and add a leek, an onion, a carrot, bay leaf and parsley and boil the goose gently for about 40 minutes. Remove and keep warm. Remove the vegetables from the stock, add a glass of cheap cooking sherry and boil very fast for 15 minutes to reduce. Use this or melted butter to serve with the bird and a variety of boiled vegetables.

Wild Goose and Venison Consommé

If you are doubtful about the age of your goose, this will save you from any embarrassment!
This recipe can also be used as a base or sauce made from any type of game carcase.

1lb/450g venison and goose meat
2lb/900g venison bones
1 goose carcase
2pt/11.2 litres medium white wine
2 celery stalks, chopped
2 tomatoes, chopped
1 leek, white part only, chopped

1 bouqet garni
1 bunch fresh mixed herbs (fennel, thyme, mint)
1 bunch parsley
4 egg whites
2 tablespoons olive oil
¼pt/150ml port
freshly ground sea salt and black peppercorns

Brown the venison bones and goose carcase for an hour in a moderate oven. Put the bones, wine, vegetables, herbs, garlic, pepper and two of the egg whites in a very large saucepan, add 5 pints (3 litres) water, bring to the boil and simmer for one hour, with the lid off, until the liquid is reduced by half. The egg whites will rise to the top to form a crust – do not disturb. Strain through a very fine nylon sieve, or alternatively a sieve lined with muslin, into another very large pan and leave to cool. Leave to cool to room temperature and then add the other two egg whites. Bring the stock to the boil slowly, simmer for another 20 minutes. The egg whites should have risen to the top again, collecting any left over 'bits' and the liquid should now be completely clear. Strain into another pan. Cut the meat into delicate strips, sauté quickly in the oil, leaving the flesh pink. Add a dash of port, then remove with a slotted spoon and keep warm. Add the rest of the port to the consommé, season to taste. Arrange a few strips of meat on the bottom of each soup plate, pour the consommé on top, and serve piping hot.

Cholent

As cooking is forbidden on the Jewish Sabbath, casseroles made of a variety of dried beans which could be prepared the day before are very much part of the culinary culture of Central Europe. This dish, known as *solet* in Hungary, originated from Transylvania and is a Jewish, East European version of the French provincial *cassoulet*. If you cannot get your goose smoked, use ordinary wild goose and add smoked sausage or bacon for the extra flavour.
Serves 8-10

3lb/1½kg smoked goose, or
2lb/1kg wild goose and 1lb/½kg smoked sausage
*   or bacon*
1½lb/675g dried white beans (haricot, chick
*   peas, butter beans, navy, lima)*
12oz/350g barley
3 onions, peeled and chopped

3 tablespoons oil
2 teaspoons oil
½ teaspoon black pepper
½ teaspoon ground ginger
2 tablespoons flour
2 teaspoons hot paprika

Soak the mixture of beans overnight (a single variety will do if others are not available). Heat the oil in a flameproof casserole. Cut the meat into neat cubes and brown in the fat together with the onions. Sprinkle with the spices and add the beans and barley and sprinkle with flour and paprika. Add enough boiling water to cover the ingredients by 1 inch (2cm) and stir all together. Cover tightly with a lid and cook in a very slow simmering oven (150C/300F/Gas Mark 2) for up to 24 hours. Serve with cabbage.

Rich Goose Pâté

Many recipes for wild goose pâté call for it to be combined with minced pork or veal. I prefer the taste unadulterated and use exactly the same recipe as for duck pâté (see page 58).

SNIPE

Gallinago gallinago
& Lymnocryptes minimus

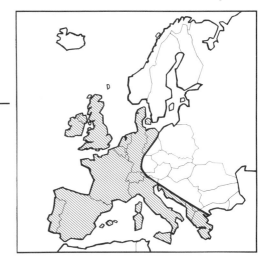

Habitat:	Bogland, marsh and moorland
Length:	10½ ins (26cm)
Weight:	4oz (125g)
British open season:	12 August-31 January

French: *la becassine*
German: *die Schnepfe*
Italian: *il beccaccino*
Spanish: *la agachadiza*
Greek: *to bekanoto*
Portuguese: *a narceja*

Serbo-Croat: *sljuka*
Romanian: *becaţă*
Bulgarian: *bekasína*
Russian: *bekasína*
Czech: *sluka*
Polish: *bekas*

Dutch: *snip*
Flemish: *de snip*
Norwegian: *en bekkasin*
Danish: *bekkasin*
Swedish: *beckasin, snappa*
Hungarian: *szalonka*

Along with the quail, the Common snipe and the Jack Snipe are quite the smallest sporting birds which will present themselves to the European sportsman. Both are smallish waders, with the long legs, racy build and long bills which characterises the type. Size, however, is no indication of sporting potential, and the birds of the snipe family probably provide more universal sporting and culinary admiration and excitement than any other quarry species.

Sniping, the definition of pinpoint-accuracy shooting, may derive from the name of these agile little birds, that can swerve and jink and zigzag in an effortlessly elusive way, leaving even the best shots spluttering in frustration as their quarry weaves away unscathed.

Snipe occur widely across the Old World and the New, and throughout both hemispheres. They are wedded closely to marshy, waterlogged habitats, in which they are happy to wade and feed in standing water an inch or more deep, and that can embrace anything from an Indonesian rice paddy to a Dutch polder or an Irish bog.

Like woodcock, snipe feed by probing with their long and highly sensitive bills, searching the liquid mud and ooze for freshwater invertebrates, snails, insect larvae and small worms. This diet is rich in easily digestible proteins, and snipe are eager, active feeders. After their late summer moulting time they quickly regain plumpness and vigour, and the onset of the first winter frosts impels them to still more vigorous feeding, laying down reserves of physical condition against the lean times that may lie ahead. But while sharp snaps of night frost can stimulate the keen feeding that ensures plumpness, long spells of unbroken frost will cause snipe to lose weight rapidly, with emaciation and death the inevitable end for snipe when freezing conditions persist continuously for more than a few days.

A good day's snipe shooting in the British Isles for one or two Guns may yield a bag of 12–18 snipe. The Common snipe is the only one that is fair game in Britain since the Jack snipe was given all-year protection in 1981, but Northern Ireland and the Republic of Ireland have retained this small winter migrant on their legitimate quarry lists, since it seems to be no less scarce than a century ago, and arguably rather more common. But a Jack snipe is tiny, barely a morsel on the plate and seldom a testing shot when the Guns are walking-up, when it rises silently with a weak, direct flight, very different from the bold *scaap*-ing, zig-zagging getaway of the common snipe. A Jack snipe driven forwards on a stiff breeze, however, is an altogether different proposition, and can be as high, fast and testing as a any Common snipe. This, plus the near impossibility of identifying a driven Jack snipe with certainty on a dull winter's day, means that a few Jacks will inevitably be bagged inadvertently on driven days when the principal quarry is its larger cousin.

In most of Europe snipe shooting begins quite early in autumn, and the British open season begins on 12th

August, a date better known for signalling the opening of the red grouse shooting. A good many snipe are shot each year on heather moorland, but an August snipe is a poor test for the shooter and a meagre contribution to the larder, compared with the plump and well-conditioned snipe of late autumn and winter. In late summer the birds are deep in the moult after the stresses of the breeding season, while young snipe are still growing and have low body weights.

A great many snipe that breed in Scandinavia and northern Europe begin to move southwards in August and early September, stopping in western Europe to moult en route to their eventual wintering grounds. Historically, the wetlands of Denmark, the Netherlands and northern Germany have been very important moulting grounds for migrant snipe, but the numbers stopping there have decreased dramatically in recent times, owing to the drainage and cultivation that has meant the disappearance of thousands of hectares of good snipe habitat. Many snipe now migrate directly to the British Isles, moulting there and remaining throughout the ensuing winter.

By mid-September snipe have begun to put on weight in preparation for the onset of winter, and like woodcock they react positively to cold weather, feeding vigorously and putting on weight quickly. Their relatively large breast and thigh muscles enable snipe to spring into fast and agile flight, and this makes them a testing sporting quarry – and these same muscles provide most of their delicious flesh.

Because snipe, like woodcock, eat foods that are soft in consistency, high in protein and low in indigestible matter, a bird that is shot is likely to have little or no gut contents – hence the tradition of not "drawing" them before cooking. When roasted in a hot oven, snipe and woodcock entrails simply melt away and become part of the natural gravy which can be caught on a slice of toast placed underneath the cooking bird – and very delicious it is, too.

Snipe flesh is delicate in taste and pale in colour, and very rich and readily digested, with a high nutritional value, which is why these little birds were especially recommended in the past for invalids and convalescents.

Snipe appear neither to benefit nor suffer from being left to hang for a short time, and there is no reason why a snipe shooter who comes in muddy and tired after a day's bog-trotting should not enjoy his birds at breakfast the next morning, or even for supper the same night. If the birds are hung they should be suspended singly and bill upwards. To serve snipe in the grand manner, the birds' heads and necks should be left in place (and sometimes they are left unplucked), and doubled back so that the long bills can be used as skewers when trussing the birds. Traditionalists and connoisseurs eat the brains, which are accounted a particular delicacy.

A snipe has barely two ounces of meat on it, and a single bird per person will suffice as a first course or a savoury, served on a crouton or a slice of toast, and suitably garnished. Allow 2-3 snipe per person for a main course. For a dinner party at which you intend to serve snipe, make absolutely certain that your Guns or your game dealer can guarantee you sufficient birds.

Snipe are still a rare enough treat these days that one can afford to be thoroughly selfish and not share them with anyone. Because of their tiny size and delicate flavour they are best cooked simply and enjoyed over a kitchen supper and a good bottle of wine. Equally, if you can get enough from a game-dealer, you can make a very pretty presentation for a dinner party.

Snipe (like woodcock) are best when they have rested a week or two from their long migration, and again at the first frost. They are usually hung from 5-8 days and because they are often cooked undrawn they should not be allowed to become too high. Check there isn't an unpleasant smell around the beak. To prepare the bird for cooking, pluck the birds and wipe them outside with a damp cloth, but do not draw. Twist the legs and squeeze them close into the body. Skin the neck and the head and pass the long beak through the legs and body instead of a skewer.

Snipe do not need more than 10-12 minutes for roasting, and it is usually advisable to lard them (either with bacon or a bard of back pork fat or simply butter and foil) to prevent them from drying out. In the Mediterranean countries you are quite likely to find them wrapped in vine leaves for protection against dehydration. When the birds are ready the entrails or 'trail' are removed, and mixed with salt, pepper, wine or brandy or even lemon juice or cream according to taste and spread on toast or served as a sauce. If the birds are cooked on a spit pieces of bread or toast can be put underneath to catch the rich juices which the French call *'les honneurs'*.

Salmis of Snipe recipes abound (the basis is the same as for other game birds), but I have not included any, as I feel snipe are best left whole, as they are so tiny. The exception is an old English recipe for Snipe Pudding and for game pie, both of which require taking the flesh off the bone.

Roast Snipe

Simplest is best!
Serves 4

4 snipe
butter
4 slices streaky bacon, cut in half

4 slices toast, crusts trimmed off
salt and pepper

Brush each bird over with warm butter, cover each breast with half length of streaky bacon and place in a moderate oven (180C/350F/Gas Mark 4), with a slice of toast under each to catch the drippings from the trail. Baste frequently with butter and cook for 10-15 minutes depending on whether you like them well done or not. Allow one bird per person. Serve on the toast and garnish with watercress. Accompany with good rich gravy.

Snipe with Cream and Cider

I often use cider; I like it for its softness. Here is a recipe in which it works very well with snipe.
Serves 2

4 snipe
4 rindless rashers smoked bacon
2oz/50g butter
a bit of flour
4 tablespoons double cream

¼pt/150ml medium-sweet cider
1 tablespoon freshly chopped fennel or dill
1 tablespoon chopped fresh parsley
salt and pepper
4 slices toast, trimmed

Smear each bird with butter, sprinkle with salt and pepper, and wrap with a rasher of bacon. Lightly butter each slice of toast, place a bird on it, then place on a tray in the oven (220C/425F/Gas Mark 7). Cook for 20 minutes basting frequently. Place on a serving dish and keep warm. Remove any excess fat from the pan, add cider, bring to the boil and simmer for a few minutes. Add cream and herbs and bring to the boil again. Simmer for a few minutes, adjust seasoning, then pour 1 tablespoon over each bird. Serve the rest separately in a sauce boat.

Kirsten's Creamy Snipe

This is a lovely light supper dish from Denmark. It is brilliantly easy to make, with a scrummy sauce and is a sure way of keeping the little birds succulent. You could serve it with some brown rice, but I like it best simply with some hot French bread and a fresh green salad.
Serves 2

4 whole snipe, with gizzard trimmed off
margarine

single cream
salt and pepper

In a heavy saucepan brown a good dollop of margarine. Then brown your snipe in it. Add a generous measure of single cream and simmer slowly for 10 minutes. Remove snipe, season sauce. Arrange the birds on toast on a dish and serve with sauce poured over or separately in a sauce boat.

Beccaccini al Nido
Snipe in their nests

This is an old country recipe from Liguria. There they use huge red mushrooms that grow wild in the area, but here we can use the large horse mushrooms that are readily available nowadays in the supermarket.

Serves 4

4 snipe
4 horse mushrooms

olive oil
salt and pepper

Cut the stalks from the mushrooms and place a snipe on the frilled underside of each one. Pour a tablespoon of olive oil over each, sprinkle all over with salt and pepper and put each bird in its nest in a covered casserole. Bake in a low oven (150C/300F/Gas Mark 2) for 20-30 minutes according to taste.

Beccaccini alla Spieda
Snipe on a Spit

If you haven't got a proper roasting spit, then this recipe works equally well over a low barbecue. Just spike a few birds onto a skewer and follow the recipe below.

Serves 6

12 snipe
6oz/175g butter, melted

6 slices toast, crusts trimmed off
salt and freshly ground black pepper

Impale the snipe on a spit (or skewer), brush generously with butter and grill for about 10 minutes about 5 inches above a hot charcoal fire. Remove from the spit, slit open and scoop out the entrails with a spoon, and mash each with a little of the melted butter. Spread some of this mixture on each slice of toast and then cut in half and arrange a snipe on each half. Pour over any remaining melted butter and sprinkle with salt and pepper.

Snipe in Nests
Szalonka

A Hungarian friend reckons this is the 'best possible Hungarian recipe for snipe'. It is also very good looking!

Serves 8

8 snipe, dressed and gutted
4 large potatoes
8 slices smoked bacon

rosemary, oil, salt, pepper
1 bunch parsley

Clean the snipe very carefully, sprinkle with salt and put aside for 30 minutes. Wash the potatoes thoroughly, wipe dry and cut in half lengthwise. Remove the middle of each half, making a hollow big enough for a snipe to fit into. Sprinkle the potato 'nest' with a little salt. Place 1 or 2 sprigs of parsley inside each snipe, roll each up in a slice of bacon and place in the potato halves. Sprinkle with freshly ground pepper.

Arrange in a deep, greased baking tray or flameproof dish. Cover with foil and bake for 20 minutes in a pre-heated oven at 200C/400F/Gas Mark 6. Remove the foil, sprinkle with finely chopped fresh rosemary and continue to bake until golden brown.

Serve hot with steamed red cabbage, mixed pickles, pickled fruit (plums or sour cherries) or with a fresh mixed salad.

Forester's Snipe
Waldschnepfen Forsterin Art

I love the way the Germans and Austrians cook game and this recipe from southern Germany is hard to beat – and hard to get wrong! Sour cream/crème frâiche/mild yoghurt go brilliantly well with game, and you will find them widely used in game recipes in Germany, Austria, Switzerland and Scandinavia. This is a fine example.

Serves 4

8 snipe
pinches of thyme, salt and pepper
4 thin slices streaky bacon
3 dessertspoons butter
6fl oz/180ml red wine
8 dessertspoons crème frâiche *or sour cream or yoghurt*

For the sauce
2 dessertspoons butter
4oz/100g mushrooms, washed and sliced
1 dessertspoon parsley
2 dessertspoons game stock

Clean the snipe, removing head and gizzard. Using a small spoon take out the trails, pass through a sieve and keep on one side. Preheat oven to 220C/425F/Gas Mark 7. Sprinkle each snipe with thyme, salt and pepper, and bard with the bacon. Melt the butter in the bottom of the casserole, place the snipe in the casserole and cook for 30 minutes in the oven, basting often. Remove the bacon and put to one side. Add the red wine and *crème frâiche*, put back in the oven and cook for another 15 minutes stirring the sauce now and then.

For the sauce, heat the other 2 dessertspoons of butter in a heavy pan and cook the mushrooms and parsley in it. Take snipe from casserole, put to one side and keep warm. Add the sieved trail to the sauce, and stir, then add the mushrooms and season to taste. Fry 4 slices of bread in 2 more dessertspoons butter till golden. Snip the slices of bacon into tiny bits, lay on the fried bread and arrange snipe on top. Serve the sauce separately.

Snipe in Brandy
Beccaccini al brandy

The Italians love eating little game birds of all sorts and they usually roast or grill them. Sometimes they are served with polenta (in the north), sometimes with rice, sometimes with bread fried in the fat they were cooked in. The use of brandy is popular with such little birds, and I have come across a similar recipe from Corsica as well.

Serves 6

12 snipe
6 tablespoons butter
2 tablespoons chopped onion

¼pt/150ml brandy
salt and freshly ground pepper

Heat the butter in a large frying pan over a high flame till melted, add the onion, stirring for one minute, add snipe and brown all over. Reduce heat and keep turning birds for about 10 minutes. Heat brandy, ignite and pour over the snipe shaking the pan until the flames have subsided. Arrange on a dish, sprinkle with salt and pepper, and pour juices from pan all over.

Hungarian Wood Snipe

No paprika, but definitely evocative of the vast Hungarian marshlands east of the Danube.

Serves 5

10 snipe
10oz/380g approx streaky bacon
1½ teaspoons salt
3½oz/100g approx lard
5oz/150g chicken liver
1oz/25g onion, finely chopped
pinch freshly ground black pepper
pinch marjoram

8fl oz/250ml brandy
5 white rolls
2oz/50g butter
2oz/50g rice
8fl oz/200ml gravy
5fl oz/150ml chicken or grouse stock

Clean the snipe and dry without cutting open, sprinkle with salt and pepper, and cover with thin slices of streaky bacon. Leave the head and neck, but prick out the eyes (if you can!) and pierce the legs with the beak so that the birds retain their shape while cooking. Put the birds in a pan and roast in a medium oven (180C/350F/Gas Mark 4) with some fat. Baste often in their own gravy. When ready (after 10-15 minutes) add a little good stock and a little brandy, remove from the heat and cover. Cut open the birds into halves, remove the gizzards, hearts and livers, cutting up the remaining intestines together with the chicken liver. Then fry all together with the chopped bacon, butter and onion, salt, pepper, marjoram and rest of the brandy. Slice the rolls, fry and spread with this mixture. Place the snipe attractively round a pyramid of rice in the middle of a large serving dish, surround with the fried croûtons spread with the *salmis* and slices of bacon. Boil up the prepared gravy, seasoning to taste, and pour over the snipe.

Snipe Pudding

This can be made ahead and is a very warming dish from great-grandmother's days.

Serves 6

12 snipe
cayenne pepper
lemon juice
1 dessertspoon chopped parsley
pinch nutmeg
¼pt/150ml red wine
¼pt/150ml stock

2 onions
truffles (optional)
4oz/100g chopped mushrooms
½ clove garlic, crushed
pinch dried herbs to taste
suet crust (see below)

Halve the birds and remove the gizzard and the trail (innards). Cut breasts off carcass. Put the trail on one side. Cover carcases with water and boil up with 1 onion and 1 carrot. Chop the onion and sauté in butter till golden, then add the mushrooms, herbs and seasonings, stock and wine, and cook all together for 10 minutes. Add the trail and rub the lot through a sieve or put it in an electric blender. Season the snipe with lemon juice and cayenne. Line an pudding basin with thin suet crust (see below) and put in the birds, with truffles if available. Pour all the sauce in and cover with pastry lid. Steam for 1½ hours.

Suet Crust

3-4oz/100-125g shredded suet
¼ teaspoon salt
½lb/225g plain flour

1 teaspoon baking powder
cold water to mix

Mix the shredded suet with a little flour. Then sift the rest of the flour, salt and baking powder and mix with suet. Using as much water as necessary, mix all to a firm dough and use when necessary.

WOODLAND

GUINEA FOWL

Numida meleagns

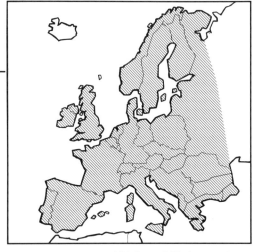

Mainly available from Poulterers

Habitat:	woodland and rough open land
Length:	20 ins (50cm)
Weight:	3lb (1½kg)
Best time for eating:	all year round

French: *la pintade*
German: *das Perlhuhn*
Italian: *la gallina faraona*
Spanish: *la pintada*
Greek: *i fragkokotta*
Portuguese: *a galinha da Guiné*

Serbo-Croat: *morska kokos*
Romanian: *bibilica*
Bularian: *tokáchka*
Russian: *tokáchka*
Czech: *perlicka*
Polish: *ptak dziki*

Dutch: *parelhoen*
Flemish: *parelhoen*
Norwegian: *perlehøiis*
Danish: *perlehöns*
Swedish: *pärlhöns*
Hungarian: *gyöngytyúk*

As their name suggests, guinea fowl are not indigenous gamebirds of Europe, and unlike other introduced species such as the pheasant they have never become established in truly wild populations either in the British Isles or continental Europe. However, their excellence as table birds and the relative simplicity of keeping them rather like farmyard poultry has made them widely popular as a domesticated species. They tend to range widely in search of wild foods, much moreso than domesticated fowl, and this wandering habit frequently leads to guinea fowl taking up a semi-feral life in woodland and among hedgerows at some distance from any farm or house.

Where coverts are stocked with pheasants, and cereal foods are provided at feeding hoppers and on strawed rides, guinea fowl will readily join their distant cousins for communal feeding, and often come to adopt the woods as their permanent home, roosting in the trees alongside the pheasants. Gamekeepers and shoot managers seldom discourage this tendency, since guinea fowl make useful allies because of their alertness and the highly vocal way in which they will announce the presence of any intruders in the vicinity of the woods. Many a poacher has found himself betrayed by the squawking vigilance of guinea fowl, which can kick up a very loud fuss when they detect a stranger. The cost of the pheasant feed they take is a small price to pay for such good lookouts.

Yet this characteristic can be a mixed blessing, and I have often had good cause to curse the birds' noisy alertness when I have been trying to stalk deer, either with a rifle or a camera. Time and again I have sighted deer in woodland or on farmland close to woods and have begun to edge my way closer, only to have the stalk ruined by the sudden caterwauling of guinea fowl. The deer always flee at once, taking the birds' alarm calls as a signal that all is not well, and so the stalk is ruined – and many a time I have been sorely tempted to line up my sights on one of those wretched birds out of sheer frustration!

Frustration can also arise when a keeper of guinea fowl wants to fetch one for the pot. Unless they are cooped up in roofed enclosure, their wandering ways mean they often cannot be readily located, and desperate measures have to be adopted. You either set off with a shotgun in search of one, or, if matters are not that urgent, invite the Guns at the next pheasant shoot to try and bag a guinea fowl for you. And so we have the slightly comic sight of a decidedly exotic, bulky and rather lumbering bird being driven from the woods by the beaters and potted by one of the Guns. And the chances are it will turn out not to be the toothsome and tender young bird that the cook really wants, but a tough and stringy veteran that can only be made palatable by long marinading and slow cooking in a casserole. Guinea fowl are not exactly testing birds for the Guns, but sometimes that may be the only way to cull those that have gone native in the woods.

Guinea fowl are not deemed to be legitimate game in the same category as pheasants, partridges or grouse, but can occasionally be obtained from a gamekeeper or a shoot manager – but be sure you are getting a young bird. Far better to play safe, and buy from someone who keeps a captive flock, or from a poulterer or supermarket, many of which have guineafowl for sale, or will take orders for them.

It is always assumed that the guinea fowl is a native of Africa, but the earliest known fossil guinea fowl is of *Numida meleagris* of the upper Pleistocene Epoch (which began 2½ *million* years ago) of Czechoslovakia, which indicates that it was once a native of Europe. Certainly nowadays they run wild in Africa, whereas they have been very much domesticated in Europe, either farmed for food, or kept as watchdogs over other game birds in woods or in a farmyard. The French name for the guine fowl *pintade* is supposedly derived from the Spanish word *pintada* meaning 'painted', which is suggested by the striking white markings on the blue-grey plumage. And there is a Greek legend which tells how the sisters of the poet Meleager wept for their dead brother until they died of grief so that Artemis changed them into guinea fowl whose plumage bore the trace of the tears they had shed.

Guinea fowl scratch on insects, seeds and tubers, and their flesh tastes somewhere between a chicken and a pheasant, but not as plump as either. You have to be careful when cooking that they don't dry out, which on the whole means that they can be very lightly cooked. Since any guinea fowl you are likely to get now will probably be farmed, there is no question of hanging; in fact you should just treat them rather like a delicate and rather svelte chicken. Once the magnificent plumage is stripped you will find a body verging on the scrawny at times, and weighing somewhere under 2lb (1kg) as opposed to 3lb (1½kg) with the feathers. One bird feeds two people.

Guinea Fowl with Raspberries

This recipe, another unusual combination of berries and game comes from Sweden.
It almost sounds too clever by half, but it is sensational. The tartness wakes up the bland meat
of the guinea fowl.
Serves 2-4

1 guinea fowl
1oz/25g butter
2 twigs of rosemary
6oz/175g fresh or frozen raspberries
1 tablespoon oil
4 tablespoons raspberry vinegar
4 tablespoons double cream

Garnish
2oz/50g raspberries
2 stalks of parsley
laurel leaves

Season the bird, inside and out, and then place half the butter, the rosemary and 2oz/50g of raspberries inside. Heat the rest of the butter with the oil in a flameproof casserole and brown the bird lightly all over. Then add the vinegar and cook the bird for 20 minutes on each side. Remove from the heat and place on a warm serving dish to keep warm. To the juices in the casserole add the cream and seasoning, stirring hard on the bottom of the pan to pick up any residue. Add the remaining raspberries and heat up without stirring. Using a large spoon carefully ladle the sauce onto the serving dish around the bird. Garnish with the final 2oz/50g of raspberries and herbs and serve with a fresh green salad. If available, this is much better made with fresh raspberries.

Guinea Fowl with Raspberries.

Stuffed Guinea Fowl Breasts

This is the recipe with which my brother-in-law, Derek Johns, won the finals of *Masterchef 1993*. His title doesn't do justice to the dish, which is a sublime combination of all the bits of the bird prettily presented in an elegant roll on a bed of *beurre rouge*. It also works with pheasant. It is really worth making the effort to use Vin Santo if possible, though another sweet substitute – sherry or marsala – would do.

Serves 4

2 guinea fowl
2 carrots
4 shallots
2 cloves
4fl oz/125ml Vin Santo
chopped fresh thyme

chopped fresh rosemary
chopped fresh marjoram
1 egg
Salt and freshly ground black pepper
1oz/25g butter

Skin the guinea fowl, and remove both breasts, slicing down the carcase from the breastbone with a sharp knife. Strip the flesh (without any fatty tissue) from the wings, legs and carcase. In a baking dish arrange a base of finely chopped carrot, 4 shallots, 2 garlic cloves, cover this with the chopped wings and legs and meat from the carcase, season with salt and freshly ground pepper, sprinkle all over with $\frac{1}{2}$ wine glass of *Vin Santo* (or, if not available, a sweet Sauternes) and cook in a medium oven (180C/350F/Gas Mark 4) for 15 minutes.

Remove and place this mixture in a food processor. Add fresh thyme, rosemary, marjoram and a pinch of dried oregano to your own taste, one raw egg and mince to a coarse cream. Hold the breast down on the work surface with the left hand, take a sharp knife and slice into the breast horizontally and make a pocket, open up carefully and place between a polythene bag/sheet, beat slowly out until it is almost 5ins (13cm) in diameter, without splitting in half. Mound two tablespoonfuls of stuffing into each breast, roll up and tie neatly together with string. Put back into the same uncleaned baking tray, brush the skins with a little garlic butter, season to taste and place a thin slice of blanched strips of red cabbage or blanched chives as the 'cooked string' across the centre, and sprinkle with 1fl oz of *Vin Santo*. Roast in an oven at 180C/350F/Gas Mark 4 for 20 minutes.

Make a *Beurre Rouge* Sauce. Melt the finely, chopped shallots in a little butter, add $1\frac{1}{2}$ glasses of red wine and any of the stock squeezed from the remaining stuffing by putting under pressure through a fine sieve; reduce the liquid until the chopped shallots are just visible. Take off the heat, and beat in with a whisk small knobs of ice cold butter making certain that you only add the next knob as the former is almost melted away. Continue whisking until after about 3-4oz of butter has been added and you achieve the same thickness to a mayonnaise.

Cut the real string off the panels and either serve whole or cut into a fan, serve with the *Beurre Rouge* and Rösti Celeriac (page 190).

Guinea Fowl Breasts in Coriander and Thyme

Guinea fowl is usually so tender that there shouldn't be problems with it turning into rubber under the grill. Recipes like this are my favourite – quick and easy to make, light and clean to eat.

Serves 4

the breasts of two 2-3lb/1-1½kg guinea fowl
5fl oz/150ml extra virgin olive oil
2 teaspoons freshly chopped coriander
1 medium onion, peeled and chopped
1 clove of garlic, peeled and chopped

the leaves from a bunch of fresh thyme (if not available try mint)
½ teaspoon salt
freshly ground black pepper

Into a large bowl pour the olive oil and add the onion, garlic, herbs and seasoning and mix well. Lay the guinea fowl breasts in this, making sure they are completely submerged. Leave to marinate for 12-24 hours, turning the breasts once. To cook, heat the grill so that it is hot rather than very hot, remove any excess marinade off the breasts and grill for 15-20 minutes, turning till they are done.

Guinea Fowl en Brochette

Using the same marinade as above, remove the breasts from the liquid, wipe off excess marinade and cut into cubes. Skewer these onto wooden skewers, alternating with red and yellow peppers, button mushrooms and squares of bacon and cook under a hot grill or in a hot oven.

Hacienda Guinea Fowl

This recipe comes from Spain and is amazingly rich and delicious. I have added thyme to the original version as it breaks down the richness a bit – and it always reminds me of the interior of Spain with its vast tracts of land and its distant sprawling *haciendas*. In fact this sauce would also go with most of the other game birds with stronger flavoured meat as it contrives to be both soft and strong all at once.

Serves 4-6

2 guinea fowl
2 dessertspoons soft butter
freshly ground salt and mixed black and white peppercorns
1½pt/900mls double cream

4oz/100g raisins
2 tablespoons beef stock
4fl oz/100ml port
1-2 dessertspoons fresh or dried thyme

Rub the guinea fowl all over with the softened butter and sprinkle with salt and pepper. Roast in a medium oven (190C/375F/Gas Mark 5) for 30 minutes, basting during this time. Remove and keep warm. Meanwhile in a saucepan mix half the port, the raisins, the cream, the thyme and salt and pepper to taste. Bring to the boil and reduce the liquid by half. Once the guinea fowl have been cooked and as you set them aside to keep warm drain off the pan juices into the above mixture, together with the rest of the port and bring to the boil again. Add more salt and pepper if necessary and then pour over the birds taking care that the raisins stay uppermost over the dish.

Guinea Fowl with Lemon and Rosemary

This is a very light sauce and best not left to sit too long, but a busy hostess can get away with preparing it in advance and then letting the whole dish warm up (but not cook or boil) again slowly but thoroughly. Everybody loves it!

Serves 6-8

2 guinea fowl
dessertspoon butter
freshly ground salt and mixed black and white
*   peppercorns*
2 teaspoons grated lemon rind
5 sprigs rosemary
half a lemon
2 stalks celery
2 large sprigs parsley

2 cloves garlic
large knob butter
10 tablespoons butter
1 glass dry white wine
2 glasses stock
more salt and pepper
4 egg yolks
juice of 2 lemons
5 or 6 knobs butter

Rub the skins of the guinea fowl with the dessertspoon of butter, sprinkle all over with salt and pepper, the grated lemon rind and the chopped leaves of 2 sprigs of rosemary. Season the inside of the birds with salt and pepper and stuff with the celery, garlic, parsley, quarter of a lemon each, and half the knob of butter. Truss the legs into the breast and secure. Rub the skins of the guinea fowl with the dessertspoon of butter, sprinkle all over with the salt and pepper and grated lemon rind. Melt the 10 tablespoons butter in a flameproof casserole and brown the birds lightly in the fat, turning constantly. Pour in the wine and let it reduce almost completely. Add the stock, cover securely and let it simmer for half an hour. Take out the birds, remove the stuffing and cut into neat quarters. Arrange in shallow ovenproof dish and keep warm but not hot (so they don't continue to cook). Next mix the egg yolks and lemon in a bowl adding a few drops of the cooking liquid. Mix well. Pour the sauce back into the casserole, whisk in the last few knobs of butter, keep the heat very low so that it doesn't curdle. Keep stirring until the sauce has thickened, but not boiled, pour over the birds and garnish with finely chopped parsley sprinkled all over and wedges of lemon.

PHEASANT

Phasianus colchicus, P. torquatus,
P. versicolor

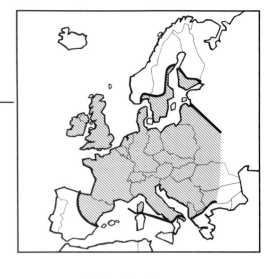

Habitat:	woodlands, hedgerows
Length:	28 ins (70cm)
Weight:	3lb (1.5kg)
Best time for eating:	October-December

French: *la faisan*
German: *der fasan*
Italian: *il fagiano*
Spanish: *el faisan*
Greek: *o fasianos*
Portuguese: *o faisão*

Serbo-croat: *fazan*
Romanian: *fazan*
Bulgarian: *fazán*
Russian: *fazán*
Czech: *bazant*
Polish: *bazant*

Dutch: *fazant*
Flemish: *de fazant*
Norwegian: *en fasan*
Danish: *fasan*
Swedish: *fasan*
Hungarian: *facan*

Legend has it that the first pheasants seen in Europe came back to Greece with Jason and his Argonauts as they returned from their quest for the Golden Fleece in eastern Asia. The pheasant's Latin name recalls the region of the Phasis river and Colchis in what is now the Republic of Georgia.

The first pheasants were undoubtedly kept by the Greeks and Romans as domestic poultry, confined within pens and cages as a handy source of meat, and of eggs too. The spread of the species across western and northern Europe is usually attributed to the influence of the colonising Romans, with their wealthier officials taking pheasants along with them as culinary treats to the remoter provinces of the Roman empire. Mosaics from Roman times clearly indicate that pheasants were known in Gaul and Britain.

Today the pheasant occupies a prominence in the game shooting world that earlier generations could not have imagined. Throughout Europe it is admired for its splendidly dramatic appearance (especially the mature cock bird), for its excellence as a sporting quarry, and for its qualities of flavour and texture. In Great Britain pheasants constitute around 85% of all game shot each year, and more than 16 million pheasants are reared and released each summer to augment the wild stocks, which could not otherwise withstand the pressures of organised shooting.

A glance along the rows of pheasants on a shoot game cart or in a game dealer's larder will reveal the variety of plumage coloration to be found among wild and feral pheasants. The hen birds are rather sombre and uniform in colour, their chief variations ranging from a pale creamy-buff to a rich brown speckling somewhat reminiscent of a red grouse. Occasional albino individuals also occur. But the cock birds are altogether more colourful and varied. The iridescent dark green feathering of the head is universal, and extends down the neck in the case of the 'black-necked' or 'Old English' strains, which exhibit the plumage typical of the wild pheasants of the *colchicus* race of western Asia. Others have a bright white ring or collar, which refers them to the 'ring-necked' or *torquatus* species whose natural range is in eastern Asia.

The feathers of the cock pheasant's back and flanks are typically a rich reddish-bronze, but very light individuals also occur, often with pale-coloured primary wing feathers, the so-called Bohemian pheasant. At the other end of the spectrum are the very dark birds, usually lacking any trace of a white collar, and with a predominantly blackish and dark iridescent green hue. These are often referred to as the melanistic mutant strain, but many of this type also display clear signs of Japanese ancestry, from the Green Pheasant of the islands of eastern Asia. But these are only hints of the original strains which have gone to make up the thoroughly hybridised and crossbred stock which has been promoted by modern game farming methods.

Like all Europe's gallinaceous (i.e. hen-like) gamebirds, the pheasant has rather short, rounded wings, capable of sudden bursts of quick acceleration into fast flight, rather than steadily sustained flight over long distances. This in turn is a function of their massive breast muscles, which are the powerhouse that propels a relatively heavy, rounded bird into a fast, rocketing flight. Good shoot management will flush the birds towards the Guns so as to present fast and testing shots as the birds reach maximum height and speed. Those large breast muscles are of course the main source of flesh on the carcase of a pheasant. Wings and thighs are well fleshed too, as with all gallinaceous birds, but the breast meat remains the primary object of the cook's attention and the diner's pleasure.

Since the mid-1980s the price paid by commercial game dealers for shot pheasants has been remarkably low, with average prices in 1991-92 in the region of £1.50-£2.50 per brace for fresh birds in the feather. This is an astonishingly low price to pay for 4-5lbs of top quality game, or indeed for any such source of protein, and is far below the very cheapest kinds of fish, red meat or cheese. It therefore constitutes one of the finest food bargains, provided you make sure to buy directly from a gamekeeper or shoot manager. Pheasants sold at this price off the game cart can end up in a poulterer's shop next day with a £7-£8 price tag per bird.

When they cost so little, it is not surprising that many families in game shooting areas eat pheasants regularly during the season, and often well into the spring, thanks to deep-freeze storage. *Toujours faisan!* might now be the lament of a visitor to a British country house or farm in the winter months, were it not for the diversity of recipes which can present pheasant in so many interesting ways.

Pheasants are best eaten before they are fifteen months old, and are generally hung for a week to 10 days to heighten the gamey flavour. Some people like their pheasant really high, when the skin develops a greenish tinge on the stomach, but for more moderate palates, the bird is ready to cook as soon as the tail feathers come away. Prepare pheasant for cooking as you would a chicken, cleaning it inside and out with a damp cloth and reserving the gizzard and giblets for stock.

The pheasant is also just about as versatile as chicken when it comes to recipes, and anything you can do with chicken you can just about do with pheasant. Traditionally it is served roast, however, and the classic accompaniments in Britain for pheasant served this way are game chips, clear gravy, fried breadcrumbs, bread sauce and a garnish of watercress and lemon wedges. All the winter root vegetables make very good accompaniments to pheasant, either served separately or combined in a casserole. Glazed chestnuts, or chestnut purée and any hedgerow fruit jelly make a good complement.

Roast Pheasant

A classic, all too often considered boring. But a good roast pheasant can be really delicious and, with all its bits and pieces, makes a perfect Sunday lunch. Nowadays pheasant is very often 'mucked up', in a disguise, but it can be so good totally unadulterated and just roasted simply.

Serves 4-6

a brace of pheasant	*bunch of parsley*
3oz/75g butter	*1 onion*
4 rashers streaky smoked bacon	*salt and pepper*
2 cloves garlic	

Clean the pheasants well inside and out. Place 1 clove garlic, half an onion and half a bunch of parsley inside each – these will flavour the juices which you drain out of the bird at the end of cooking and use for the gravy. Smear the bodies with butter, sprinkle with salt and pepper, cover each with two rashers of bacon. Place in a baking tray and roast in a pre-heated oven at 400F/200C/Gas Mark 6 for 30 minutes, basting every 10 minutes. Take out of the oven, remove the bacon, baste and return for another 10 minutes or so until they are golden brown. Remove the birds to a warm serving dish, tipping them up and draining the juices out of their stomachs into the roasting pan as you do so. Set aside and keep warm. Deglaze the pan with a good glass of port and game stock, strain into a small saucepan and reduce to make a delicious gravy. Serve with redcurrant tartlets (see page 187), roast potatoes, and Brussels sprout purée.

Pheasant Goujons

This was a family recipe I inherited on my marriage. It is our family's favourite. It can be made just before dinner and left quite safely in a warm oven without drying out. These goujons are also delicious cold and very easy to transport for picnics. My mother-in-law used to serve them with melted butter, but I like to accompany them with sauce tartare, or a tomato coulis (see page 180 and 184). For people who have overdosed on pheasant it is also a good disguise; some can't tell whether they are eating veal, pork or chicken! It is also very economical – one pheasant done as goujons seems to feed twice as many people as it does either roast or casseroled.

Serves 6-8

1 brace of pheasant	*6-8oz/175-225g butter*
3-4 eggs, beaten with salt and pepper	*6-8 tablespoons vegetable oil*
8oz/225g fine white breadcrumbs, toasted in the oven till dry	

Skin the pheasant and cut the meat off the carcase, including legs and thighs, in short strips – not too fat or too thick. Melt the butter and oil together in batches – one ounce (25g) butter to every tablespoon oil. Dip the pheasant goujons into the beaten egg, and dip into a bowl of breadcrumbs till evenly and lightly covered all over. Fry gently in the fats – about a minute or two each side will do so that they don't dry out while you are keeping them warm. Arrange in a wide shallow dish, garnished with lemon wedges and parsley. Serve with Sauce Tartare (page 179) or Tomato Coulis (page 180 and 184).

Wokked Pheasant

Crisp, clean, and quick to make. I adapted this from a Chinese recipe for chicken when I was trying to do something different with pheasant. It is as light as a casserole is filling. Not European, I admit, but stir-fry pheasant is another family favourite.

Serves 4

8oz/225g pheasant breast meat, boned and
  skinned
1/2 teaspoon salt
1 egg white
1 tablespoon cornflour
1 stick celery
1 green pepper

6 balls stem ginger or
4 slices ginger root, peeled
2 spring onions
4 tablespoons light vegetable oil
2 tablespoons soy sauce
1 tablespoon sherry

Slice the pheasant meat into fine slivers, using a very sharp knife. Mix the slivers with first the salt, then the egg white and finally the cornflour – in that order. Cut the celery, green pepper, ginger and spring onions into matchstick-sized slivers the same size as the pheasant. Heat the oil in a wok (or frying pan) and stir-fry the pheasant shreds over a moderate heat until the pieces are lightly coloured. Remove the pheasant with a perforated spoon. Increase the heat, and when the oil is very hot, put in the ginger and spring onions followed by the celery and green pepper. Stir for about 30 seconds, then add the pheasant shreds with the soy sauce and the sherry. Mix all together well and cook for a further 1-1½ minutes, stirring all the time. Serve instantly, very hot.

Barbecued Pheasant

In the summer we barbecue whenever we can. Given a choice, my young sons would rather have barbecued pheasant than anything else – especially in the lemon and herb marinade. I dissect the birds into six – two breasts, two legs, two wings and then leave in the marinade for anything from 3-24 hours. Usually I then cook them in the marinade in a medium oven for half an hour or so and then put straight onto the barbecue and cook, turning, till they are done right through.

Lemon and herb marinade
Into a large bowl pour and mix the following: 1 pint/600ml vegetable oil, juice of two lemons, liberal quantities of salt and pepper, a handful of mixed herbs, 6-8 cloves pressed garlic.

Sweet and spicy marinade
Into a large bowl pour and mix the following: a huge dollop of tomato ketchup, two tablespoons golden syrup, two tablespoons honey, 8 or more cloves pressed garlic, a dash of Worcester sauce, a dash of soy sauce, a dash of Tabasco, two dessertspoons soft dark brown sugar, ½-1pt/300-600ml vegetable oil, depending on the quantity being marinaded. Taste and adjust by adding any more of the above. Place the pheasant joints in the marinade and turn, making sure they are all coated. Leave to marinade for about 3 hours, barbecue and serve with hot garlic bread.

Pheasant Sausage

This is another of Matthew Fort's wondrous creations during the time he cooked for us. He actually made it with chicken but I have made it since with pheasant with great success. The secret is not to grind the meat too fine, and not to overcook. It is also excellent cold for picnics, buffets etc.

Serves 6-8

2 pheasant
8-10 slices prosciutto
1 teaspoon vegetable oil
¾lb/350g pork (fillet or pork belly or chops, but
    not too fatty)
1 cup double cream
1 generous handful pistachio nuts (shelled)
salt and freshly ground pepper

For the rich stock
    pheasant carcases, trimmed of all fat
    pork knuckle
    4 chicken drum sticks
    2 large carrots
    1 onion
    1 bouquet garni
    6 peppercorns
    1 stick celery or a teaspoon celery seasoning

Remove all the pheasant meat off the bone and keep to one side. Put the carcases into a large saucepan, with the pork knuckle, chicken bones and vegetables, bring to the boil and simmer for at least one hour – even up to two. Strain and reserve. Next take a large sheet of foil, spread the teaspoon of oil over the centre of it and on top of the oil carefully lay the slices of *prosciutto* side by side. These will form the 'skin' of the sausage so you can have them overlapping slightly to ensure that none of the filling escapes during the cooking. Put all the pheasant meat into a food processor and whizz for a few seconds until the meat is broken down but still chunky (this is to supply texture to the sausage). Remove and put into a bowl. Repeat with the pork, then remove and add to the bowl of pheasant meat. Mix well together with the cream and pistachio nuts and plenty of seasoning. Transfer to the centre of the two of *prosciutto* slices, spreading the mixture from end to end. Then roll the *prosciutto* around and shape the sausage by massaging it to make one big long sausage about 3-4 inches thick. Wrap the foil tightly around the sausage, seal the edges and ends and place on a flat baking tray. Refrigerate until needed – at least 1 hour. When you are ready bake the whole sausage in a pre-heated medium oven (180C/350F/Gas Mark 4) for 40 minutes, turning the package once. Remove the foil – or just open it up – to let the skin crisp up a bit and then turn off the oven, or remove to a cool oven and let it rest, until needed, for at least half an hour. Cut the sausages into slices about ½ inch thick and serve with the stock which you have meanwhile reduced to about half. If you want, you can add a dash (or more) of sherry to the stock before you start reducing. This gives a thin but deep tasting sauce with the sausage. Serve with a hot salad of mixed winter root vegetables. If you make this with chicken you can use the chicken skin to surround the sausage, but pheasant skin often has an acrid taste and it is therefore better to use the *prosciutto*.

Pheasant and Chicory

This is quite different from the normal run of pheasant casseroles – another of Matthew Fort's
creations for us – and is lovely and light.
Serves 8

4 pheasant
8 chicory
1 bottle cider

2oz/50g butter
salt and pepper

Season the inside of the birds with salt and pepper. Brown the pheasants in the butter in a frying pan and
then transfer to a casserole large enough to hold them all. Slice the chicories in half and tuck in, around and
over the pheasants. Pour the bottle of cider over the lot. It should more or less cover everything. If not, add
more cider, or a little water, or even some chicken stock. Bring to the boil on top of the oven and then simmer
gently for 40 minutes. Remove from the heat, and strain off the cooking liquid into a saucepan and then boil
till it is reduced by about three quarters. This should produce a really good taste. Meanwhile, carve the birds,
arrange on a serving dish with the chicories and when the sauce is ready pour over and rejoice!

A variant of this dish is to replace the chicories with white cabbage sliced up very finely. Put some in the
bottom of the casserole and the rest on top of the birds. When the birds are cooked, take them out and keep
them warm, but leave the cabbage in with the liquid while you are reducing it. The cabbage will continue to
cook to a suitable consistency.

Pheasant Breasts with Basil Sauce

This sauce is to die for and combines to make a lovely light main course.
Serves 8

8 pheasant breasts
¹/₂pt/300ml chicken stock
2 dessertspoons English mustard
1 tablespoon chopped fresh basil leaves
2 tablespoons double cream

freshly ground sea salt and black and white
   peppercorns
1oz/25g butter
1oz/25g flour

Beat the pheasant breasts to flatten like veal escalopes, spread with 1 dessertspoon mustard, sprinkle with
salt and pepper and put in a frying pan with half the stock. Cook over a gentle heat till just cooked through
lightly. Remove from the pan, arrange in a shallow ovenproof dish and keep warm. Melt the butter, add the
flour, then add the pan juices and the rest of the stock bit by bit stirring constantly to avoid lumps forming and
bring to the boil. Add the other dessertspoon of mustard (or more according to taste), basil and cream and
simmer till well amalgamated. Pour over the pheasant and garnish with a few fresh basil leaves.

Insalata di Fagiano

This really is a different way of having pheasant – clean light and fresh. I adapted it from a recipe of Matthew Fort's for capons and find it invaluable as a starter. The seasonings in the marinade can of course be varied according to taste and for a lighter taste altogether you could substitute the olive oil for vegetable oil. This will keep several days in a tightly sealed jar and therefore also comes into the 'useful' as well as 'yummy' category.
Serves 4-8, depending on whether it is a first course or main course.

2 pheasant (about 4lb)
1 whole onion, peeled
1 celery stalk
1 scraped large carrot
5 sprigs parsley
coarse grained salt

Marinade
3-4 cups olive oil
juice of 1 lemon

2 tablespoons red wine vinegar
3 whole cloves
2 whole bay leaves
3 tablespoons pine kernels
3 tablespoons raisins
freshly ground sea salt and mixed black and
*   white peppercorns*
1 tablespoon granulated sugar
large pinch hot red pepper flakes or crushed
*   chillies*

Clean the pheasant well and put into a saucepan with the onion, carrot, celery and parsley. Cover with water, bring to the boil and add the coarse grained salt. Simmer for 40 minutes, and then remove the pheasants, placing each on a separate plate to cool. Leave them to stand until completely cold. Then remove each breast whole and carefully cut into thick strips. Place these in a large china or glass bowl. Remove any meat off the legs carefully, shaping these into nice strips which will blend in with the breast meat. Add to the bowl. Pour the oil into a small bowl, and add the squeezed lemon juice. Next add the vinegar, cloves, bay leaves, pine nuts and raisins and season with plenty of salt and pepper to taste. Mix all the ingredients together, add the sugar and hot red pepper flakes, mix again and pour all over the pheasant strips. Mix everything very well together ensuring that every bit of meat is well coated, then either cover or transfer to a spring-lid tightly sealed jar and refrigerate for at least 12 hours before serving. When needed, remove the jar from the fridge and let it stand until it reaches room temperature. Discard the bay leaves and serve on a nest of bitter mixed salad on individual plates.

Roast Pheasant with Braised Celeriac

A different sort of wintery accompaniment to the classic roast pheasant.
Serves 4-6

2 pheasant
freshly ground sea salt and black and white
*   peppercorns*
4oz/100g melted butter
1 large celeriac, peeled and cut into matchsticks

juice of ½ lemon
2oz/50g butter
1 or 2 2oz/50g tins anchovy fillets to taste
chopped parsley to garnish

Brush the trussed pheasants with melted butter and sprinkle with salt and pepper and place in a roasting tin. Roast in a moderate oven (350F/180C/Gas Mark 5) for 45 minutes to one hour, basting occasionally with the butter. Meanwhile blanch the celeriac for 4 minutes in boiling salted water with lemon juice. Drain well and dry. Remove the pheasant from the oven, quarter and keep warm in a shallow ovenproof dish. Add the celeriac sticks to the roasting butter with the extra butter. Mix well with the pan juices. Add the anchovies with their oil. Cover with foil and cook gently on top of the stove until the celeriac has softened, remove and arrange in a ring around the pheasant. Sprinkle with parsley and serve.

Faisan en Filets au Jus d'Orange et Coriande

This is another very clean, fresh way of doing pheasant.
Serves 4

1 large pheasant
1 large bunch fresh coriander
1 large orange
2oz/50g butter
1 tablespoon mixed dried herbs

¹/₄pt/150ml dry white wine
¹/₂pt/300ml veal or chicken stock
salt and freshly ground black pepper

Wash the orange and using a zester use the entire skin to make very fine long *juliennes*. Place them in a small saucepan of water, and boil for a couple of minutes. Strain and rinse immediately under cold water. Set to one side. Take all the meat off the pheasant and cut into neat thin strips. Melt the butter in a heavy-bottomed pan and toss the pheasant till it is lightly cooked – only a matter of minutes. Remove from the fat and keep to one side. Meanwhile chop the coriander very finely, reserving some leaves for decoration. Put the carcase into a saucepan with the wine and stock and salt and pepper and boil till the liquid is reduced by half. Strain and pour into another clean pan. Remove any grease on top by soaking it up with kitchen paper and then add the pheasant. Stir in the orange juice and bring to just below boiling point. Transfer to a serving dish, sprinkle with the chopped coriander, decorate with spare coriander leaves and orange *juliennes,* and serve.

Little Hot Mousses of Pheasant in a Leek Case

This starter always brings gasps. I have made it with salmon as well as pheasant, and also chicken and sole. Guinea fowl, sea trout and trout would also do well.
Serves 8

2 pheasant breasts (about 5oz/150g)
2 clean leeks
1 teaspoon butter
1 egg, plus 1 yolk
7fl oz/200ml milk

¹/₄pt/150ml double cream
salt and freshly ground pepper
4 sprigs chervil (optional)
1 teaspoon butter

Take 8 ramekins and grease with butter. Set to one side to keep cool. Boil a large pan of salted water. Trim the tops of the leeks, peel away any tough outer layers and trim off the root. Separate the leaves, slicing any fat ones lengthways to make ribbons about ¹/₂ inch/1cm wide. Plunge into the boiling water and blanch for one minute. Remove from the pan with a slotted spoon and plunge the leek ribbons immediately into iced cold water, then drain and dry with kitchen paper. Take the ramekins and line them with the leek ribbons, laying four or five across each other to form a star and leaving the ends hanging over the edge of the ramekins. Make sure that you have used green as well as white in each arrangement as this will give the overall effect at the end. Cover each ramekin with clingwrap and refrigerate. This can be done half a day ahead. Dice the pheasant breasts and place in a food processor with the chervil, egg and egg yok, milk and a good teaspoon of salt and generous sprinkling of white pepper. Whizz till you achieve a fine purée and add the cream. Adjust seasoning if necessary. Spoon the mixture into the ramekins, fold the overhanging edges of the leeks over to enclose the mousse and place the ramekins in a *bain marie* reaching two thirds of the way up the ramekin dishes. Place in a pre-heated moderate oven (170C/350F/Gas Mark 3) and cook for 20-25 minutes. Gently press with your finger tip to check that they are cooked and then turn out onto individual plates. Carefully pour some hot Lemon Cream Butter Sauce (page 176) or Tomato Butter (page 178) round the base of each mousse and garnish the top of each with chervil leaves.

Braised Pheasant with Sauerkraut

We normally associate *sauerkraut* with Austria and Germany, but it is also very popular in the Netherlands, and this is a typically Dutch dish – though you will find similar versions in both Germany and Austria too.

Serves 4

5oz/150g smoked streaky bacon, diced
one pheasant cut into portions (about 2lb/1kg)
freshly ground sea salt and black and white
    peppercorns
¼pt/150ml white wine

a few juniper berries
1½lb/675g sauerkraut
mashed potato made from 2lb/1kg potatoes
a little cornflour

Melt a little butter in a flame-proof casserole and fry the diced bacon for 5-10 minutes until cooked through, then remove bacon from the casserole. Sprinkle the pheasant portions with salt and pepper and turn in the bacon fat till golden all over. Add the wine, bacon, juniper berries, and cover all evenly with the *sauerkraut*. Braise for about 1½ hours in a medium oven (180C/350F/Gas Mark 5). Arrange the *sauerkraut* in the middle of a pre-heated serving dish, arrange the pheasant on top. Pipe the mashed potato (made from potatoes, milk, salt, pepper and a pinch of nutmeg) around the *sauerkraut*. Thicken the pan juices with a little cornflour and pour over the pheasant.

Sauerkraut

Very popular in Germany, and called *choucroûte* in French, *sauerkraut* is a form of fermented cabbage which has been used for centuries as a way of preserving cabbage – important in the long snow-bound winters of northern Europe before the days of canning and freezing. Traditionally it has been the classic accompaniment to boiled ham or bacon, game, sausages and knuckle of pork, as its sourness offsets the richness of these foods. You can buy it ready made nowadays, but it is also easy to make at home. To do so you must use a solid white cabbage. Cut the cabbage into quarters and then shred into wafer-thin strips. Take a large jar and layer the cabbage alternately with salt and coriander (optional). Cover with muslin, then a large plate and a heavy weight and leave to ferment for 4-6 weeks turning every few days.

Pheasant with Boursin and Apricots

The Swedes use the lovely golden cloudberries *(Hjortron)* which grow almost exclusively there as accompaniment with game. These are almost impossible to find here, so this recipe takes its tanginess and colour from the apricots instead.

Serves 4-6

2 pheasant
freshly ground sea salt and black and white
    peppercorns
1oz/25g butter
1 tablespoon olive oil
50 pine kernels

8oz/225g Boursin *cheese*
8oz/225g dried apricots, finely cut
4 slices bacon
4 tablespoons stock (see page 00)
watercress or parsley to garnish

Sprinkle the birds inside and out with salt and pepper to taste. Heat the butter and oil in flameproof casserole and brown all over for about 10 minutes. Remove from the casserole and allow to cool slightly. Next place the pine kernels in the casserole and brown slightly (they turn very quickly). Remove with a slotted spoon and put one third to the side. Mix the remaining two thirds of the kernels with the Boursin and apricots and fill the birds. Wrap two bacon slices, rind removed, around each bird and tie with string. Bake covered for 45-50 minutes in a moderate oven (350F/180C/Gas Mark 5). Skim all the fat from the casserole and pour in the stock with the pan juices and boil rapidly for 5-10 minutes till reduced a bit. Pour all over the birds and serve, covered with remaining pinenuts, garnished with watercress or parsley.

Pheasant Brochettes

A really easy, no-work recipe, the sort of thing I love to do for supper parties so that I can get everything ready beforehand and not abandon my guests for the kitchen all evening.

Serves 6

6 skinless pheasant breasts
18 thin rashers smoked bacon
36 small mushrooms

Soy sauce
1/2pt/300ml coconut milk
1 tablespoon bottled chilli and ginger sauce

Cut each pheasant breast into 9 pieces. Stretch each rasher of bacon slightly with the side of a knife blade and cut into half. Using thin metal or bamboo skewers thread on a piece of pheasant, then a mushroom wrapped in bacon and continue until each stick holds 3 pieces of chicken and 2 mushrooms. Drizzle a little Soy sauce onto each brochette and turn the grill to high. Grill the brochettes for about 5 minutes each side or until the bacon is crisp and sizzling. Meanwhile make the sauce by putting the coconut milk and chilli and ginger sauce into a small saucepan. Bring to the boil and simmer for 5 minutes. Serve 3 brochettes per person on warm plates which you have previously flooded with some of the hot sauce. If you are using wooden skewers wet them thoroughly in cold water before threading the meat on. This prevents them burning under the heat. A simpler alternative is to thread the diced pheasant breasts with whatever variations take your fancy (bacon, mushrooms, peppers, onions, etc) and simply marinate for half an hour or so in the lemon and herb mixture used for Barbecued Pheasant (see page 83). Grill as above, or bake briefly on a rack in a very hot oven.

Casseroled Pheasant

Faisan en barbouille

If you're not quite sure of the provenance (or age) of your pheasants, this recipe is guaranteed to do a grand cover-up job.

Serves 6

1-1 1/2lb/450-675g cooked chestnuts (fresh or
*   tinned)*
2 pheasants
2 tablespoons butter
2 tablespoons vegetable oil
2 tablespoons Armagnac or Cognac
4 carrots, peeled and diced
2 onions, peeled and finely chopped
3 tablespoons flour
a pinch of dried thyme

2 bay leaves
bouquet garni
2 cloves garlic, crushed
1 teaspoon salt
freshly ground white and black peppercorns
1pt/300ml red wine
12 small boiling onions
18 mushrooms
2 thick slices fat salt pork, diced

Prepare the chestnuts by dropping into a pan of cold water, bringing it to the boil and quickly removing the nuts and peeling off the outer and inner skins. If they start to cool and the skins are difficult to take off, drop back into the water to warm up and start again. Alternatively use tinned chestnuts! Quarter the pheasant, reserving the rib cages for game stock. Sauté these sections in the butter and oil in a large flameproof casserole until lightly browned. Pour the Armagnac over them and set alight. When the flame dies down, remove the pheasant from the pan. Into the remaining fat in the pan, add the carrots and onions and sauté until browned. Stir in the flour and cook a minute. Add the thyme and bouquet garni, garlic, salt and pepper, then pour in the wine and stir until the sauce thickens. Add the onions and return the pheasant to the casserole. Cover and simmer for about 40 minutes, then add the mushrooms (with stems cut off), and the cooked chestnuts, and the sautéed diced salt pork. Simmer for a further 30 minutes, or until the pheasant is tender. Thicken the sauce if desired with some *beurre manié* (equal quantities of butter and flour – a teaspoon flour mixed with a teaspoon butter, for example, dropped into the sauce and stirred till amalgamated). Adjust seasoning to taste, then serve on a platter with boiled potatoes.

Curried Pheasant Tartlets

This was a recipe for chicken that I have adapted for pheasant, adding mango and taking away the walnuts. But that is just a matter of taste. You could equally well use a mixture of meat from any cold game birds and this will still be ideal for buffets, or lunch *al fresco*.

Makes 8

12oz/350g shortcrust pastry (see page 187)
1¹/₂lb/800g cooked pheasant or other game bird
  meat, cut into fine   strips
¹/₂pt/300ml mayonnaise
4 teaspoons curry powder
4 teaspoons mango chutney, the mango chopped
  small

4 tablespoons lemon juice
freshly ground sea salt and mixed black and
  white peppercorns
snipped chives for decoration

I always use Saxby's shortcrust pastry when I'm cooking. You can't beat it, and it does save so much time! However for the purists the recipe is set out on page 187. Roll out the pastry, divide into eight and line 8 loose bottomed tartlet cases. Line with greaseproof and ceramic baking beans. Bake blind for 15 minutes in a moderate oven (350F/180C/Gas Mark 4) and allow to cool. Stir the curry powder, lemon juice and mango chutney into the mayonnaise, fold in the pheasant and season to taste with salt and pepper. Remove the greaseproof paper and baking beans from the cases and fill with the mixture. Sprinkle with snipped chives to garnish.

Winter Pheasant

The sweetness of all the winter root vegetables goes very well with pheasant, and I love this combination. The traditional manner in Czechoslovakia is to purée all the vegetables and serve this as a rich, thick sauce with the bird. I also like to leave the vegetables intact and serve the bird sitting in the midst of them. I have also resorted to the good old British compromise and puréed half the vegetables into a sauce, and served the bird nestling in the middle of the other half. Whichever way you like to do it, it's delicious!

Serves 4

1 pheasant
3 carrots, cut into small sticks
3 parsnip, cut into small sticks
¹/₂lb/225g turnip
1 fat or 2 thin leeks
or any combination of winter root vegetables in
  those quantities

1 dessertspoon plain flour
¹/₂pt/300ml stock
18 juniper berries
5fl oz/160ml sour cream
2oz/50g butter

Fry all the root vegetables together in a heavy frying pan until just turning golden and then arrange in the bottom of a casserole that can also be placed over the heat. Place the pheasant in the middle of the bed of vegetables and sprinkle with salt and pepper. Pour the half pint of stock over the vegetables and cover the casserole tightly with the lid. Cook in a pre-heated moderate oven (180C/350F/Gas Mark 4) for ¹/₂ hour. Remove the bird and keep warm on one side. Add some of the juices from the casserole to 1 dessertspoon flour in a cup, mix together and then stir into the vegetables. Add the juniper berries and sour cream. Cook on top of a low to medium heat for 5-10 minutes until well blended. Sieve or liquidise the vegetables and then serve in a sauceboat with the pheasant. Alternatively joint the pheasant, arrange on a dish and pour sauce over. If you want to thin the sauce down a bit, add some more soured cream. Serve with boiled potatoes, shaped into small cubes, lozenges or 'apple slices' (see page 192) and sprinkle liberally with parsley.
Can also be used for hare and any other game.

Boned Pheasant with Lemon Cream Cheese and Spinach Filling

Boning is not nearly as difficult as most people imagine. It does take a bit of time, but with practice you can get quite speedy. It really is worth trying out – a boned stuffed bird is spectacular, filled with all sorts of tempting stuffings. The varieties are endless – cream cheese and mushrooms or leeks or with pinenuts added; or more conventional 'turkey-type' stuffings – sage and onion, chestnut etc; or fruity stuffings with raisins and apricots and nuts; there is no end. Best of all is that this is an excellent way of eating the bird cold – for light summer lunches or for picnics – as it is so easy to carve. It also freezes very well, and can be eaten hot or cold after it has thawed. Just remember to have a pair of pliers at hand to pull out the most resistent sinews in the legs.

1 bird serves 2-3

1 plump pheasant
4oz/100g cream cheese
6oz/175g cooked spinach leaves
grated rind of half a lemon

1-2 cloves garlic, crushed
freshly ground salt and pepper
1 tablespoons melted butter

Bone the pheasant, using pliers to extract the sinews from the lower thigh. Set the boned bird aside, opened up and breast side down. In a small bowl mix the grated lemon rind, crushed garlic and salt and pepper into a cream cheese. Lay this mixture in the centre of the open bird, covering just out to the breasts. Over this arrange the cooked spinach leaves. Fold the bird back over this mixture which will plump it out to its original size. Pinch the two flaps of skin together and tuck under the bird when you turn it back, breast uppermost, on to its back. The skin will stay together during the cooking without having to be skewered. Rearrange the legs to the correct position, and gently mould the whole bird into its erstwhile shape. Add some salt and pepper to the melted butter and paint over the whole bird. Cook in a medium oven (180C/350F/Gas Mark 4) for 40 minutes, raising the heat to high (230C/450F/Gas Mark 8) to brown off the bird for 5 minutes. Some of the cream cheese might have oozed out from the apertures into the natural juices in the pan, and can be used just like that as a simple and delicious sauce. Serve either hot with the sauce or cold without.

Chaudfroid de faisan à l'éstragon
Chaudfroid of pheasant with tarragon

This is definitely a party dish, good for dinner after the theatre or for a summer lunch. It is very pretty to look at and easy to eat since only the breasts are used. With very small, young pheasants one breast per person is probably manageable, but with larger birds you will probably have to cut the breasts in half on the diagonal (to keep an attractive trapezoid – if you can remember your geometry! – shape). This always looks extremely professional, but is much easier to make than it looks. Don't be daunted. It can score lots of brownie points! Traditionally the chaudfroid sauce is made with a béchamel base, but it can also be made with mayonnaise. Both variations are below.

2 large, tender and plump pheasant
1 large bunch fresh tarragon
salt and freshly ground pepper
1oz/25g butter, melted
2 egg yolks
juice of 1½ lemons

1 teaspoon sugar
½pt/300ml oil
white pepper
1 x 2½oz pkt aspic jelly powder
¾pt/425ml water

Wipe the pheasants inside and out, and brush outside with the melted butter. Sprinkle all over with salt and pepper. Add a sprig or two of tarragon inside keeping 8 small sprigs to garnish each breast with at the end. Roast in a medium oven (280C/350F/Gas Mark 4) for ½-1 hour, depending on size, making sure that the meat is properly cooked but still very moist. Remove and leave to cool. Meanwhile make the mayonnaise and aspic mixture with which you will coat each half breast. To make the mayonnaise, beat the eggs with salt, pepper and sugar, then add the oil drop by drop until the mixture thickens. Once half the oil has been added this way, add the rest in a slow steady trickle. Taste, adjust the seasoning if necessary and set to one side. Make up the aspic jelly following the recipe on page 94 or according to instructions on the packet adding the water. This amount of water will produce a stiffer jelly than normal, so don't worry – it helps to set the mayonnaise. Leave the jelly to one side, reserving 4 tablespoons, and leave to cool. Remove the four breasts from the pheasants, cut diagonally in half, remove the skin and lay out on a board. When the aspic is almost at setting point, fold it carefully into the mayonnaise and then coat each half breast. Place in the fridge and allow to set completely. Remove and arrange a small sprig of blanched and dried tarragon leaves in the centre of each breast. Cover with a coating of the reserved aspic (still not quite set – so make sure it has been kept in a warmish place), replace in the fridge until it is set again. You can, of course, use other garnishes for the decoration under the glaze – delicate slivers of lemon or cucumber or tomato or carrot, or any other fresh herb leaves – coriander, parsley etc. They will all bring murmurs of admiration!

Chaudfroid of Pheasant II

This is the recipe using the more conventional base of a béchamel sauce which you might find sets more easily in warm weather and is less likely to run in the sun if you are eating outside.

2 large, tender and plump pheasant breasts
1 large bunch fresh tarragon
salt and freshly ground pepper
1oz/25g butter, melted

Chaudfroid sauce
1¼oz/35g flour
1¼oz/35g butter
3/4/45ml milk
1 small onion, peeled

1 bouquet garni
½ celery stalk, chopped
pinch mace
pinch white pepper
pinch salt
1 small carrot, chopped
¼/10g gelatine powder ((or 1 rounded teaspoon)
2pt/200ml aspic (see below)
2 tablespoons double cream
salt and pepper to taste

Wipe the pheasants inside and out, brush the outside with the melted butter and sprinkle all over with salt and pepper. Add a sprig or two of tarragon inside, keeping 8 small sprigs to garnish each breast with at the end. Roast in a medium oven (180C/350F/Gas Mark 4) for ¾-1 hour depending on the size of the birds and making sure that the meat is properly cooked but still very moist. Remove and leave to cook. Meanwhile make the béchamel. First flavour the milk by putting it in a saucepan together with the onion, bouquet garni, celery stalk, mace, white pepper, salt and carrot, bringing just to the boil and then setting to one side to steep and cool. When it is completely cool, sieve to catch the vegetables and skin. Then in a non-stick pan melt the butter, stir in the flour and slowly mix in the flavoured milk to make a smooth thick white sauce. Leave to cool and then stir in the gelatine dissolved in ¾/100ml aspic (see page 94 for aspic if you aren't using it out of a packet). Adjust the seasoning and then carefully fold in the cream. Set to one side while you remove the breasts from the birds, remove the skin and cut each in half on the diagonal to keep a diamond-like shape. Set on a board and then coat each breast with the chaudfroid sauce just as it is on the point of setting. Chill in the fridge and if necessary add another layer of sauce, but it should really be thick enough for one coat only. When it is completely set arrange the reserved sprigs of tarragon on the centre of each breast and glaze with the rest of the cool aspic. Return to the fridge to set, and if necessary repeat the coating of aspic again to make a good glaze. Let any remaining aspic set in a flat dish, and once it is firm chop it up and use for garnishing each breast or on a large dish.

Aspic Jelly

If you can't cheat with instant packet-made aspic, this is the homemade alternative using gelatine. It will make about 2pts/1200ml.

*1³/₄pts/1 litre good chicken or veal stock (or
    pheasant)
4 tablespoons dry white wine
4 tablespoons sherry*

*2 tablespoons tarragon vinegar
2oz/50g powdered gelatine
2 egg whites, whipped*

First make sure that your stock is *completely* free of any trace of grease or fat. This is very important. Then pour it, with the wine, sherry and vinegar into a very large saucepan so that it is only about a third full (this is because the liquid will rise with the addition of the egg whites). Gently warm up the liquids and when they are hot, sprinkle the gelatine over the surface allowing it to sink and then dissolve. Stir once it looks as though it has vanished to make sure that it is completely dissolved and then add the whipped egg whites and, using a large whisk, whisk anti-clockwise till it comes to the boil. Let the mixture boil till it reaches the top of the pan and then draw to one side to let it subside. Repeat the process twice more (as for consommé). Leave to settle for a few minutes and then strain through muslin or a fine nylon sieve lined with a couple of layers of kitchen paper. Allow to cool and use as directed above.

Pheasant in Cream and Mango Chutney

The sauce for this is really rich, and you just want more and more! It is one of these foolproof recipes which was given to me by a great friend. Not for anyone on a diet, but brilliant for kitchen suppers, and will keep very happily in a warm oven for a good time without spoiling.
Serves 8

*3 pheasant
3oz/75g butter, melted
salt and pepper
1pt/600ml double cream*

*1 teaspoon paprika
4 tablespoons Worcester sauce
4 tablespoons sweet Mango chutney
salt and pepper to taste*

Wipe the pheasant inside and out, brush each with an ounce (25g) melted butter, sprinkle with salt and pepper and roast in a medium oven (180C/350F/Gas Mark 4) for an hour or so until cooked through, but still very moist. Remove and allow to cool. Once cool, take off the bone, cut into pieces or slices, and arrange in a deep ovenproof dish. In a large bowl whip the cream until it is firm and then fold in all the other ingredients. Spoon the mixture over the pheasant and bake in a moderate oven (as above) for about 45 minutes until golden and just bubbling.

Pheasant Croquettes

One of the easiest and best disguises for those bored with pheasant, the sort of food you use children as an excuse for but adults really love too (especially with un-grown-up stuff like ketchup!). The secret of making really good croquettes is to let the mixture get really cold and clammy, and fry without touching each other in smoking hot fat to ensure ultimate crispness.

Serves 6

2oz/50g plain flour
2oz/50g butter
¹/₂pt/300ml milk
12oz/350g leftover cooked pheasant, very finely
  chopped
5-6 mushrooms, finely chopped

1 teaspoon chopped parsley
salt and pepper to taste
1 tablespoon flour
1-2 eggs, beaten
2-3oz/50-75g toasted breadcrumbs

First make the white sauce by melting the butter in a small non-stick saucepan and stirring in the flour. When it is all absorbed add the milk bit by bit, stirring all the time to make a very thick sauce. (If it is too thick add a drop or two more milk). Add the pheasant, mushrooms and parsley to the mixture and season to taste. Allow to go completely cold. Using a dessert spoon, take spoonfuls of the mixture out and roll into balls or lozenge shapes. Dip each into flour, coat liberally with beaten egg and then roll in the breadcrumbs. Leave to stand in the fridge for another half hour or so, then plunge into boiling fat, a few at a time so that they are not touching and can crisp all over. Remove when golden, drain and serve on a large platter, garnished with parsley. They are very good with tomato sauce ('real' or from the bottle!) or Sauce Tartare (page 179) or Sauce Verte (page 181). You can, of course, improvise with any other leftovers in the fridge and add bacon or ham to the mixture, capers, onions, whatever takes your fancy.

Chilled Pheasant Mousse

Another good disguise and a change from all the varieties of pheasant slop that abound. This is good for picnics, buffets, light lunch or supper and can be made either in individual moulds or in one big one.

Serves 8

1 x 2¹/₂oz/65g pkt aspic jelly powder
(if unavailable use gelatine powder)
1pt/600ml stock (chicken or pheasant)
1lb/500g cooked pheasant meat, very finely
  chopped
3fl oz/75ml sherry

pinch cayenne
pinch sugar
2 teaspoons tomato purée
1 clove garlic, crushed
¹/₂pt/300ml double cream
salt and pepper to taste

Following the instructions on the packet, make up the aspic with the stock and then allow to cool till it starts to set. Alternatively, make your own aspic following the recipe on page 94. Mix together with the pheasant meat, sherry, cayenne, sugar, and whizz in a food processor until smooth and fine. Fold in the cream and tomato purée and turn into wet ring mould or soufflé mould (or individual moulds) with a capacity of 2¹/₂ pints or 1¹/₂ litres. Allow to chill until set and then turn out and garnish with watercress. Serve with warm brown bread or toast.

Pâté de Campagne de Faisan

A standby which never lets you down – good for first course for Sunday lunch, or a picnic, or kitchen supper. Serve with something sweet and tart – a Cumberland sauce, or plum sauce, or even dried apricots in vinaigrette.

Serves 8-10

8oz/225g butter
2 onions, very finely chopped
2 garlic cloves, crushed
1½lb/675g pheasant meat, minced
10oz/275g chicken livers, minced
1 dessertspoon redcurrent jelly

1 dessertspoon tomato purée
¼pt/150ml red wine
1 tablespoon mixed dried herbs
¼pt/150ml chicken or pheasant stock
10 rashers streaky bacon
2 bay leaves

First flatten the bacon rashers till they are thin and pliable. Arrange the two bay leaves, upside down, in the centre of a terrine dish and then line the whole terrine with the rashers of bacon, covering the bay leaves. Melt 1 ounce/25g butter in a small frying pan and soften the garlic and onions in it. Melt the rest of the butter and in one large bowl mix all the ingredients together with it, including the garlic and onion. Press into the terrine, cover with foil or with its own tight-fitting lid, place in a bain marie of water half way up the side of the terrine and cook in a medium oven (350F/180C/Gas Mark 4) for 2½ hours. Remove, cover with weights and allow to cool. Serve with any sauce to taste and hot bread or toast.

WINES

PHEASANT

The traditional British way of serving pheasant, and perhaps still the best, is roasted with a full accompaniment of roast potatoes, Brussels sprouts, roast parsnips, bread sauce and fried breadcrumbs, with a nice bottle of claret or Burgundy to hand. Claret is especially suitable for pheasant in almost all forms, and the final choice will probably be dictated by your budget. All but the heaviest Rhone wines are also excellent choices, with Crozes Hermitage and Chateauneuf-du-Pape among my personal favourites. Rich oaky Riojas are also very suitable, and there is a wide choice of appealing eastern European Cabernet Sauvignons, not forgetting their equivalents from California, Chile and South Africa.

When pheasant is served cold, the lighter clarets or a Beaujolais are ideal, and a number of white and rosé wines should also be considered. White Burgundy is excellent, and so are the best white Riojas. Rosés – Tavel, Loire and Alsace – come into their own with cold pheasant too.

WOODPIGEON, TURTLE DOVE & COLLARED DOVE

Columba palumbus, Streptopelia turtur, &
Streptopelia decaocto

Length:	16 ins (40cm)
Weight:	1¼lb (600g)
Open season:	all year round
Best time for eating:	April-October

French: *le pigeon*	Serbo-Croat: *golub*	Dutch: *duif*
German: *die Waldtaube*	Romanian: *porumbel*	Flemish: *de hautduif*
Italian: *il piccione*	Bulgarian: *gálab*	Norwegian: *en due*
Spanish: *el pichón*	Russian: *gálab*	Danish: *due*
Greek: *to peristeri*	Czech: *holub*	Swedish: *duva*
Portuguese: *o pombo*	Polish: *golab*	Hungarian: *galamb*

The soft, plangent cooing of a woodpigeon in the leafy cover of a tree in summer sounds like the very epitome of rural innocence – which only goes to show how appearances can be deceptive! In reality, the woodpigeon is one of Europe's most serious agricultural pests, which annually devours many millions of pounds worth of arable crops. Pigeons are gluttonous feeders, whose high metabolic rate requires them to eat at least one-fifth their own body weight in vegetable matter each day, and more in cold weather. Their crops can contain prodigious quantities of food, and will easily accommodate 30-40 whole acorns.

But happily for sportsmen, diners and cooks, the woodpigeon is also a very desirable sporting bird, testing for the Guns and with delicious flesh. Woodpigeon shooting therefore combines essential crop protection and pest control with excellent sport and the prospect of excellent eating. Every country in Europe can produce fine recipes for preparing and enjoying this ubiquitous bird.

In temperate areas of Europe woodpigeons are fairly sedentary in their habits, forming sizeable flocks in autumn and winter, and moving about only as far as is necessary to locate suitable feeding. Except when there is thick snow cover, woodpigeons usually have no difficulty in finding fields of winter greens such as oilseed rape and kale. But in other parts of Europe woodpigeons are birds of passage, migrating long distances with the changing seasons. In south-western France, for example, there are massive annual passages of migrant *palombes* through the high passes of the Pyrenees as the birds move northwards in spring to Scandinavia and north-west Russia, and south again to Spain in the autumn. The shooting of migrant woodpigeons is an annual tradition there, attended by excitement and ritual every bit the equal of the Twelfth of August on British grouse moors.

The turtle dove is a smaller bird than the woodpigeon, and it is a common bird of southern and eastern Europe, and of the lands around the Mediterranean. It occasionally forms large flocks, and large migrations take place in certain areas, where seasonal shooting takes place, similar to that of the woodpigeon in the Pyrenees.

The little collared dove is a recent arrival in most of western Europe and the British Isles, having been unknown west of Turkey and the Balkans up to the 1920s. It was not introduced by man, but came as the result of natural dispersal and by migrants wandering far off course in adverse weather. What had been a rare or unknown bird soon became a frequent sight and eventually commonplace and numerous, as the birds found and exploited a vacant niche in the western European bird world. Initial protection soon gave way to partial shooting seasons and finally to year-round pest status as these greedy little doves demonstrated their destructive effect on crops and seeds. The first British breeding was confirmed in the 1950s, and by the early 1970s the British resident breeding population was estimated at around 40,000 breeding pairs. And if the soft coo-ing of a woodpigeon sounds deceptively soothing, the plaintive bleating call of the collared dove, incessantly repeated, is often supremely irritating.

Pigeon has been considered a delicacy since the Romans. In fact, the Romans thought so well of them that they built tall towers called *columbaria* to encourage them to nest near civilisation. This custom spread across Europe where many great houses had dovecotes where they would breed literally hundreds of the birds. The wild bird is a very canny creature, shying away from any movement from miles away; what enviable eyesight! Pigeon aren't strictly game birds so there is no particular season for them. They are shot all year round, especially by angry farmers to whose crops they do a fantastic amount of damage. They are now available in larger supermarkets and make excellent eating – with a rich sweetish flavour. I love them. The young birds are tender and mouthwateringly good, but an old pigeon can be tougher than almost anything else old.

Pigeons don't need to be hung, though you should empty the crop as soon as possible. They are excellent roasted if they are young, but if you're not sure casserole slowly for a long time! Many people don't bother with the whole bird, just using a sharp knife to cut off the breast. It does save plucking if you don't mind just pulling all the skin off and using the breasts alone. You can use the carcase for game stock.

Pigeons with Peas.

Devilled Pigeon Halves in Breadcrumbs
Panierte Wildtauben

This is one my favourite ways of doing pigeon. You could actually use the same recipe for most
of the other game birds (and indeed I have done it with partridge), but I like it best for pigeon as
it makes a change from the variations on salmis and stews that people normally do. It is also so
lightly cooked it doesn't get tough.

Serves 2

2 pigeons, split in half lengthways
freshly ground salt and pepper
hot, strong mustard
pinch cayenne pepper
3 tablespoons seasoned flour
1 large egg, lightly beaten
4 tablespoons fine white breadcrumbs,
*   previously baked*

2 tablespoons very finely chopped parsley
2 tablespoons very finely chopped lean smoked
*   ham or bacon*
2 cloves garlic, crushed
melted butter

Sprinkle each pigeon half with freshly ground salt and pepper, and cayenne pepper, and then spread
liberally with mustard. Mix breadcrumbs, parsley, chopped ham and crushed garlic well together. Toss each
half in the plain flour, dip into the beaten egg and turn in the breadcrumb mixture. Place on a non-stick baking
tray and bake in a medium oven for 5 minutes. Remove, then very gently pour melted butter over each half,
making sure each is covered with butter but not drowned in it! Replace in oven and cook for another 15
minutes till golden and crispy. Serve with creamed spinach or salad.

p.s. I generally allow more than two halves per person – the men usually come back for at least a third half.

Salmis of Pigeon Breasts

For many people it is only the breasts of the pigeon that are worth bothering about. Lazy eaters
don't have to fiddle about picking the meat off the bones, and presentation is also easy. If you
aren't sure of the age of the birds, then marinate them overnight first to tenderise the meat and
use the marinade in the sauce. The marinade for Grilled Pigeons (see page 104) is very good
used in this way, otherwise use the simpler marinade below.

Serves 2

2 pigeons
bones of any other roast or raw birds
4fl oz/120ml port
1pt/600ml game or chicken stock
1 onion finely chopped
1 tablespoon flour

2oz/50g mushrooms, sliced
parsley
fresh or dried thyme
12 peppercorns
freshly ground salt and pepper

First bard the pigeons with streaky bacon and bake in a moderate oven till firm, but very soft to the touch
and pink inside (about 20 minutes). Remove, cool and when cold remove the breasts. Keep these to one side
till needed. Melt the butter in a heavy pan and add the onion and mushrooms, cooking till softened. To this
add the bones, parsley, thyme, peppercorns and cook, with the lid on, for about 20 minutes. Next dredge the
flour all over, add the port, stock and boil gently for ½ hour, skimming the surface every now and then.
Remove the bones and strain, rubbing the softened vegetables through a fine sieve.

Now take the pigeon breasts, lay in a shallow ovenproof dish, cover in the sauce and bake in a moderate
oven for 10-15 minutes till they are properly warmed through. Garnish with croûton triangles, button
mushrooms and sprinkle with chopped parsley.

Easy Potted Pigeon

A wonderful standby for busy times like Christmas when the house is full and time scarce, or quieter times when you only want to cook once and then live off the proceeds for a day or two! This can be made well in advance and will keep well in the fridge. You can serve it as a starter or as a main course with other cold game, meats or sausages.

Serves 8

4 pigeons
8oz/225g butter
1 tablespoon juniper berries
2 medium onions, finely chopped

$1/2$ teaspoon grated nutmeg
4 tablespoons port
8 slices smoked streaky bacon
salt and pepper

Crush the juniper berries and add half the butter, softened. Mix well together and add the onions and nutmeg and salt and pepper. Spoon in equal quantities into the inside of each bird. Sprinkle each bird with salt and pepper, turn upside down and fit, tightly packed, into a heavy casserole with tight fitting lid. Add the port, and cover the birds over with the strips of bacon. Seal tightly with a lid and cook in a warm oven (150C/300F/Gas Mark 2) for $1/2$-$1\frac{3}{4}$ hours. Remove from the oven and tip all the pan juices into a small basin. Drain the juice from the inside of each bird into this basin before removing the breasts (without the skin). Reserve to one side and line a bowl or earthen-ware dish with the bacon. Cut the meat into small pieces and press into the dish. Remove the layer of fat off the cooled juice, reheat to let any residue fat mix back into the liquid, season to taste, and pour the liquid over the meat. Allow to cool. Melt the rest of the butter, pour over the cooled meat and refrigerate. Serve with hot brown toast and port.

Pigeons with Peas
Pigeons aux Petits Pois

This is best made with young birds. If you aren't sure of the age, marinade the birds beforehand to tenderise the meat, using a simple marinade of white wine, oil and some finely chopped onion.

Serves 2

2 pigeons
2 tablespoons butter
5-8 shallots or small onions
1 slice belly of pork
4 slices streaky bacon for bards
1 glass chicken or game stock
1lb/450g fresh or frozen petits pois

2 lettuce hearts or 2 small Cos lettuce
freshly ground salt and pepper
2 thick slices smoked bacon, diced
beurre manié, made with 2 tablespoons butter
    and 2 teaspoons flour
1-2 teaspoons caster sugar to taste

Melt the butter in a heavy pan and in it brown the onions and diced smoked bacon. Remove and put to one side. Bard the pigeons with the streaky bacon and lightly brown all over in the pan. Remove and place into an ovenproof casserole. If using frozen peas, put into a pan of boiling water, wait till the water comes to the boil again and drain immediately. Add to the casserole together with the shredded lettuce, and bacon and onions, neatly surrounding the bird. Sprinkle with sugar, and add the beurre manié, dropped in equal knobs around the bird. Pour over the stock, or if preferred the equivalent amount of marinade if used. Cover tightly with a lid to prevent evaporation of the juices while cooking, and cook slowly for $1/2$-$3/4$ hour or until tender.

Braised Pigeon with Oranges and Raisins

Like marinade for the grilled pigeons (on page 104) this makes a lovely rich casserole and all the hard work has been done by the marinade the night before. It's the sort of cooking I like as it works in well into a busy schedule with the minimum of fuss.

Serves 3

3 pigeons
4oz/100g mushrooms
1 large onion, finely chopped
1 tablespoon flour
1 teaspoon mixed dried herbs
3 slices thick smoked bacon, diced
1 tablespoon butter

Marinade
12fl oz/360ml vintage port
12fl oz/360ml red wine
4fl oz/120ml vegetable oil (like sunflower)
1 generous handful raisins
15 strips orange zest, the full length of the orange
Juice of 1½ oranges

Mix the ingredients for the marinade in a bowl and place the pigeons in it, breast side down, so that they are almost completely submerged. Leave in a fridge or cool place for at least 24 hours, even up to 2 or 3 days. Multiply the quantities in the marinade according to the number of birds used.

Cut each pigeon in half, drain and lightly fry in the butter melted in a heavy bottomed pan. Remove and set aside. Next fry the diced bacon, sliced mushrooms and chopped onion all together till softened, then dredge with the flour and herbs till well mixed. Add half to the bottom of a casserole. Transfer the birds and arrange on top. Cover with the rest of the vegetables and pour the marinade over all. Put on the lid firmly and cook in a moderate oven for 1-2 hours or until tender.

Stewed Pigeon

Unlike squab, or tame pigeon, woodpigeons can be tough little demons. On the whole they require long slow cooking and this is an excellent recipe for just that.

Serves 2

2 tablespoons butter
2 pigeon
2 slices back pork fat
salt and pepper
6oz/175g bacon or ham
a handful of black olives, preferably stoned

8-10 shallots/2 medium-large onions, finely chopped
a dozen mushrooms, sliced
thyme leaves, fresh or dried
2 teaspoons cornflour
4fl oz/120ml red wine
2fl oz/60ml stock

Season the pigeons inside with salt and pepper, and cover with a bard of back pork fat securely tied with string. Melt the butter in a heavy pan and brown the birds all over. Remove and place in an ovenproof casserole. Blanch the diced bacon and stoned olives in boiling water, drain and toss with the rest of the ingredients in the butter used for the pigeons until golden. Remove from the pan and arrange around the birds in the casserole. Sprinkle all over liberally with ground salt and pepper. Mix the cornflour slowly with the wine and the stock and pour all over the contents of the casserole. Simmer over a moderate heat for an hour or cook in a moderate oven for an hour.

Pigeon Breast in Cabbage

Wildtaubenbrüstchen in Kohl

The Germans use cabbage far more than we do as an integral part of their cooking and this is
yet another example of its flexibility as a vegetable. The other bonus of this recipe is that any
doubts as to the age – and therefore toughness – of the pigeons can be assuaged as the whole lot
gets minced up and tenderised.

Serves 10

8 pigeons
1 medium sized hard white cabbage
6oz/175g pork
freshly ground sea salt and white and black
  peppercorns
½ teaspoon of mustard

¼pt/150ml armagnac
1 tablespoon melted butter
½pt/300ml stock made from the carcase
4oz/100g finely chopped mushrooms
4oz/100g butter
For the Stock: *1 onion, 1 carrot, 1 stick celery*

Remove breasts from the carcase and boil up carcase (with onion, celery, carrot) to make stock. Remove the
skin from the breasts and put them into a food processor with the pork, salt, pepper, mustard and Armagnac.
Whizz till finely minced. Separate the leaves of the cabbage and cut in half removing the thick part of the
central vein. Blanch for an instant in boiling unsalted water, remove and rinse in cold water. Lay each half
leaf out, fill with the minced meat and wrap into neat parcels. Turn these quickly in a heavy bottomed pan in
the melted butter, arrange in a shallow ovenproof dish, and bake in a hot oven (400F/220C/Gas Mark 7) for
10 minutes. Remove and keep warm. Strain the stock and cook up again with the finely chopped mushrooms
for 10 minutes. Take off and whizz in a liquidiser with the 4oz/100g of cold butter. Cut each parcel in half in
the dish, rearrange to look pretty, and pour the sauce over them all. Serve with simple boiled potatoes.

Pigeon a l'Espagnole

This is very easy to make and brings back every memory of the tastes of the Mediterranean and
Spain in particular. The chilli pepper gives it just that extra pep, but if chillis are not easily
available it may be worth investing in a bottle of Provençal oil – olive oil steeped with southern
herbs and chillis. I use it whenever I can, in all sorts of things – and it saves going off for a
chilli whenever the recipe calls for one.

Serves 2

5 tablespoons olive oil
4 cloves garlic
parsley thyme, oregano (marjoram), dried if not
  available fresh
10 black olives (not bitter)
2 bay leaves
½ chilli pepper (if not available, use Provençal
  oil)

2 pigeon
salt and freshly ground black and white
  peppercorns, mixed
2 tablespoons vinegar
½pt/300ml chicken or game stock

Heat the oil in a flameproof casserole, then gently cook the chopped herbs and garlic, the stoned olives and
the whole bay leaves and pepper. Season the inside of the pigeons and brown them all over in the casserole
without burning. Remove the chilli, pour over the vinegar and stock, season, cover and simmer gently for up
to 2 hours or until tender. Remove the bay leaf. Cut the pigeons in half and serve them on a mound of well-
seasoned rice drenched with the juice from the casserole.

Grandmother's Pigeon and Prune Casserole

My mother and mother-in-law both share a passion for prunes. Prunes, therefore, are *de rigeur*
on the breakfast table every morning when they come to stay. And when they leave there are
always plenty left over since we don't touch them at breakfast! I concocted this dish after one of
their Christmas visits, and it is dedicated to both of them. It is a lovely rich casserole and the
prunes combine well with the rich dark meat of the pigeon.

Serves 2

2 woodpigeon
4 thickish slices of smoked bacon
1 medium onion, finely chopped
2oz/50g butter
1¹/₄pt/750ml prune juice (which the prunes were
   stewed in)
¹/₄pt/150ml red wine

¹/₄pt/150ml chicken or game stock
20 prunes (stewed, but not to the point of being
   mushy)
beurre manié *made from 2 dessertspoons*
   softened butter and 2 dessertspoons plain
   flour, well mixed with freshly ground salt and
   pepper

In a heavy frying pan melt the butter and gently fry the bacon, snipped into small pieces, with the finely
chopped onion till both are soft. Remove from pan and place in the bottom of a casserole. Sprinkle the
pigeons all over with freshly ground salt and pepper and brown in the remaining light layer of butter left in the
pan, turning over on all sides. Remove and place in the casserole. Surround with the 20 prunes. Add the three
different liquids and then drop the *beurre manié* in small blobs in the liquid around the birds. Put the casserole
in a hot oven (450F/200C/Gas Mark 7) for ten minutes until the juices bubble. Then lower the temperature to
a medium oven (350F/180C/Gas Mark 4) and cook gently for at least an hour. It can actually be left safely for
up to 2 hours. Serve with baked potatoes or noodles, red cabbage and green salad.

Pigeons in Wine

This bitter-sweet Greek combination of tomatoes and olives goes well with the strong dark
flesh of the pigeon – and makes a nice change from the variety of 'brown' sauces that
usually accompany them.

Serves 4

4 pigeon
salt and pepper
4oz/100g butter
¹/₂pt/300ml dry white wine

4 medium sized ripe tomatoes, peeled and
   chopped
8oz/225g green olives

Clean and sear the birds, smear with butter, sprinkle with salt and pepper, and roast in a moderate oven
(180C/350F/Gas Mark 4) in a flame-proof casserole until golden brown (about 20-25 minutes). Remove to the
top of the cooker over a medium to high flame, add the wine and when it has almost evaporated add the
tomatoes. Cover and cook over a very low heat until the birds are tender and the sauce is thick. Boil the olives
for five minutes and add to the pigeons 15 minutes before they are done.

Grilled Pigeon

This is a no-work, instant results recipe – the result of a hectic timetable. The marinade is dark and rich and any expense involved is compensated for by lack of time (and therefore money!) involved in the cooking. That's what I tell my husband, anyway, as I rush off with the best port! Twenty four hours marinading, five minutes grilling – and a pretty plateful of pigeons for dinner.

Serves 2

2 pigeon
1 orange
watercress
freshly ground salt and mixed white and black
* peppercorns*
1 dessertspoon soft butter per bird

Marinade
8fl oz/240ml vintage port
8fl oz/240ml red wine
4fl oz/120ml light vegetable oil (like sunflower)
1 generous handful raisins
10 strips orange zest, the full length of the
* orange*
juice of 1 orange

Mix the ingredients for the marinade in a bowl and place the pigeons in it, breast side down, so that they are almost completely submerged. Leave in a fridge or cool place for at least 24 hours. Multiply the quantities for the marinade according to the number of birds used. Remove from the marinade at least half an hour before cooking to give time to make the marinade into a sauce. To do this, pour the marinade into a saucepan and boil fast for 5-10 minutes to reduce. Season to taste with plenty of salt and pepper and keep warm in a sauceboat until the birds are ready. Next, smear the birds liberally with a dessertspoon each of soft butter, grind sea salt and peppercorns all over, and pop under a hot grill for 5-10 minutes. If there isn't space under your grill to cook them whole, split them in half and grill, turning both sides. Arrange on a dish with orange slices and watercress and serve promptly with the sauce. This marinade also makes a good base for braising (see Braised Pigeon with Oranges and Raisins page 101).

Warm Salad of Pigeon

This is another light summer recipe, suitable for any type of game bird, and takes no time at all.

Serves 2

a few leaves of iceberg lettuce, torn up
a few leaves of endive, cut across but not finely
a chunk of cucumber, peeled, slit down the centre
* and then cut thinly to form D-shaped slices*
a few spikes of chives, snipped finely
chopped parsley
1 pigeon

2oz/50g ready-to-use apricots, sliced
2 dessertspoons butter
1 dessertspoon sunflower oil
2 slices smoked bacon, diced
French dressing (see page 184)
salt and pepper

Take 1 dessertspoonful of softened butter and smear it all over the pigeon. Sprinkle the bird with salt and pepper, wrap in foil and bake in a moderate oven for 30 minutes till firm but still pink inside. Leave to one side to cool completely. When cold, remove the breasts and cut into medium sized chunks or thin slices, according to taste. Mix the lettuce, endive, cucumber and sliced apricots and arrange on individual plates. Melt the other dessertspoon of butter with the oil in a heavy-bottomed frying pan, raise the heat and then very quickly toss the diced bacon and pigeon breasts till warmed right through, but still pink. Remove from the heat and arrange immediately over the salad. Immediately, and while still hot, pour the French dressing all over and sprinkle with snipped chives and parsley. Serve instantly.

Pigeons Bonne Femme

This is absolutely delicious, but make sure your pigeons are young or you can ruin the melting vegetable concoction by having to struggle with unforgiving meat.

Serves 2

2 woodpigeon
2 tablespoons butter
4oz/100g smoked bacon, finely chopped
1 carrot, sliced very finely
1 stalk celery, cut into matchsticks
1 clove of garlic
1 bay leaf
pinch of thyme
2 bards (pork fat or 4 slices bacon)
4 tablespoons brandy
2fl oz/60ml white wine

2fl oz/60ml game or chicken stock
salt and pepper
2 tablespoons butter
4oz/100g unsmoked bacon, diced
8-10 button onions
8-10 button mushrooms
2fl oz/60ml game or chicken stock
pinch of sugar
pepper
finely chopped parsley

Wipe the pigeons inside and out and cut in half, trimming away backbone from each half to use for stock. Melt the 2 tablespoons butter in a large flameproof casserole and cook the bacon and vegetable matchsticks, the bay leaf and thyme till they are soft and golden. Place the pigeon halves in the casserole, let them warm up gently, turning all the time, pour the brandy on top of them and then set it alight. When the flames have died down add the wine, bring to the boil and let it bubble till it is reduced to almost nothing. Add the 2fl oz/60ml stock, season with salt and pepper, cover with a tight-fitting lid and let it simmer on top very gently for half an hour.

Meanwhile blanch the unsmoked bacon quickly in boiling water, rinse with cold water and drain immediately. Melt 2 tablespoons butter in a frying pan and fry the bacon, mushrooms and onions till they are golden. Add the extra 2fl oz/60ml of stock and simmer for 10 minutes. Arrange the mixture on a fireproof dish, take the pigeon halves from the casserole and arrange on top. Pour the juice from the casserole over it all and then flash under a grill to brown off. Sprinkle all over with chopped parsley before serving.

Salad of Pigeon Breasts, Apricots and Almonds

This makes a light, fresh change from the more wintery and traditional ways of cooking pigeons in casseroles. It also avoids the rubberiness that pigeons tend towards.

Serves 4

4 pigeon breasts
1 bunch watercress
1 bunch rocket lettuce
a few yellow curly wisps of chicory

4 fresh apricots (if not available substitute with
 plums)
a handful of toasted almonds
French dressing

Follow as for warm salad of pigeon (page 104).

Rich Pigeon Pâté

If you have pigeons that you are worried may be on the tough side, this is the answer – rich,
slightly sweet, and melts in the mouth. Perfect for a first course or salad lunch.
Serves 8-10, depending on whether it is first course or main course.

breast of 6 pigeons
1 largish onion, finely chopped
2oz/50g smoked bacon, finely snipped
6oz/175g lard
6oz/175g butter
¹/₄pt/150ml brandy
2 teaspoons mixed herbs
2 cloves garlic
12 juniper berries, crushed
1 dessertspoon redcurrant (or other wild fruit) jelly
2 teaspoons hot English mustard powder with a drop of water to make a paste
freshly ground sea salt and mixed black and white peppercorns to taste
6-8oz/175-225ml melted butter

Skin the pigeon breasts and dice into small cubes. Melt the butter and lard in a heavy-bottomed pan and
lightly fry the bacon and onion till they are golden. Remove from the pan and reserve in a bowl. Sauté the
diced breasts in the remaining fat till they are lightly cooked, making sure that they are still pink inside.
Remove from the fat with a slotted spoon and add to the onion and bacon. Don't worry if it looks as though
there is an awful lot of fat over; it all blends in later. Add the herbs, garlic, juniper berries, redcurrant, mustard
and brandy to the pan juices and bubble rapidly for 3-5 minutes. Put half the pigeon mixture with half the
juices into a food processor and whizz until finely ground. Repeat with the other half of the mixture. Add the
salt and pepper to taste, mixing both halves of the pâté together well. Pour into one large earthenware terrine
or individual ramekins, cover with melted clarified butter and leave to set. Cover with cling film and leave in
the fridge, preferably for 2-3 days before eating, to allow the flavour to mature. Eat at room temperature with
brown toast.

Pigeon Pie

Simple, traditional and warming. The breasts only are best for this, so cut them off first and use
the carcases for stock.

Serves 6

12 pigeon breasts, cubed
1oz/25g butter
2 tablespoons oil
½lb/225g stewing steak, cubed
4 large onions, finely chopped
6oz/175g mushrooms, sliced
4oz/100g bacon, diced
1 tablespoon flour
¾pt/450ml red wine

4 tablespoons redcurrant jelly
2 cloves garlic, crushed
1 teaspoon dried mixed herbs
freshly ground salt and mixed white and black
   peppercorns
½pt/300ml stock
1lb/450g flaky pastry
1 beaten egg to glaze

Heat the butter and oil in a heavy-bottomed pan, dredge the pigeon and steak with flour and then fry lightly
in the hot fat. Drain and remove to a flameproof casserole. Using the same fat, fry the mushrooms, bacon and
onions all together until they are cooked through and transfer to the casserole. Pour the wine into the frying
pan to collect any residual bits and flavouring left, bring to the boil and then transfer to the saucepan, adding
the stock, jelly, thyme and plenty of seasoning. Bring to the boil, then cover and simmer for about 2 hours
until tender. Turn into a large pie dish with a funnel and enough gravy to cover; keep any extra separately.
Roll out the pastry and cut off a strip wide enough to cover the lip of the pie dish. Dampen the lip with water
and press the strip to it. Brush this with water or milk and then fasten the lid to it, crimping it into place with a
fork. Decorate with leaves, brush with beaten egg to glaze and bake in a hot oven (425F/220C/Gas Mark 7)
for about 30 minutes. Reduce the heat to moderate and cook for a further 20 minutes, protecting the pastry
with a covering of greaseproof paper if it is already brown enough. Serve with the extra gravy in a sauceboat.

WINES

WOODPIGEON (and other doves)

Because woodpigeon and other doves are generally perceived as the quarry of the rough shooter and the
artisan shotgunner, they tend – very unfairly – to be relegated to a more lowly place than 'true' gamebirds like
grouse and pheasants. In fact, pigeon well presented is a dish fit for a banquet, and fully justifies really fine
red wines from Burgundy and Bordeaux. The fuller flavours of Pomerol and Saint Emilion are especially
appropriate.

For less formal occasions, try one of the New World reds, especially the oaky wines from California and
Chile, or one of the tangy Cabernets Sauvignons from Hungary or Bulgaria. Rich Rioja, Dão, Bairrada and
Chianti are also excellent choices, as are some of the delicious red wines from the eastern Pyrenees region.

WOODCOCK

Scolopax rusticola

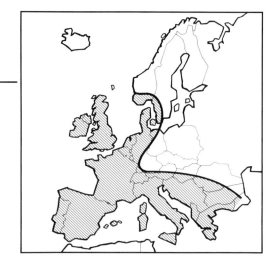

Habitat:	Woods and bogs
Length:	13 ins approx (33cm)
Weight:	11oz (325g)
British open season:	1st October – 31st January
Scottish season:	1st September – 31st January
Best time for eating:	October – December

French: *la bécasse*
German: *die Schnepfe*
Italian: *la beccaccia*
Spanish: *la chocha*
Greek: *i bekatsa*
Portuguese: *a galinhda*

Serbo-croat: *sljuka*
Romanian: *sitar*
Bulgarian: *górski bekás*
Russian: *górski bekás*
Czech: *sluka*
Dutch: *korheon*

Flemish: *de hautsnip*
Norwegian: *en rugde*
Danish: *sneppe*
Swedish: *morkulla*
Hungarian: *erdei szalonka*

The woodcock is highly regarded by sportsmen and cooks, artists and naturalists, and is interesting and unusual in many ways. It is unlikely to be mistaken for any other bird, and looks rather like a giant reddish snipe. It is in fact classed by ornithologists as 'a webless-footed woodland wader', and at some stage in its evolution this bird which feeds by probing in mud and soft ooze became adapted to a life in woodland and low shrubby cover, where it roosts silently and solitarily by day, flying out at dusk to feed through the night on open pastures, where it probes with its long and powerful bill for earthworms, invertebrates and insect larvae of many kinds.

When flushed from cover by beaters or dogs on a shooting day, a woodcock will spring into powerful flight, propelled by its muscular thighs and its broad wings. When plucked, it reveals large breast muscles and chunky thighs, and both yield some of the most delicate and subtly flavoured of all gamebird meats. Woodcock flesh is pale and dense in texture, and always delightfully tender and toothsome.

I have never heard anyone make any distinction of flavour or texture between young and old birds, although it is just possible to tell young birds (i.e. birds of the year) apart from birds aged 1 year-plus by inspection of the tips of their primary feathers and the markings on the primary covert feathers. Young birds tend to have ragged or broken primary feather tips and there is a broadish band of reddish-brown colour at the point of the covert feather, compared with the crisp and smooth "butter-knife" outline of the older bird's primary tips, and a much narrower sandy-buff margin on the coverts.

Because woodcock in the autumn and winter shooting season feed almost exclusively by night, and since their diet is of soft yet protein-rich food items, their gut contents do not require the long maceration and digestion processes which are necessary with the vegetarian grouse or the acorn-eating pigeon. Almost every woodcock flushed and shot on a normal shooting day will not have eaten anything for at least 3-4 hours, and perhaps longer. The bird's digestive tract will therefore be almost empty – hence the tradition whereby woodcock (and snipe) are not eviscerated before cooking. This practice, which may at first seem oddly repellent, is in fact a practical recognition of the birds' feeding habits, for an empty gut harbours no nasty materials which might taint the cooked dish. On the contrary, the 'trail' (i.e. entrails) of woodcock and snipe are deemed to make an important contribution to the essential flavour of the birds, and are therefore left intact. As the bird cooks, perhaps on a slice of bread, toast or a *croûton*, the trail melts and forms part of the rich juices which drip down from the cooking carcase, to form a delicately flavoured gravy to enjoy with the bird when it is served.

Another physical feature – the woodcock's bill – is also frequently taken into account when the bird is cooked and served. Most poultry and game has head and legs removed before cooking, but woodcock are often prepared with the head left intact, sometimes plucked and sometimes not. That long and sturdy bill, almost three inches long, can be doubled back and skewered through the woodcock's body, and this aspect of woodcock (and snipe) cookery is especially prominent in recipes from mainland Europe, particularly France. The retention of the head is also essential in recipes which present the whole bird to diners expecting to indulge in that special delicacy, the woodcock's brains. Like the proverbial brains of peacocks and the tongues of larks, this delicate tit-bit has a special appeal for the ardent gourmet.

Woodcock are seldom found in large numbers on a shooting day, except in certain especially favoured corners of Europe where the wintering migrant birds occur in high densities. A typical December covert shooting day in Britain, for example, may yield a bag of 200 pheasants and only two or three woodcock. So woodcock must either be enjoyed as they come, in ones or twos, or stored until eight or more are available for a dinner party. Unless you buy this number all in one go from the game dealer, the deep freeze is the only alternative. Woodcock destined for storage in a deep freeze should be frozen in the feather and without gutting, and it is then a simple matter to remove the birds the night before they are required, to thaw and be prepared.

Many people prize woodcock above all other game for its very distinctive flavour; others abhor it for the same reason. Some gun dogs, too, are averse to the smell and will refuse to retrieve a woodcock when they are quite happy to pick up other game birds. If you aren't sure about your guests' tastes, it may be easier to 'lose' any spare woodcock you may have in a steaming game pie than to serve them simply roasted in the traditional manner when their flavour is shown off at its best or worst depending on your taste! If you are an *afficionado*, this is the best way to eat them (and, indeed, most game) – simply roasted and served with their own juices and trails.

Woodcock, like snipe, are best when they have rested a couple of weeks after their long migrations. Pick ones with plump, firm flesh. They are generally hung from 5-8 days depending on how high you like your game, and traditionally cooked undrawn but with the gizzard removed. When the bird is cooked at heat, the entrail – or 'trail' – liquifies and is considered a great treat (by some) spread on toast on which the bird is then served. But if there are more squeamish friends or family amongst you, you can perfectly easily gut them like any other game bird and maybe replace the thrills of the trail with an interesting stuffing. Although snipe and woodcock each have their own special flavours, the recipes for either can usually be interchanged if you want more variations.

Roast Woodcock

Because they are the perfect size for an individual portion, woodcock roast simply look
stunning arranged in ranks on a big platter trussed in the traditional manner.
Serves 10

10 woodcock, trussed and without gizzard
butter
salt and pepper

10 slices streaky bacon, cut in half
¹/₄pt/125ml red wine or stock or water (or a
combination!)

Rub roasting pan with butter, and rub the back of each bird with butter. Sprinkle with salt and pepper, and
cover each breast with half a length of bacon. Place in a medium oven (180C/350F/Gas Mark 4) and cook for
20 minutes. Remove bacon and keep to one side for decorating the serving dish, baste the birds well and cook
uncovered for another 10 minutes – more if you prefer them better done. Add wine and/or stock to the pan
juices, bring to the boil on top for a thin gravy to be served separately.

Woodcock with Wine
Bekatsa me krassi

This is a brilliantly easy recipe if you're in a rush which most of us seem to be. No prior frying
– just throw it all in and hey presto! The generous amounts of olive oil and butter are what
make it more 'Mediterranean' than a similar English version of the recipe.
Serves 6

6 woodcock
1 large onion
4oz/100g butter
1 tablespoon olive oil

¹/₄pt/150ml water
4fl oz/120ml red wine
salt and pepper

Clean and truss the birds and put them in a deep ovenproof casserole. Add the finely chopped onion, butter,
olive oil, water and red wine. Season to taste and cover. Cook in a moderate oven and baste frequently for an
hour or until tender. Garnish with parsley and serve with brown rice.

Quail may be cooked in the same way but try wrapping each bird in a strip of streaky bacon to prevent
drying out.

Jellied Woodcock, Chicken and Ham

When there are leftovers of game at home, I like – if I've got time – to incorporate them into a jelly rather than make a pâté. I think it's a better way of highlighting the individual tastes which so often get lost in a pâté once they are mixed up with liver, or pork belly, or minced veal or whatever. The Germans like to add lots of blanched vegetables to their cold game jellies, but again I prefer the consistency of sticking to a combination of meats with green herbs chopped in for freshness as well as decoration. This recipe evolved out of one leftover woodcock I once had, and I now use it for summer lunches and suppers, made up of any left over game fowl.

Serves 6

1 cooked woodcock
4oz/100g chicken breast, flaked or cut into neat
  bits
4oz/100g cooked smoked ham, cut into neat
  chunks
1¾pt/1litre game stock
2 egg whites and 1 shell

bunch fresh coriander or chervil depending on
  availability
bunch fresh parsley
2 level tablespoons powdered gelatine
6 level tablespoons cheapest sweet sherry
  (cream)
1-2 teaspoons salt

Take whole breasts and meat from legs off the woodcock. Add the carcase to 1¾pt/1 litre stock (any combination of chicken, chicken and pheasant, pheasant and partridge, cooked with onion and carrot, will do). I always keep some stock in reserve in the deep freeze for this sort of occasion. Bring to boil and simmer for ½-1 hour. Take off the heat and strain. Set aside and cool. Now clarify as for consommé. Whisk egg whites to a light froth and add, with the one shell, to the cooled stock, plus 2 tablespoons sherry, in a saucepan. Put on heat and stirring all the time bring to the boil until the egg whites rise to the surface, forming a crust and collecting all the insoluble particles en route. Take off the heat and let the crust subside. Put back on heat, bring to the boil once more and set aside. Take a large sieve, line it with 2 sheets of kitchen paper, and strain the consommé through. You should be left with a clear amber liquid. Now add the other four tablespoons of sherry. Pour 8 tablespoons of this liquid into a small pan, bring to the boil, set to one side and sprinkle the gelatine over it. Once it has sunk to the bottom and completely dissolved, stir and then add to the rest of the liquid, stirring to ensure that it is evenly mixed. Now take a mould – oblong or ring – and pour in the first thin layer of consommé. Put in fridge and let it almost set. Take out and arrange coriander (or chervil) leaves at pretty distances. Pour over another thin layer of consommé and let almost set in the fridge. Take out and arrange the woodcock breasts, cut across in slices, in a pretty pattern, cover with another layer of consommé, return to the fridge and let almost set. Repeat this with a layer of chicken, and finish with a layer of ham. Add more chopped parsley and/or other herbs according to inclination throughout the layers. Return to fridge to set completely. Serve with salad and French bread.

Woodcock and Bean Salad

I love pulses, and I think they make a very good counter-balance to game, either hot or cold. This is, in fact, cold – the result of some left-over chick peas and haricot beans once, but it would work very well as a warm salad, and equally well with a mixture of any other left over game.

Serves 4

2 woodcock
4oz/100g haricot beans
4oz/100g chick peas
2oz/50g baby broad beans

2oz/50g French beans
4 spring onions
French dressing

Soak the chick peas and haricot beans overnight, and then cook in salted water for 1-1¼ hours till they are '*al dente*'. Liberally smear the woodcock with butter, sprinkle generously with salt and pepper and roast for 25 minutes so they are *just* cooked through. When cool, remove the breasts and any meat from the legs, and dice into small neat cubes, keeping the skin on to add extra taste to the salad. Blanch the baby broad beans in salted water and blanch the French beans in salted water. Drain and cool off immediately after taking them off the boil by holding under running cold water. This keeps the fresh green colour – very necessary with the pulses. Snip the French beans into small bits and mix the green vegetables in with the pulses and diced woodcock. Snip the spring onions into the mixture and toss generously in French dressing.

For pulse salads I make my French dressing in a different way to normal (see page 179) without any sugar which I don't think combines well in flavour in this case.

Salmis of Woodcock

The strength of the mustard in this variation on a salmis counter-balances the very strong and individual flavour of the woodcock extremely well.

Serves 4

4 woodcock and livers and giblets from the
*   inside of the birds*
4 tablespoons dry white wine
4 tablespoons rich beef or game stock
2 lemons
freshly ground sea salt, black peppercorns, and
*   nutmeg*

1-2 tablespoons dry mustard
3oz/75g mushrooms, finely sliced
1 tablespoon butter
1 tablespoon flour
2 tablespoons finely chopped parsley

Roast woodcock slightly (about 10-15 minutes) in a moderate oven until half cooked, and cut into halves. Be sure to have a dish underneath as you cut it to catch the juices and livers and giblets from the insides of the birds. Boil up the rib sections left over from the half birds quickly in the stock you are using to give extra flavour. Arrange the woodcock halves in a shallow ovenproof dish. Next crush the livers and giblets in with the juices you have caught and add to them the dry white wine, stock, and juice of 2 lemons. Stir in the finely-grated peel of 1 lemon and season to taste with salt, pepper, nutmeg and mustard. Add the sautéed sliced mushrooms (and juices) and bring to the boil. Add the *beurre manié* made of butter and flour and stir till properly amalgamated. Pour this mixture over the birds, and heat through again in a moderate oven for another 10-15 minutes. Sprinkle with finely chopped parsley and serve.

Woodcock Casseroled with Cream
Beccaccia in casseruola alla crema

This was a recipe I first came across in Italy, but it seems a fairly universal way of doing woodcock and there are variations across Europe. It is a classic.

Serves 6

6 woodcock, trussed
6 tablespoons butter
¼pt/150ml cognac

½pt/300ml double or sour cream
salt and freshly ground black pepper

Heat the butter in a flameproof heavy casserole over fairly high heat and brown the woodcock on all sides. Reduce the heat slightly and turn the birds in the hot butter for about 12 minutes. Heat the brandy, ignite and pour over the birds. Shake the casserole until the flames subside. Remove the birds to a serving dish and keep warm. Add the cream to the casserole, bubble for 3 to 4 minutes to reduce, correct the seasoning and spoon a little of this sauce over the birds.

Woodcock in Wine and Tomatoes
Bekatses krasates

In the winter months, after the tourists have gone, local Greeks love to go out with their guns after woodcock and quail. In Corfu, where we have a house, there are lots of recipes for both. This is one of them and it is a lovely easy way of cooking woodcock and a particularly succulent way of dealing with any that might have been discovered after the 'best by' date in your freezer.

Serves 4

4 woodcock and livers
4oz/100g butter
1 onion, finely chopped
1 heaped teaspoon flour
¼pt/150ml dry white wine

3 medium sized tomatoes, peeled and chopped
1 carrot, sliced
1 celery stalk, finely sliced
salt and pepper
2 cloves garlic

Clean and sear the birds. Keep aside the liver. Heat half the butter in a saucepan and lightly brown the birds. Add the onion, salt, pepper, carrot, celery and livers (chopped). Cook for a few minutes. Sprinkle with the flour, then add the wine and tomatoes. Cover and cook in a moderate oven until the birds are tender (about 1 hour). Remove onto a dish and keep warm. Rub the sauce through a sieve, or liquidise, heat and pour over birds.

Woodcock with Oysters

Sheer sybaritic indulgence here, from my co-author, Colin McKelvie, author of two books about woodcock, who is irreconcilably opposed to the very idea of *cuisine minceur*! Oddly for such a rich dish, this combination was originally a European favourite in Lent, since woodcock were believed to feed "by suction" i.e. by sucking nourishment from the mud — and therefore did not count as flesh at times of fasting. (Barnacle geese were also deemed to be edible in Lent, since medieval man thought they grew from barnacle shellfish!).

*One woodcock per person, trailed inside, heads
   on and unplucked, trussed and skewered with
   the bird's bill*
8 oysters per portion
2 anchovy fillets per portion
1 crouton per portion
1 lemon, sliced

grated nutmeg
olive oil
breadcrumbs
3 eggs, beaten
pepper
salt
brandy or armagnac

Stuff each undrawn woodcock with 4 oysters, 2 finely minced anchovy fillets, nutmeg, pepper and salt, with a dash of lemon juice. Roast for about 20 minutes in a medium hot oven, then place each bird on a crouton fried in olive oil. Mix the woodcock juices from the roasting tin with a dash of brandy or armagnac, melt in 3 ounces of butter, and pour over each bird. Remaining 4 oysters per bird can *either* be served cold, in shells to surround the birds on the plate, *or* can be dipped in beaten eggs, covered with breadcrumbs and fried quickly. Serve with a chunky slice of lemon on each dish. (A good Burgundy or Cotes-du-Rhone is almost compulsory with this dish!).

If the idea of undrawn birds strikes you as repellent, you can always clean them out if preferred, although the oyster and entrail sauce will not be as rich or flavoursome. Likewise, heads may be removd, but this will not suit the purist who regards the brains as the finest mouthful of all. You will also lose the useful and traditional skewer bill.

WINES
WOODCOCK

With its white flesh, fine texture and delicate flavour, woodcock can be enjoyed with both white and red wines, provided these are selected with care and do not overwhelm the special qualities of this bird. It is surprising how often woodcock is served with a wine that is too assertively rich. Anyone preferring a white wine should consider some of the Alsace options. Gewurztraminer may be just a little too tangy and spicy, but the gentler kabinetts and ausleses can be very suitable.

Among the red wines, a light claret is excellent, and for real authenticity, why not serve a bottle of Chateau le Becasse. Tanner's of Shrewsbury also have a pleasant and aptly named Becasse Rouge, a quaffable red wine from the eastern Pyrenees. A personal choice would also be a Chateau Puygeraud, a stylish claret from the Cotes de Francs, an underrated sector of Bordeaux.

DEER & BOAR

VENISON

Roe Deer *Capreolus capreolus*
Height: 24 ins (60cm)
Weight: 4 stone (25kg)
Open season: *bucks*, 1 April-30 October;
                         does, 1 November - 28/29 February
                         Scotland: bucks, 1 May - 20 October;
                         does, 21 October - 28/29 February
Best time for eating: *bucks*, October; *does*, December-February

Fallow deer *Dama dama*
Height: 34 ins (85cm)
Weight: 12 stone (76kg)
Open season: *bucks*, 1 August - 20 April;
                         does, 1 November - 28/29 February
                         Scotland: bucks, 1 August - 30 April;
                         does, 21 October - 15 February
Best time for eating: *bucks, October-November*
                         does, December-February

Red deer *Cervus elaphus*
Height: 48 ins (120cm)
Weight: 20 stone (127kg)
Open season: *stags*, 1 August - 30 April;
                         hinds, 1 November - 28/29 February
                         Scotland: stags, 1 July - 20 October;
                         hinds, 21 October - 15 February
Best time for eating: *stags*, July-August;
                         hinds, December-February

French: *la venaison, le chevreuil (roe deer)*
German: *das Wildbret*
Italian: *la carne di cervo*
Spanish: *la carne de venado*
Greek: *to elaphi*
Portuguese: *a carne de veado*

Serbo-Croat: **srnetina**
Romanian: *vânat*
Bulgarian: *elénsko mesó*
Russian: *elénsko mesó*
Czech: *divocina*
Polish: *dziczyzna*
Dutch: *hertevlees*

Flemish: *het hert*
Norwegian: *en hjort (m), hind (f)*
Danish: *kronvildt*
Swedish: *kött av rådjur (roe deer)*
     kött av kronhjort (red)
     kött av dovhjort (fallow)
Hungarian: *vad*

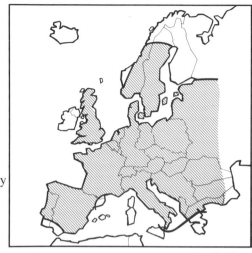

Roe Deer

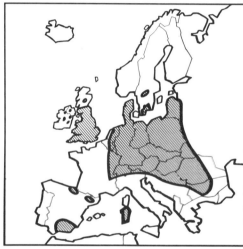

Fallow Deer

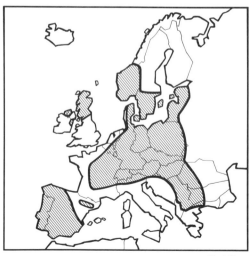

Red Deer

RED DEER

Cervus elaphus

William the Conqueror, it is said, 'loved the tall red deer as if he were their father', and this handsome native deer of European woodlands has been a prize for Europe's keenest hunters since the Dark Ages. The gaelic chieftains of medieval Scotland had their *tainchells*, mass deer hunts, which usually ended with a great slaughter of red deer driven into a pass in the hills. In Norman England and across Europe the hunting aristocracy and royalty passed hideously severe Forest Laws to protect their red deer from poachers, and to punish peasants who dared to harm their highly prized quarry. More recently, senior Communist Party members did much the same in their 'democratic' states in eastern Europe, setting aside large hunting reserves and preserving deer and all game for themselves, regardless of the damage that was done to trees and arable crops.

More genuinely democratic conditions prevail today, when the hunter of red deer has no need to demonstrate aristocratic lineage or party loyalties. All he or she needs to do is sign a large cheque! To ride to hounds in pursuit of the great woodland red deer of French and Belgian forests, a sport still carried on with pre-revolutionary Bourbon pageantry, is an expensive sport, while the stalking of one of the truly massive stags of Hungary or Czechoslovakia can cost tens of thousands of pounds.

The red deer of the Scottish highlands are a dwarf race of these large woodland deer, driven by the clearance of the old Caledonian forests to adapt to life on the bare hills. A Scottish highland stag will do well to exceed 200lb (90kg), while many specimens from central Europe run to 600lb (270kg) and more.

Red deer on the open hills of Scotland feed almost exclusively by grazing on hill grasses and heather, but deer in woodland will feed by both grazing and browsing, eating twigs and shoots, and sometimes stripping and eating the bark of trees, a characteristic which does not endear them to foresters. Red deer will also readily descend from the hills and emerge from the forests to raid by night on arable crops in the fields, both root and cereals.

Red deer numbers in Britain, especially Scotland, are increasing, and there are calls for a heavy cull. Massive culling has also had to be carried out in various eastern European countries to reduce red deer populations to manageable levels after years of excessive numbers to provide sport for senior party members. Low market prices for venison are the result, especially if you buy direct from an estate stalker or forester, and red deer venison is excellent value.

FALLOW DEER
Dama dama

A favourite of great landowners and their landscape gardeners, of Oxbridge dons and scholars, the fallow deer has long been admired for its elegance in a park and its flavour and texture at the dinner table. Although fallow have sometimes been hunted with hounds, and are nowadays usually managed by selective shooting, they have always been regarded primarily as ornamental deer, and a useful source of good meat on the hoof.

Originally a native of south-west Asia, the fallow deer came to Europe with the Romans and the Phoenicians, and it is now such an established part of the European fauna that it has good claims to be considered a genuinely European game species.

Fallow herd happily and adapt readily to an enclosed life within a deer park, a fact which led to the creation of many enclosed herds in the parklands of the gentry, at large religious houses, and at universities, to serve both as a pleasant addition to the scenery and as a ready source of meat on the hoof. Fallow venison is usually moist and tender, and a good herd of well marked deer always looks handsome in a parkland setting.

Fallow occur in a range of pelage, varying from almost pure white to a near-black donkey colour, and there is considerable variation from herd to herd, and between individual animals in the same herd. The preferred coloration of most deer park owners, and of wildlife painters depicting fallow deer, is the so-called "common" pelage, with strikingly contrasting large white flecks on a reddish-brown coat.

A mature buck, distinguished from all other medium sized European deer by the flattened palmations of his antlers, can weigh up to 220lb (99kg), while a well grown doe may weigh up to 130lb (58.5kg). A young buck or doe aged 1-3 years – the best age when selecting a beast for the larder – will weigh around 70-100lb (31.5-45kg).

ROE DEER
Capreolus capreolus

The roe is the smallest native deer found in Europe, and it is widespread across the central and northern latitudes from the Urals westwards. Ireland has no roe, however, since it became an island before the westward colonisation of roe after the last Ice Age. More than any other deer species, the roe embodies all the qualities of Bambi, in its delicate charm and elegance.

Roe have a long sporting history, and are coveted quarry for both hound enthusiast and rifleman. Roebuck hunting with hounds, which is still practised by a number of organised packs in France and Belgium, has been compared to hare hunting, as both animals will tend to dodge and circle as the pursuit goes on. Modern wildlife management involves the careful culling of roe, and other deer, by capable riflemen, since man has largely eliminated their original enemies such as wolves and lynx, and so the capable deer stalker is both a sportsman and an active conservationist.

In Britain roe have only recently attained their deserved sporting status, having been denied the prestige enjoyed by red deer and fallow deer under the medieval forest laws, and having been widely regarded as little more than vermin until the 1960s. Their numbers and range have increased across most of Britain, assisted by the spread of commercial conifer afforestation in many areas. They often constitute a menace for the forester who is anxious to get his new young trees established, but they provide a superb quarry for the sporting rifleman, and a wonderful source of delicious venison, which has always had a high culinary status in Europe and is now increasingly appreciated by British palates. The carcase of a roe taken from an area of good feeding will typically weigh around 25lb (11.25kg) after cleaning and skinning, and yields small and easily manageable joints for the modern kitchen.

Like other European deer, male roe have antlers, but these are shed in the late autumn, and not in spring like red deer and fallow. The buck is in season as a sporting quarry from early spring until late autumn when his antlers are hard and clean of velvet, and all roe venison tastes good after the animals have had a good period of rich summer and autumn feeding. Roe are woodland and farmland deer, and in summer they often live a secretive hidden life in fields of standing wheat, barley and oilseed rape.

Venison is, of course, the generic word covering the meat of the deer family and in Britain it generally refers to red deer, roe deer and fallow deer, the three best known and most commonly eaten of the seven species altogether in this country. Of course in Scandanavia it also refers to reindeer, elk and/or mousse (see recipe, page 122). In France (where else?!) they make a distinction between *venaison* which is the generic name for venison, and *chevreuil* which is usually for roe deer. And they refer to the meat of hares and rabbits as *basse venaison*. Which meat of the three is the best is a matter of taste: roe deer is the most tender and least gamey; red has the strongest and most gamey flavour; but many people consider fallow to be the best – maybe just because it is not as common!

One great plus point about venison is that it is wonderfully lean; young animals (known as fawns up to 18 months) need not be marinated. In fact, I think there is a tendency to over-marinate. Venison is such superb meat that it is best left totally unadulterated unless you are pretty sure that it is going to be old, tough and dried out. The only problem is that it might need some extra larding because of its own lack of fat, but I don't even bother with that too much – a covering of bacon is usually enough protection for a saddle or a haunch. The finest parts of the animal are, of course, the haunch, saddle and loin which can be cut into chops and cutlets. The rest, and any meat which has been damaged by shot, can be made into rich deep dark casseroles and stews or pâtés and terrines. Venison meat is also good for kebabs and barbecues and make the most meltingly tender steaks – easily as good as the best fillet – but again may need a bit more butter in the cooking than you would need for beef. The liver (usually considered part of the keeper's perks) is also quite delicious, and if you can get hold of it should be eaten as soon as possible, either simply fried or devilled. If it is not quite petal fresh, make it into a rich, smooth pâté.

The youngest venison can do without hanging as it can do without marinating. But on the whole venison should be well hung from a week to a fortnight, depending on the age of the beast and the coolness of the weather. The meat should be clean and dry, and you can test it by sticking a skewer in by the bone. If there isn't a smell, the meat is in good condition. If the meat does smell at all, you can wash it with some lukewarm vinegar before cooking. Unless you are making a stew, venison can also get away with less cooking then people imagine – it should be served pink like beef. Traditional game accompaniments – redcurrant and rowan jellies, sour cream sauce – go very well with venison. Winter vegetables – red cabbage, braised endive and celery, roast roots, glazed onions also work well, as do the sweet/sharp tastes of ginger, pink peppers, mango, paprika.

Venison Steaks in Creamy Sauce.

Roe Deer Steaks in Creamy Sauce

The Scandinavians, like the Austrians and Germans, are past masters at drool-worthy dishes of venison, very often steeped in cream or sour cream. This is one such recipe, from Sweden.

Serves 4

4 roe deer fillet steaks, each about 6oz/175g
sea salt
8 juniper berries, crushed
2 tablespoons oil
1oz/25g butter

1 tablespoon honey
2 tablespoons mild French mustard
4 tablespoons double cream
1oz/25g toasted flaked almonds
watercress or parsley to garnish

Trim and remove any traces of membrane or fat from each steak, then rub with sea salt and crushed juniper berries, and brush with oil. Heat the rest of the oil and the butter in a heavy-bottomed frying pan until golden. Place the steaks in the pan and fry for a minute on each side, or more to taste, pressing them against the pan. Remove and reserve on a serving dish to keep warm. Next, add the honey, mustard and cream to the pan, heating them up slowly together and stirring until the sauce becomes smooth. Pour the sauce over the steaks and sprinkle the toasted flaked almonds on the top. Serve with boiled potatoes and crisp green vegetables.

Roast Saddle of Venison

This is one of the ultimate treats for carnivores – tender, lean meat which literally melts in the mouth. I think it is best cooked as simply as possible to let it speak for itself, and really does not need marinating either, unless you're truly worried that it might be a tough old beast. For young red deer, or any sort of roe deer, marinating is gilding the lily. Roe deer legs can also be cooked in the same way.

Serves 8

1 saddle of venison
8 rashers streaky bacon
sprig of rosemary
1/4pt/150ml port

beurre manié *made of 1oz/25g flour and 1oz/25g*
   butter
1 tablespoon butter with salt and pepper mixed in

Remove any membrane from the meat, using a very sharp knife to cut under it and ease it off. Smear the seasoned butter all over the meat and then sprinkle with leaves off the sprig of rosemary. Cover with the bacon, add half the port to the pan and place in a hot oven (220C/425F/Gas Mark 7) for 10 minutes. Reduce the heat to moderate (160C/325F/Gas Mark 3) and cook for another 20 minutes. Remove the bacon and set to one side to keep warm and cook the saddle for another 10-20 minutes depending on how pink you like it. Transfer the meat to a serving dish and keep warm. Meanwhile scrape the juices in the pan, add a dash of water to the scrapings and bring to the boil. Add the rest of the port and, if you like a thicker gravy, add the *beurre manié* and boil for another five minutes or so. Season and boil again and serve separately in a sauceboat.

Very Rich and Yummy Venison Casserole

This does take time – but you can split it up into short periods over several days. It is well worth every minute spent. I use any of the meat from the carcase, feeling that the saddle is so delicious it should be reserved for roasting, or cutting into steaks.

Serves 10-12

6-7lb/3½kg venison meat (saddle, shoulder, legs etc)
4 tablespoons butter
4 tablespoons oil
(or 8 tablespoons Golden Crown which I use a lot)
½lb/225g smoked streaky bacon, snipped in pieces (ideally you should use salt pork but this is very difficult to find these days)

1 tablespoon dried thyme
6 bay leaves
6 cloves garlic
15 black peppercorns
6 juniper berries, crushed
a handful of whole cloves
a handful of raisins

Marinade
3 bottles red wine
½pt/300ml vegetable oil
3 large onions, sliced
6 carrots, diced
3 sprigs parsley
3 bouquet garni

Sauce
marinade juices (reduced)
beurre manié *(made of 3 tablespoons soft butter, 3 tablespoons flour, mixed together)*
12fl oz/350ml port
6 tablespoons redcurrant or elderberry jelly (apple is a bit tart)

To make the marinade: sweat the onion and carrots in a little oil till softened, add all the herbs and spices, and mix together. Transfer to a very large crockery or pyrex bowl (avoid using a metal container if at all possible) and pour over the oil and wine. Stir all together and mix well. Take all the venison off the bone, removing membrances where possible and leave to steep in the marinade for at least three days in a cool place. If you can leave it longer it will be even better – the longer you leave it, the gamier the flavour and the tenderer the meat. It will keep quite happily for a week but make sure to turn regularly so that the meat is evenly marinated.

When you are ready, remove the meat from the marinade with a slotted spoon making sure you drip as much excess liquid off the meat back into the marinade. Taking a sharp knife dice the meat into even cubes, removing any further membrane you may find on the way – you may find it easier (as I do) to use scissors than a knife for this. Also remove any cloves or other bits of the marinade that may be clinging to the meat and return to the marinade. Take a heavy-bottomed pan and melt the butter and oil in it, and then lightly sauté all the meat – you will probably need to do this in about three batches but keep using the same fat in the pan for each batch. Keep the meat to one side in a bowl. Return the juices from the frying pan to the marinade, pour the whole mixture into a flameproof casserole (preferably a cast iron one), place over a high heat and boil rapidly till the liquid is reduced by half. Strain the liquid, removing all the bits and bobs in the marinade. Place all the cooked meat back into the casserole, pour the strained liquid over it and cook for about 1½-3 hours or until tender. Remove from the liquid and keep to one side (not necessarily warm as it will heat up again very quickly once you have made the sauce).

To make the sauce, boil the liquid in the pan very rapidly for about 10-15 minutes to reduce by about a quarter. Then add the *beurre manié*, stirring all the time to make sure it is well amalgamated and keeping the sauce simmering. Next add the jelly and the port and keep stirring till the jelly is dissolved. Boil all together for five minutes. By now the sauce should be rich and thick and dark. Pour over the venison, and garnish with sautéed whole mushrooms, or triangles of fried bread, or glazed chestnuts and sprinkle with chopped parsley. It reheats well if you want to make it a day in advance.

Venison Fillet with Chanterelle Sauce

Chanterelles are those exquisite slender yellow fungi which can be found in the woodlands of Great Britain, but are more commonly found (and eaten) in other parts of Europe. You can, nowadays, find them fresh in specialist greengrocers and dried or frozen in the better delicatessens and grocers. The Swedes make this sauce to go with elk, but it does just as well with roe and red deer – and, once again, the sauce is sublime.

Serves 8

3lb/1.3kg venison fillet
freshly ground black pepper
2 tablespoons butter
1¹/₂-2 teaspoons salt

For the sauce
¹/₂lb/225g parboiled chanterelles, frozen, dried or
  fresh

3 medium spring onions
¹/₂ teaspoon salt
1 tablespoon butter
7fl oz/200ml gin
7fl oz/200ml water, plus the juice from the
  chanterelles
1 beef stock cube
14fl oz/400ml double cream

Cut the chanterelles into pieces, fry lightly in butter and allow the juices to reduce a little. Chop the spring onions and add them to the chanterelles, frying for a couple of minutes till soft. Season with salt and remove to one side. Trim the fillet of any vestige of membrane, sinew or fat, season with salt and pepper and lightly fry in the 2 tablespoons of melted butter until it is golden but still pink inside. This depends on the thickness of the fillet; roe deer will take 5-10 minutes; elk or red deer 10-15. Cook for longer if you do not like it pink, but be careful not to let it dry out as it has no marbling of fat through it. Remove the meat from the pan, wrap in foil to keep moist and keep warm. In a separate pan combine the stock cube, gin, cream and water and bring to the boil, stirring till the cube is dissolved. Boil for another 5-10 minutes to reduce and then add the chanterelles. Season to taste and allow to simmer for a few more minutes. Remove the fillet, slice and arrange on a serving dish with the sauce poured over or around. Serve with boiled potatoes and a sauce of blueberries (cranberries will do!)

Venison Fillet Steaks in Armagnac

Roe deer or red deer, these should melt in the mouth – really exquisite morsels of meat. And they are almost totally fat free! What perfection.

Serves 4-6

3lb/1.3kg venison fillet
5fl oz/150ml Armagnac
5oz/150g butter
2 sticks celery, chopped

2 carrots, diced
1 onion chopped
10fl oz/500ml red wine
salt and freshly ground pepper

Cut the fillet away from the saddle and carefully trim away any vestige of membrane or fat, then slice into neat, fat little pieces about 1 inch/2cm thick. Place the slices in a bowl and cover with the Armagnac. Leave to marinate for some 3-4 hours. Meanwhile break up the saddle carcase, brown in the butter and place it in a pan with the chopped vegetables. Cover with red wine and simmer till the liquid is reduced by half. Remove the venison fillets from the Armagnac and drain any excess juices back into the Armagnac which you have kept to one side. Pat the fillets dry with kitchen paper and then toss in a pan of melted butter at a highish heat to seal. Remove to a serving dish and keep warm. Pour the Armagnac into the frying pan and stir in all the scrapings. Add the reduced red wine stock, boil for a further 5 minutes to reduce by half, season with salt and pepper to taste and pour over the fillets. Serve garnished with little sprigs of fresh rosemary.

Tjälknöl

This is rather a special Swedish way of preserving venison meat (in this case elk)
Serves 8-10

4.4lb/2kg rolled shoulder or loin of elk or any
other venison meat

Preserving mixture
18fl oz/500ml water
4oz/100g sea salt
1 teaspoon sugar
1 tablespoon crushed black pepper

Place the meat in an ovenproof dish in a moderate oven (160C/325F/Gas Mark 3) and cook for 1½-2 hours till the meat is pink but cooked. If you prefer your meat better cooked, leave it for another half hour. Insert a thermometer, to test; at 60C the meat is pink, at 75C it is well cooked. Make sure the thermometer is completely submerged. Meanwhile put all the ingredients for the preserving mixture into a pan and bring to the boil. Remove and cool till it is completely cold. Remove the meat from the oven when it is ready and cover with the cold preserving mixture. Leave to stand for 5 hours. To serve, cut the meat in very thin slices and accompany with boiled potatoes and soured cream with mashed gorgonzola added to taste. Or serve with potato gratin and salad.

Saddle of Venison with Game Sauce

Another Swedish recipe for elk, but which can be adapted for any type of venison,
especially red deer.
Serves 8-10

2 whole red deer fillets
1 carrot, chopped
1 onion, chopped
1 celery stalk, chopped
2oz/50g butter
12 crushed juniper berries
a good pinch mixed herbs
salt and freshly ground black pepper

Sauce
7fl oz/200ml venison stock
4fl oz/100ml white wine
2 tablespoons white wine vinegar
2 tablespoons redcurrant or rowan jelly
2oz/50g butter mixed with 2oz/50g flour to make
  beurre manié
salt and pepper

Remove the fillets from the saddle and break up the carcase. Put the bones into a large saucepan, add the carrot, onion and celery and cover with water. Bring to the boil and simmer for 1½ hours to make a good stock. Trim the fillets of any membrane and sinews, rub with salt, pepper, crushed juniper berries and mixed herbs. Keep cool till the stock is ready. Then melt the butter in a heavy-bottomed frying pan and turn the fillet in it until golden brown, but still very pink in the middle. Wrap the meat in thick foil and keep warm in a very low oven (110C/225F/Gas Mark ½) for an hour, making the meat extra juicy and tender. Reduce the 7fl oz/200ml venison stock by two thirds and then add the wine, vinegar and jelly. Season to taste and simmer for 20-30 minutes. Add the *beurre manié*, stirring until it is completely amalgamated. Remove the meat from the oven, pour off the juices into the sauce, bring to the boil and then pour over the meat – or serve separately.

Chargrilled Venison Steaks

These can be out of this world; they can also be jaw-breakers. The secret is to eat them as quickly as possible after they have been cooked as they toughen as they sit. The other trick is to slice the steaks thinly rather than into hefty chunks. If you have marinated the saddle before removing the loin, you can use the marinade, combined with cream and redcurrant jelly, for sauce.

Serves 6

1³⁄₄lb/800g venison loin or fillet   *knob of butter*
salt and freshly ground pepper

Slice the loin or fillet equally to allow one steak per person. Sprinkle liberally with salt and pepper and refrigerate until needed. Take a heavy bottomed griddle pan, and heat till it is very hot with enough butter to just moisten the surface, and not allow the meat to stick to the griddles. Sear the meat for 1-2 minutes each side till scarred with black lines and serve immediately with green salad, wild fruit jelly or chutney, and baked potatoes.

Roe Deer Butterfly Steaks

This is my husband's absolute favourite. I'm pretty keen on it too as it can be done in a jiffy.
The recipe is Swedish – and both the angostura and grated radish give a novel touch.

Serves 4

4 roe deer fillets about 4oz/100g each   **Radish butter**
angostura bitters   *1oz/25g soft butter*
1¹⁄₂oz/40g butter   *2 tablespoons chopped chives*
1 tablespoon oil   *2 tablespoons grated radishes*
2 tablespoons Cognac
salt and white pepper

Begin by preparing the radish butter. Mix the ingredients together and then roll into a fattish sausage. Refrigerate until it has gone hard and then cut into 4 slices.

Cut each fillet off the saddle, removing any membrane very carefully. Split each fillet down the middle, cutting with a very sharp knife from the wider side into the pointed side. Open up and press with your hand into a butterfly shape. Sprinkle a little angostura on each side of each fillet and then season to taste. Heat the butter and olive oil in a thick-bottomed pan and fry the fillets for 15 seconds on each side, pressing towards the bottom of the pan. Remove from the pan, place in a flat shallow serving dish and keep warm. Remove the pan from the heat and add the cognac, stirring hard to collect the scrapings in the pan. Replace pan, bring to the boil and pour immediately over the fillets. Garnish with a slice of radish butter, and serve with redcurrant tartlets (see page 187), mange touts and potato and celeriac purée (see page 191).

P.S. If you prefer your meat better done, fry the fillets for 30-45 seconds each side, but certainly not more.

Fried Roe Deer Liver

This is a delicious supper dish, quick and easy to make. It is best to eat the liver as soon as possible after the beast is shot as it goes off very quickly, even in the fridge. As a variation, you could add this to make a salade tiède (see page 104 for pigeon) for lunch.

Serves 2

1 roe deer liver
2 tablespoons ground medium oatmeal
4oz/100g butter

1 dessertspoon crushed juniper berries
1 teaspoon chopped thyme (dried or fresh)
6 slices smoked bacon

Cut the bacon into smallish pieces and fry in the butter till just done and keep warm in the plate oven. Mix together the oatmeal, crushed juniper berries and chopped thyme. Slice the liver into thin slivers, dip into the oatmeal mixture and fry lightly in the butter which the bacon was cooked in. Remove from the heat and combine with the bacon, all lightly tossed together, on a serving dish. Sprinkle with finely chopped parsley and serve with salad and hot French bread.

Venison and Mixed Herb Crumble

Crumbles are suddenly back in fashion, and this makes a change from variations of stew and casserole, good as they are, and may be more palatable for children who could be slightly dubious about game. You can, of course, alternate the toppings – using mashed potato, as in shepherd's pie, or lightly creamed parsnip and potato.

Serves 6

2lb/1kg stewing venison, minced
2oz/50g butter
1 large onion, red if possible, finely chopped
4oz/100g mushrooms, chopped
1½ level tablespoons flour
3 tablespoons port or 3 tablespoons jelly
6 juniper berries, crushed

¾-1pt/450-600ml venison or beef stock
pinch coriander
salt and pepper
6oz/175g plain flour
3 tablespoons butter or margarine
2-3 tablespoons mixed dried herbs (any
   combination to taste)

Melt the butter in a large pan and soften the mushrooms and onions over a low heat until softened. Add the meat and cook, stirring till well browned. Sprinkle all over with flour and stir until completely absorbed, season with salt and pepper, and slowly add the stock, stirring continuously to ensure even mixing. Bring to the boil and simmer for 5 minutes. Add the herbs, spices and port or jelly. Cook gently for a further 20-30 minutes and transfer to a large pie dish. To make the crumble, mix with your fingertips the flour and fat till they resemble breadcrumbs. Stir in the herbs and plenty of seasoning and sprinkle all over the meat. Bake in a hottish oven (200C/400F/Gas Mark 6) for half an hour or until golden brown. Alternatively mash a mixture of boiled potatoes and parsnips (1lb/500g potatoes, 8oz/225g parsnips) together, add 4fl oz/125ml cream mixed with one beaten egg, add plenty of salt and pepper and cover the mince. Cook for 20-25 minutes as above.

Loin of Roe Deer in Cream Sauce
Rehbraten in Rahmsauce

Having lived in Austria for so long, I could quite easily be accused of bias! But that is not the reason why I think this is one of the best recipes ever. It's just that the sauce is absolutely irresistible – smooth, rich and luscious. My mother got the recipe from an Austrian friend who got it from an Austrian cook book – and I have adapted it a bit.

Serves 4

1 saddle of roe deer, and butter to spread over
24 juniper berries, crushed
pinch nutmeg
freshly ground salt and pepper
1 onion
2 carrots
1 celeriac (or 2 parsnips, or ½ turnip, or any combination of these three)
1 tablespoon butter

1 teaspoon French mustard
1 bay leaf
pinch thyme
6 cloves
grated rind of ½ lemon
1 cup water or stock
¼pt/150ml red wine
¼pt/150ml sour cream

Remove membrane from meat and spread all over with butter. Sprinkle on top the salt, pepper, crushed juniper berries and a little nutmeg. Slice the onion, carrots and celeriac. Melt the tablespoon butter in a heavy frying pan, and lightly brown all the vegetables in it. Add the meat, brown a little on both sides, then transfer meat and vegetables to a casserole. Add a teaspoon French mustard, a bay leaf, a pinch thyme, the cloves and grated lemon rind and one cup water or good stock. Cover the casserole with a lid and cook for half an hour at 180C/350F/Gas Mark 4. Take out meat, remove to a separate platter and keep warm in a warm oven covered with buttered paper. Put casserole on to medium heat and to the vegetables add first the wine, then the cream, stirring well together. Bring to the boil and then simmer for 10 minutes until slightly reduced. Sieve the sauce, *without* puréeing the vegetables through the sieve (*on no account* liquidise all together). Now take out meat, cut off the bone and slice into small medallions, and arrange prettily onto dish. Pour sauce over sliced meat. Serve with noodles and cranberry sauce.

WINES

VENISON

Venison is generally thought of as a particularly rich form of red meat, requiring a sturdy red wine to accompany it. Mighty Rhones and powerful Burgundies are often chosen on special occasions. But as the recipes show, there is a considerable range of styles in which to present venison at the table, and a powerful tasting red wine that might be ideal for a roast of rich red deer venison would be in danger of overpowering the subtler flavours of a saddle of fallow, especially if it comes from a youngish animal. Fully flavoured sauces can also stand up to massively flavoured wines, while gentler flavours require something more restrained in your glass.

Claret always goes well with venison, and the rounded and richly flavoured wines of Pomerol and Saint Emilion are ideal. The Californian and Chilean Cabernet Sauvignons, and some of the vintage estate bottled growths from Hungary and Bulgaria, can be superb with venison, which is nicely complemented by their oaky characteristics. Also good are Côtes du Rhone and Crozes Hermitage. The amazing Château Musar from Lebanon is a personal favourite of mine with fully flavoured venison, and good Burgundy seldom fails to suit it very well, too. For the milder cuts and gentler sauces, consider a Beaujolais, Dão or Chianti.

With venison served cold, perhaps as a salad when using up the remains of a roast, claret or Beaujolais is ideal, and some white wines come into their own here, too. Try a rich Gewürztraminer from Alsace, or a fully flavoured white Macon.

WILD BOAR

Sus scrofa

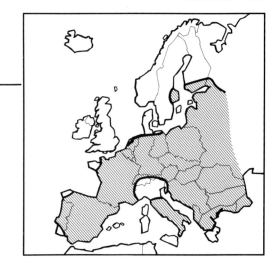

Habitat:	Woodland
Length:	3ft/1 metre and upwards
Weight:	50-70lb/22.5-31.5kg and upwards
Open season:	September-March
Best time for eating:	September-Christmas

French: *le sanglier*
German: *das Wildschwein*
Italian: *il cinghiale*
Spanish: *el jabali*
Greek: *o agriochiros*
Portuguese: *o javalin*

Serbo-Croat: *divlja svinja*
Romanian: *miskret*
Bulgarian: *gligán*
Russian: *gligán*
Czech: *divoke prase*
Polish: *dzik*

Dutch: *wild zwijn*
Flemish: *het everzwijn*
Norwegian: *et willsvin*
Danish: *vildsvin*
Swedish: *vildsvin*
Hungarian: *vaddizznó*

Hairy and horrible, black and bristling, tusked and mad-eyed, the wild boar haunts the imagination in ways redolent of the most ancient folktales of Europe. Whether in early stories, classical myths, medieval tapestries, renaissance manuscripts or modern sporting paintings, the wild boar of Europe recurs constantly as an icon denoting savagery and menace, second only perhaps to the wolf as a symbol of primaeval brute energy.

But, if correct in our terminology, we should reserve the words 'wild boar' only for the adult male of this native Eurasian species of wild pig, the ancestor of all our domesticated breeds of swine. But usage has decreed that all these wild swine of European woodland and farmland should be commonly known as wild boar.

These are creatures of Europe's great forests, foraging in extended family groups of 'sounders' of up to 25 adults, immature animals and laterally striped young, and often travelling considerable distances in a single night to feast in arable fields and vineyards before the first hints of dawn drive them back to their daytime resting places.

Wild boar, like their domesticated counterparts, are catholic in their feeding habits, rooting and delving with restless energy for foods of many kinds. Where they are numerous they can do great damage to growing crops, especially if fields of potatoes, turnips, maize and vines are within close range of the woodlands where they lie up by day. Their importance as a sporting quarry runs parallel to their status as a serious agricultural pest over much of Europe. In the countries of eastern Europe their recent impact on farming has been very serious, especially where large acreages were set aside as the hunting grounds of former Communist party chiefs, just as earlier generations of European aristocracy used to preserve game for their sport, regardless of the serious losses incurred by peasant farmers when sounders of boar invaded their fields. Since the reunification of Germany and the opening up of other former Eastern Bloc countries after the fall of communism, many areas have had to embark on large scale culls of wild boar, to reduce the animals' depredations on farmland to manageable levels.

Wild boar are hunted with packs of hounds in France and Belgium, while in Scandanavia, Germany and eastern Europe they are almost exclusively the quarry of the sporting rifleman, who shoots as one of a line of Guns when the forests are beaten out, or who waits and watches from a high seat in chilly dawns and dusks, alert for families of wild boar moving between their nighttime feeding grounds and their woodland refuges by day.

Wild boar became extinct in Britain in the seventeenth century due to over-hunting and the whittling away of the forest habitat, but in recent years has started to reappear in the kitchen as enterprising people have taken to farming it in pockets over the country (see list below). On the Continent, however, wild boar have always continued to be enjoyed both on the table and out hunting. Horace advised the ancient Romans that their tables should 'groan with the weight of an Umbrian wild boar fed on acorns', and in the Middle Ages the hunting of wild boar, with lance and spear, was a popular sport amongst the king and his court, and often depicted on tapestries of the 16th-18th centuries. Even now in Spain and in France early morning shooting parties set out at dawn to hunt the wild boar and stop for lavish picnic/barbecue breakfasts in the forests by 9am.

Wild boar suffers from an endemic virus called *trichinosis*, which in its milder forms leads to sickness and headaches but which can also be fatal. Should you chance to eat one that has been shot and taken straight out of the forest, it is advisable to cook it well through to avoid any unfortunate hiccups with *trichinosis*. Any other wild boar, however, is perfectly safe. Most wild boar shot on hunts, and certainly all farmed wild boar, goes through the slaughter house where it is checked for the virus. With that stamp of approval it can quite happily be eaten pink, as it usually is in France. This is only really possible with young wild boar which are tender enough to cook and eat like domestic pork; adult animals (they live up to 30 years old and can weigh as much as 300lb) can be very tough and are only palatable after long marinating and stewing, if then! The eating of wild boar in France is such an art that it has developed its own vocabulary for the various ages and stages of the beast. Up to the age of six months they are known as *marcassin*, and make excellent eating. From six months to one year old they are known as *bête rousse* and are still good eating. From 1-2 years they are called *bête de compagnie* and need marinating and careful cooking - useful additions to game pies or terrines. After two years (when they cease to make good eating and are best as hunting trophies only) a wild boar is known as a *ragot*; at three years *sanglier à son tiers ans*, at four a *quartenier*; after that a *porc entier*, when he is very advanced a *solitaire* or *ermite*. The growth rate of the farmed wild boar is at least half that of a domestic pig but that means that they reach their prime at 12-15 months.

The meat of the wild boar, unlike that of pork, is dark with most of the fat being concentrated under the skin. The flavour is, quite naturally, more gamey than pork and owes much to their predilection for foraging. Wild boar is best hung (depending on the weather) for a minimum of a week, preferably two, and is also best marinated for 3-5 days. If you want to eat the meat sooner, use a boiled marinade which will penetrate the meat more quickly, but only use a little in the sauce if you have incorporated much vinegar. It can be roasted in the same way as venison, but allow 15-20 minutes to the pound (half kilo). If you are buying your wild boar from a farm, you will find that most will butcher for you as the haunch and saddle, and prime cuts, are on the big size for most cooks to cut up at home. They will also dice for casseroles, and some sell sausages and pâté and home-smoked hams. Home-made Spiced Wild Boar (see page 130) makes a rich and interesting change for cold meats over a busy period like Christmas as well as a return to older, more traditional forms of cooking.

Wild Boar Farms/Suppliers

Mr and Mrs Gilroy,
The Factor's House,
Auchenfad,
Auchencairn, Castle Douglas,
Scotland
Tel: Auchencairn (055 664) 333

Holmbrush Farm,
Faygate,
Horsham, W. Sussex RH12 4SE
Tel: 0293 51000/851700

The Real Meat Co.,
East Hill Farm,
Heytesbury,
Warminster, Wiltshire BA12 0HR
Tel: 0985 40436/40060

Heal Farm,
Kings Nympton,
Umberleigh,
Devon EX37 9TB
Tel: 0767 572077

Robert Spencer Bernard,
Estate Office,
Nether Winchendon,
Aylesbury,
Buckinghamshire HP18 0DY
Tel: 0844 290101

Leg of Wild Boar, Portuguese Fashion

In the last couple of years the Portuguese have noted an invasion of wild boar *('javalin')* from Spain. Ecological explanations for the phenomenon vary, but changing agricultural practices in both countries are probably responsible. A landowner in the Ribatijo district says that the boar come over for the fruit of the Portuguese cork trees which had previously been 'grazed' by roving bands of domestic pigs. Whatever the reason, it has given rise to this recipe.

Serves 8-10

1 leg of wild boar (about 5lbs/2.5kg)

Marinade
3pt/1.75 litres dry white wine
¹/₂pt/300ml vinegar
7fl oz/200ml olive oil
3 carrots, finely chopped
1 onion, finely chopped
3 shallots, finely chopped
2 cloves garlic, finely chopped
small bunch parsley
generous pinch salt

6 bay leaves
generous pinch fresh or dried thyme
10 peppercorns
3 whole cloves

Sauce
4fl oz/120ml Madeira
2oz/50g toasted pine nuts
2oz/50g raisins or sultanas
1 tablespoon flour
1oz/25g diced butter

Lightly sauté the vegetables and herbs and spices in three tablespoons of the olive oil. Add the wine and vinegar and simmer slowly for 30 minutes. Cool, then add the remaining olive oil and mix well together. Rub salt all over the leg and then place in a crockery bowl (not metal) large enough to hold it so that it can be completely covered by the marinade. Cover with the marinade and leave to steep for 4 or 5 days, turning frequently. Remove the leg from the marinade and pat dry with a kitchen paper towel. Melt the bacon in a very large frying pan and fry the leg lightly all over in the fat. Move into a large roasting pan practically filled with the strained marinade, reserving the remainder, and roast for 1 hour 40 minutes (20 minutes per lb/ ¹/₂ kilo) in a medium oven (180C/350F/Gas Mark 4). Turn several times during the roasting, basting each time. Halfway through the cooking, cover the pan with a large sheet of foil. When it is done, baste the leg one more time and set aside to a cooler oven to keep warm but not cook while you make the gravy. For this, take off the pan juices and pour into a large saucepan. Add the remainder of the marinade and boil over a high heat until reduced to half. Strain again and add a little freshly ground pepper if necessary.

To make the sauce, take the reduced marinade off the heat and add 4fl oz/120ml lukewarm Madeira wine in which you have already soaked 2oz/50g toasted pinenuts and 2oz/50g of raisins or sultanas. In Portugal the sauce then gets thickened with a little 'fecula' or potato flour dissolved in water - 1 tablespoon flour, to 2 tablespoons water - but here you could just use ordinary flour. Add to the mixture and bring to the boil, stirring all the time to ensure there are no lumps. Just before serving take off the heat and beat in 1oz/25g of diced butter to make a smooth velvety sauce. Serve the leg accompanied by a purée made of one third celery, one third potato and one third apples cooked in butter.

Cinghiale a la Siciliana

This is a rich Italian casserole with all the purigency of game and Mediterranean ingredients in one.

Serves 6-8

2¼lb/1¼kg wild boar
1pt/600ml red wine
1pt/600ml vinegar
2 tablespoons olive oil
3 onions, chopped
4-5 tomatoes
1 head garlic
peel of one orange
½pt/300ml water

3 tablespoons tomato purée
1 small hot red pepper
½ teaspoon caster sugar
salt and pepper
handful of green olives, stoned and blanched
3 stalks of celery, chopped
3 leaves basil
2 tablespoons capers

Make a simple marinade combining the wine and vinegar. Dice the wild boar meat and marinate for 2 days. Remove from the marinade, drain and pat dry with kitchen paper. Heat the oil in a heavy flameproof casserole, add the onions and cook till translucent. Skin and chop the tomatoes and garlic cloves, chop both roughly and add to the onions. Tie the orange peel in a small piece of muslin to make a bouquet garni and add to the pan with the water, tomato purée, pepper, sugar and seasoning. Simmer gently for an hour with the lid off and when the sauce is thick remove the garlic, pepper and orange peel. Move to one side. In a deep heavy frying pan, heat the 2 tablespoons of olive oil and sauté the meat. Remove the meat with a slotted spoon to the casserole. Add a glass of the marinade and reboil for a couple of minutes till the liquid in the pan is reduced by half. Add to the sauce in the casserole together with the chopped celery and olives and simmer, very gently, for another two hours adding water if the sauce starts getting too thick and concentrated. Just before serving, chop the basil and add to the sauce with the capers. Serve with noodles.

Spiced Wild Boar

This makes a change from ham at Christmas or other festive occasions. Saltpetre is available at chemists' shops and makes the basis of a very easy form of pickling. The sweet/savoury/spicy flavour of this meat makes an interesting and delicious addition to the cold table.

Serves 8-10

5lb/2.5kg rolled leg or loin of wild boar, skin
   removed
3oz/75g soft pale brown sugar
1 tablespoon black peppercorns
1 dessertspoon pink peppercorns
1 tablespoon juniper berries

1 teaspoon whole cloves
pinch ground cinnamon
1 teaspoon saltpetre
4oz/100g coarse sea salt
½pt/300ml water

Rub the joint all over with the sugar and leave for two days in a crockery or glass bowl, *never metal*. Roughly crush the dried peppercorns, juniper berries and cloves, add the salt and saltpetre and cinnamon and mix all together. Rub over the wild boar and keep turning the joint and rubbing the mixture in for the next week to ten days in a cool place. The salt and sugar will cause the meat to exude rich aromatic juices. Before cooking, rub the ground spices off the meat, but do not rinse to clean. Place the joint into a close fitting heavy casserole, fill with the water, cover with greaseproof paper to prevent evaporation and place in a low oven (140C/275F/Gas Mark 1) for five hours. Leave to cool in the liquid for two hours or so and before the fat sets, remove, wrap in foil and set overnight in another container with heavy weights on a plate on top (about 3-4lbs/1.5-2kg). The meat will keep for several days in the fridge. Carve very thinly and serve with salad and baked potatoes.

Marcassin a l'Ardennaise

Wild boar are prevalent even in the highly populated regions of France (Normandy, the Ardennes, Ile-de-France) because they love foraging amongst the crops. Roasting a wild boar joint is only for young, tender animals. If there is any doubt about the age, use a cooked marinade which penetrates the meat more deeply. This is a country roast, with the joint served on a bed of diced celeriac or any other root vegetables mixed with diced bacon.
Serves 6-8

1³/₄pt/1 litre cooked marinade (page 186)
1 leg of wild boar (about 5lb/2¹/₂kg)
5 tablespoons oil
3oz/75g butter
1 tablespoon flour
1¹/₄pt/750ml stock (game or beef)

salt and pepper
8oz/225g bacon, finely snipped
3¹/₂lb/1.5kg celeriac diced (or a mixture of root
  vegetables carrots, parsnip, turnip, celeriac,
  all diced)
1 lemon

Cook the marinade (see page 186) and allow to cool. Marinate the leg of boar for 2-3 days, turning every so often. Drain and dry the meat, and strain the vegetables from the marinade, reserving the liquid. In a heavy-bottomed pan melt 2¹/₂ tablespoons oil and 2oz/50g butter and toss the marinade vegetables in the fats till soft. Add the flour and stir into the vegetables until it turns golden. Add the marinade liquid and seasoning, then bring to the boil and simmer for 1-1¹/₂ hours until reduced by half. Take off the heat and reserve. Meanwhile brush the joint with the remaining oil and roast in a preheated hot oven (220C/375F/Gas Mark 7) in a very large roasting pan for 20-25 minutes. Peel the celeriac, dice and sprinkle with lemon juice to prevent discolouring. Remove the meat from the dish and pour off any fat. Add just over half the remaining butter, celeriac, bacon, pepper and very little salt. Reduce the oven to 180C/350F/Gas Mark 4 and cook for another 30-40 minutes to taste. Strain and taste the sauce, whisking in the rest of the butter, chilled and diced. Arrange the vegetables on a serving dish, and place the joint on top. Add any more pan juices to the sauce and serve separately in a sauceboat.

Boiled Wild Boar with Rose-Hip Syrup

This is a recipe from Hungary and a combination that works wonderfully. If you can't get rose-hip syrup, melt down some rose-hip jelly with water, or another wild fruit jelly.

Serves 4

2¹/₂lb/1.5kg haunch of wild boar
7oz/200g carrots, cut into sticks
4oz/100g parsnips, cut into sticks
2 large onions, chopped
15 peppercorns
5 juniper berries

1 bay leaf
7¹/₂fl oz/200ml red wine
5oz/150g fresh grated horseradish
4 tablespoons rose-hip syrup
1 head garlic, each clove peeled, but whole

Fill a large pan with salted water, place the wild boar in it and simmer gently till half cooked (about 45 minutes). Then add the carrots cut into strips, the parsnips, onions, garlic and red wine. Also add the pepper, bay leaf and juniper berries and continue to simmer until tender. Grate the horseradish and add to the warmed rose-hip syrup. Serve the syrup with the boiled haunch, thinly sliced.

FISH

SALMON

Salmo salar

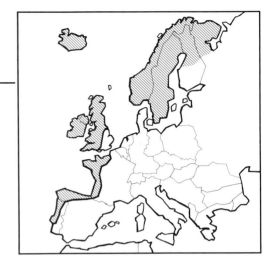

Habitat: the sea and rivers
Length: average 30-48ins (75cm-1.2 metres)
Weight: average 5-12lbs (2½-6kg)
Season: wild salmon, February - August
                                farmed salmon, all year
Best time for eating: as above

French: *le saumon*   Serbo-Croat: *losos*   Dutch: *zalm*
German: *der Lachs/Salm*   Romanian: *somou*   Flemish: *de zalm*
Italian: *il salmone*   Bulgarian: *syómga*   Norwegian: *en laks*
Spanish: *el salmón*   Russian: *syómga*   Danish: *laks*
Greek: *o solomós*   Czech: *losos*   Swedish: *lax*
Portuguese: *o salmão*   Polish: *losos*   Hungarian: *lazac*

The salmon is 'the leaper' – his official Latin name proclaims it – and in every month of the year salmon can be found battling their way upstream from the sea in every major river system on Europe's Atlantic seaboard, from Portugal to Finland and north-west Russia. But pollution and impassable barriers have spelt the end of salmon in some European waters. The Rhine, formerly Europe's greatest salmon river, up which returning fish ran as far as Switzerland, is now devoid of them. Elsewhere, wonderful recovery has occurred, and the Tyne, once heavily polluted by industrial waste, is now England's most productive salmon river.

The salmon's rich, moist flesh of subtle pink is the product of its life at sea. This begins when the river-reared young fish begins to turn into a silver smolt and drops gradually downstream, moving from the relatively impoverished freshwater environment of the river to the rich feeding grounds at sea. In a typical Scottish river it will have taken some four years for the young salmon to develop through the successive freshwater stages of egg, alevin, fry, parr and smolt, by which time it will be all of six inches long and weighing perhaps 3 ounces. A year later it may return from the sea as a grilse weighing 4-6 lbs, an astonishing surge of growth. Fish that spend two or three winters at sea before returning to the rivers of their birth often achieve weights of 25-35lbs and more.

The salmon that finds its way into the kitchen will come from one of four main sources – the creel of the rod-and-line fisherman; the nets of the estuary commercial fisher; the hold of a boat that fishes with drift-nets offshore and on the salmon's high seas feeding grounds; and, increasingly, from the cages of a commercial fish farm. At its best, farmed salmon is indistinguishable in taste and texture from its wild counterpart, and an increasingly high proportion of the salmon offered for sale by fishmongers and in restaurants have been farmed. This is good conservation, taking commercial fishing pressure off the wild stocks. Like all types of fish reared in confinement, a farmed salmon will lack the fully developed tail and fins of the wild fish, and these are signs to watch for it you are offered allegedly 'wild' salmon at a premium price. Farmed salmon usually have markedly smaller tails and fins, which are rounded and sometimes ragged in outline.

Smoking salmon is another practical and traditional way of preserving this wonderful fish, and it also brings out a whole new character in the texture and taste of the flesh. So too does the Scandinavian *gravadlax* treatment, which is increasingly popular across the rest of Europe.

A silvery salmon fresh from up from the sea is a magnificent sight, and it can be a magnificent sight at the table, too, if presented with skin, head and tail intact. But a salmon taken late in the season, or one which has been in fresh water for some time, may have lost most of that pristine silvery glory, turning darker in colour and looking less appealing. Many salmon fishers select such fish to go for smoking or as *gravadlax*.

However your salmon may have been caught or treated or cooked, spare a generous thought for this miraculous fish that begins life as a tiny egg in the gravelly headwaters of a river, that goes to sea and swims 3,000 miles and more to its feeding grounds off Greenland and back again, to return unerringly and despite every obstacle and hazard to spawn in the selfsame stream where its life began.

Everyone knows what an extraordinary fish the salmon is; it is beautiful to look at, delicious to eat and its courage and energy knows no bounds. From the vast open waters of the big seas it finds its way up all our rivers to spawn in the tiniest of tributaries before it swims out to the oceans again. What is less well known is that it wasn't classified until the late 19th century when the eminent natural historian Sir William Jardine, Bart, of South West Scotland, wrote the definitive classification: *British Salmonidae*. It seems strange that a fish that was king of the table for centuries from Russia through the Baltics, Scandinavia and right down through southern and Eastern Europe should have taken so long to be 'discovered'. Although Sir William's classification, published between 1839-1841, was the first British attempt of its kind and widely accepted in mid-Victorian times, it has often been disputed subsequently. Freshwater biologists are still squabbling over the exact relationships of salmon, trout and sea-trout etc, but cooks are unanimous that they are all delicious, whatever their official Latin names!

Wild salmon are caught by anglers from February to August and there is still more cachet to eating wild salmon than farmed. But farmed salmon are everywhere; most supermarkets stock them, though usually in cutlets rather than the whole fish. Young salmon (grilse) are considered the best eating, usually weighing in at somewhere around 5lb (2½kg). Bigger salmon weigh up to 12lb/6k and still make good eating. Thereafter the weight can escalate into the 20s and 30s, but these are better smoked or made into Gravad Lax, the method the Scandinavians favour (see page 134). The British record is still held by one Miss Ballantyne who in October 1922 caught a 64lb salmon off the side of her father's fishing boat in the Tay. Apparently her arm ached for a week after!

The usual way to cook a whole salmon is to poach it in a *court-bouillon* (see page 174), but many people don't have fish kettles big enough to hold a decent sized salmon. The alternative is to bake or roast, curving it to fit into a roasting pan, and if you are careful there is no more danger of the fish drying out than if you poached it. The flesh is very oily so it doesn't need extra marinating if you want to use it for kebabs for barbecuing. Any leftovers from a whole fish can be made into a multitude of dishes – kedgeree or fish pie – as popular with children as they are with adults. It is also fashionable nowadays to eat salmon raw – either marinated as *seviche* or as salmon tartare.

BROWN TROUT and SEA-TROUT: RAINBOW TROUT
Salmo trutta & Oncorhyncus mykiss

Throughout Europe the most universally admired resident freshwater fish, for anglers and gourmets alike, is the brown trout. Wherever there are lakes and rivers with pure cool water and adequate supplies of suitable food items, there will be trout. In the chilly glacial lakes of the Alps and Scandinavia, and in the peaty hill lochs and loughs of Scotland and Ireland, they may remain small and hungry, eager to snatch at whatever food they can find – and at the flyfisher's offering, too. Elsewhere, in food-rich alkaline waters, they grow big and muscular, and have a well deserved reputation among anglers for being fastidiously selective feeders, difficult to tempt with fly or bait.

A brown trout of 12-14 inches and weighing about the same number of ounces – 'breakfast size' – makes an ideal main course portion for one person. But there are small rivers and acidic lakes where such a trout would be a monster, and the flyfisher's basket will reveal fish averaging no more than 8-10 ounces – in which case serve two per hungry person. A brown trout of 5-6lbs from a rich lake can make a superb fish for a lunch or dinner party, but a large old fish from poorer waters is best consigned to a glass case, or, increasingly these days, released gently back into the water, where it may have taken as much as 15 years to reach its present weight.

The flesh colour of brown trout is variable, and can be anything between a near-white and a rich salmon-pink. This is a direct reflection of the individual fish's feeding. A small trout from a hill loch may have lived chiefly on small insects and reveal a pallid flesh, but still firm and flavoursome, while a trout from a rich limestone lough or a chalk stream is more likely to have the pink flesh which betokens a diet of freshwater shrimps and other crustaceans, rich in the carotene which imparts that pinkish tint. Not unexpectedly, commercial fish farmers have devised ways to create this attractive pink colour in the flesh of their product by feeding special foods that have carotene additives.

It could be tempting to try and describe the trout as a member of the salmon family which does not migrate to sea. But it does, or at any rate some of them do, and thereby become sea trout. Fisheries experts are still uncertain why one trout goes to sea while another remains in the river or lake all its days, but they are at least certain that both belong to the same species. Earlier generations of scientists and most fishermen believed that they were quite distinct species, and the eager 'splitters' of nineteenth century biology conferred separate Latin names upon them. Sea trout is often – but quite wrongly – described by fishmongers and restaurateurs as 'salmon-trout', a term never used by anglers or fisheries experts. It presumably stems from the silvery hue of sea trout fresh from the sea, and from their pinkish flesh, both of which are rather similar to fresh salmon.

Like salmon, sea trout enjoy the benefits of abundant rich feeding in salt water. A trout that goes downstream as a five-inch smolt may return from the North Sea or the Irish Sea a year later as a splendidly muscular sea trout weighing 3-4lbs. But their marine lives do not involve the great journeys across the Atlantic that salmon undertake. Sea trout stay closer inshore, and may move frequently in and out of the river estuary as the tides ebb and flow.

The rainbow trout, now familiar in countless fisheries and on fishmonger's slabs throughout Europe, is an introduced species from North America. Its name derives from the vivid iridescent band of colouring that runs along its flanks, especially conspicuous in the truly wild specimens, and fading quickly after death. In its home waters in the U.S.A. and Canada it exists in both sedentary and migratory ('steelhead') forms, the New World equivalents of the European brown trout and sea trout. In Europe, however, it is particularly popular with commercial fish farmers and managers of commercial sporting fisheries. It grows much faster and to heavier weights than the brown trout, and in the weight range 14-18 ounces it is a popular item on supermarket shelves and in restaurants, to the extent that any fish described there as simply 'trout' is now almost sure to be a rainbow trout.

SEA TROUT: *Salmonidae*

Habitat: sea and rivers
Length: 1ft-3ft (24cm-1 metre)
Weight: 3lb-7lb (1¹/₂-3¹/₂kg)
Season: February to August
Best time for eating: as above

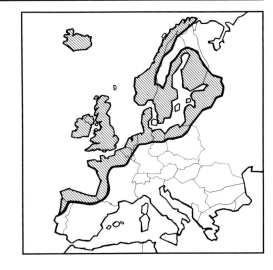

French: *le truite de mer*
German: *die Seeforelle*
Italian: *la trota salmonata*
Spanish: *trucha asalmonada/salmonada*
Greek: *i pestrofa thalassis*
Portuguese: *a truta salmoneja*

Serbo-Croat: *pastárva*
Romanian: *craisor*
Bulgarian: *mórska pastárva*
Russian: *mórska pastárva*
Czech: *pstruh mórsky*
Polish: *osioso pstrag*
Dutch: *zee forel*

Flemish: *de zeeforel*
Norwegian: *en støørret*
Danish: *hav ørred/lakse ørred*
Swedish: *hauslax o ring*
Hungarian: *tengeri pisztráng*

Often known as salmon trout, especially at the fishmonger, the sea trout, to my mind combines the best of the salmon and the trout: the flavour is as good as the salmon's but the flesh is as fine as the trout's – and light and moist to boot. For this reason it really is best eaten totally unadulterated – not 'mucked up' as my father might say – poached or baked in foil. There is no logical reason why it shouldn't be smoked as salmon and trout are, but somehow it never is. It does, however, translate superbly into *seviche* (see page 148 for salmon marinated in line and coriander), cut into slim fillets and very lightly marinated. I only ever use leftovers for pie, quiche or soufflé. (It is sacrilege to turn fresh sea trout into any of these dishes).

Poached Salmon

This has always been the traditional way of cooking salmon for eating either hot or cold. The problem about it, though, is that you can only poach a fish that is small enough to fit into your fish kettle – even if it is a big one. Fish kettles are as bulky as they are expensive – not an item to buy in quantity! Fish that are too large for poaching in a fish kettle can be just as successfully baked in the oven, covered in foil, or simply roasted in their skin in a high oven, or curved to fit into a large roasting tray. A whole cold poached salmon is a perfect answer to a large summer party, or buffet at any time of year. Many people like to decorate the fish with a coating of aspic and/or decorations of sliced cucumber, radish, lemon etc in a variety of combinations and patterns. I personally like to see the fish lying simply skinned, with a fresh sprig of dill for garnish at the head and/or tail, some shredded lettuce to partly fill empty space on the serving dish, and a few slim wedges of lemon.

Serves 10

2½pt/1.5 lites court bouillon (see page 00)
a whole 5lb/2.5kg salmon, gutted

fresh dill, lettuce, lemon, parsley, cucumber etc
for garnish

Make sure the fish is properly cleaned and gutted and remove the gills which can give a bitter taste to the water of *court bouillon* (page 174) you use for poaching. If you are using a fish kettle to cook the fish in, place a smaller fish on the rack and lower it carefully into the *court bouillon* or water. If you are cooking a very big fish (about 8lb/3.6kg) curve it carefully into the empty fish kettle, then pour cold *court bouillon* or cold water water over it to ensure even cooking. In both cases make sure the fish is completely covered. Bring the liquid up to the boil and then simmer so that the water is just on the move for about 5 minutes. Take off the heat and leave the fish in the water until it has cooled completely at room temperature (not warm!). The fish will be cooked right through but be really moist and succulent. Now lift the fish out of the kettle on the rack. It will have set in the shape you cooked it in – curved or straight – and that is the shape it will keep on the serving dish. While it is still has strength from the skin, lift it directly onto the serving dish you are using. Keeping a roll of kitchen paper beside you, carefully peel off the skin, leaving the head and tail intact and untouched, and mopping up any escaped liquid or scales or other mess with the kitchen paper as you go along. I usually try to curve my fish in the pan so that it stands upright on its tummy on the dish, rather than flat on its side. This not only looks more stunning, but it also makes it easier to skin without having to turn the whole thing from one side to the other. Garnish to taste and serve with Mayonnaise (page 176) or Sauce Verte (page 181), if you are eating the fish cold. If you want hot poached salmon, let the liquid simmer so that it is just moving for 40 minutes (about 8 minutes to the pound/half kilo), then remove from the pan, skin carefully and serve with Sauce Hollandaise (page 175), or Quick Butter, Lemon and Cream sauce (page 176) or Sauce Mousseline (page 175). For whole baked salmon turn to pages 139 and 142).

Baked Salmon, Sea Trout or Trout

Baking in foil is a foolproof way of cooking any of the game fish and ensuring they stay moist. It also gets over any problems with squeezing large fish into fish kettles as any monster can be wrapped in foil and then curved to fit into a roasting pan. You can also stuff the fish with practically any combination of fresh herbs and/or citrus fruit (lemon, lime or orange) that takes your fancy. Bay leaves, fresh sprigs of thyme, fennel, parsley, sticks of celery, a bunch of spring onions, watercress, sorrel, chervil: the variations and combinations are endless, the results simple and delicious.

Serves 10-12

1 7lb/3.5kg salmon
salt
1 tablespoon butter

stuffing to taste or whim – any combination of the above citrus fruit and/or herbs

Cut the salmon, clean and wipe dry. Sprinkle salt along the spine and then dot the length of the fish internally with butter. Stuff with any herbs or citrus fruit according to taste and/or availability. Place the fish in the middle of a well-oiled sheet of foil, wrap completely and stand the fish on its tummy in a roasting pan, curving if necessary to fit it in. Bake in a moderately slow oven (170C/325F/Gas Mark 3) for about 15 minutes to the pound. If you want to eat the fish cold, leave it to cool in the foil in a very cool place. Once it is cold remove the foil and the fish will hold its shape in a curve and stand on its tummy – I find this far more attractive than serving a fish lying flat on its side. Serve hot with Hollandaise (page 175), Mousseline (page 175) or Lemon, Butter and Cream sauces (page 176) or cold with Mayonnaise (page 176).

Salmon and Turbot in an Emerald Jacket

This is one of Matthew Fort's creations. It is wonderfully showy and wonderfully simple. You can, of course, make it just with salmon, or with salmon combined with other fish than turbot. Serve it with Beurre Blanc or Saffron Sauce – or any variation of basic fish sauce.

Serves 8

8 small salmon steaks off the skin, approx 2ins x
¹/₂in (about 1lb/900g)
8 small turbot steaks off the skin, approx 2ins x
¹/₂in (about 1lb/900g)

16 Savoy cabbage leaves
salt and freshly ground pepper

You will need a steamer to make this, so if you haven't already got one, put it on the shopping list along with the fish. Select 16 cabbage leaves, making sure that they aren't the tough outer ones, but still big enough to fold over and make into little parcels. Cut the spine out of each leaf and then blanch the leaves in salted water for one minute. Drain and cool immediately in a basin of ice cold water. Pat dry. Lay enough cabbage leaf on a piece of clingfilm to make one parcel. Place the salmon and turbot steaklets either side by side or on top of each other on the cabbage leaves. Sprinkle each piece of fish with salt and pepper and then wrap the leaves around the fish. Wrap the clingfilm tightly around the lot, and then leave in the fridge until needed. Arrange the parcels in the steamer and then steam the parcels for 7-10 minutes. Take off the heat and leave to finish cooking for 3-4 minutes. Peel off the clingfilm, arrange on individual plates and serve with a creamy sauce (Beurre Blanc, page 185; Saffron Sauce page 180). The beauty of this is that it can be prepared in the morning and left to steam during the first course of dinner.

Salmon Steaks in Filo Parcels

I have filleted and wrapped a whole fish in filo pastry before now; it makes for quite a spectacular entrance but the slicing can get out of hand and the general effect is fairly messy fairly quickly! This is a much neater solution all round.

Serves 4

4 salmon fillets, boned and skinned
1 packet filo pastry, thawed
1/4pt/150ml sour cream
1oz/25g butter, melted

2 tablespoons chopped dill
salt and freshly ground mixed black and white
   peppercorns

If you haven't worked with filo pastry before, it is worth remembering to have a damp cloth at hand as it dries out quickly. Then mix the dill and some seasoning into the sour cream. Paint a sheet of filo with melted butter and cover with another sheet. Paint this again with butter, very thinly. Place the salmon fillet at one end and spoon a quarter of the sour cream on top. Roll the fillet once over in the filo, then turn in the outside edges, and finish rolling to the end to make a neat parcel. Seal the edges with melted butter. Repeat with the other fillets and place each parcel on a baking sheet. Paint the top of each parcel with some more melted butter and bake for 20 minutes in a hottish oven (220C/425F/Gas Mark 7). Serve with Beurre Blanc (see page 185) and 'spaghetti' cucumber (cucumber cut into thin long strands and sautéed in butter with salt and pepper).

Frittura di Pesci Misti del Pescatore

This is a wonderful sort of 'fisherman's fish fry', based on the perenially popular *Frito Misto* that appears on the menu in most Italian trattorias. You can use it for any combination of fish, and fillets or chunks from any of the game fish in this chapter. Serve with a good Sauce Tartare or *Salsa all'aglio* (better known as the Provençal Aioli!)

Serves 4

2 1/2lb/1kg mixed fish fillets (salmon, trout, pike,
   eel, etc)
8oz/225g well seasoned flour

oil
lemon wedges
parsley

Clean and dry the fish fillets and cut them into roughly equal sized cubes or slivers. Season the flour well with plenty of fresh ground salt and pepper (add a few dried herbs, too, for a change) and dip each piece of fish in this making sure it is evenly coated. Take a large, deep heavy-bottomed frying pan and heat a generous amount of oil to smoking point. Add the fish, toss quickly in the oil for about 2 minutes and remove, to keep warm on a serving dish. Repeat with the rest of the fish – or alternatively use two pans at the same time so that the fish can be eaten as soon as it is cooked rather than having to wait. Pile onto a large serving platter, garnish with lemon wedges and parsley and serve with Sauce Tartare (page 179) or *Salsa all'aglio* (page 183).

Terrine of River Fish

This is a favourite – and stunning to look at. You can, of course, vary the types of fish used, or just make the whole terrine from only one – just salmon, or trout, or pike or carp (or haddock or whiting from the shops!) But it is truly sensational – ideal for a first course, or on a cold buffet table.
Serves 12-16 (makes about 4lb/2kg)

For the trout layer
10oz/300g trout fillets
4 tablespoons double cream
2 tablespoons white wine
salt
2oz/50g onions, finely chopped
1oz/25g each of fresh chives and chervil, finely snipped
1 tablespoon tarragon, finely snipped
1 egg
5oz/150g butter

For the pike layer
10oz/300g pike fillets
1 egg
1 tablespoon double cream

salt
1/2 teaspoon powdered saffron
5oz/150g softened butter
1/4oz/10g green peppercorns in brine

For the salmon layer
10oz/300g salmon fillets
4 tablespoons double cream
salt
2 tablespoons white wine
2oz/50g leek, very finely sliced, white part only
juice of 1/2 lemon, strained
1 egg
5oz/150g butter, softened
cayenne pepper

For the trout layer, place in a small pan the cream, wine, a pinch of salt and the shallots. Bring to the boil, cook for 5 minutes and allow to cool. Add the chives, chervil and tarragon. Place the trout in a food processor or liquidiser with the egg and butter, blend thoroughly and mix with the herb mixture. Adjust the seasoning.

Next put the pike into the food processor and whizz with the egg, salt, saffron and butter till it is smooth and fine. Remove, and stir in the green peppercorns.

For the salmon layer, cook the cream, a pinch of salt, the wine and the leek together for 10 minutes. Allow to cool. Put the salmon into the food processor with the lemon juice, egg, pinch of salt and butter, and whizz till smooth. Remove and turn into a bowl, and carefully fold in the cream and leek mixture.

Butter a rectangular porcelain terrine. Fill first with the trout, then the pike and then the salmon layers to make the effect of a pink and white sandwich. Cover first with foil, and then with a lid. Cook in a *bain marie* in a pre-heated oven at 180C/350F/Gas Mark 4 for 1½ hours. Turn off the oven and allow the terrine to cool in the oven so that it finishes cooking slowly. Do not weight the terrine. Leave for 24 hours before eating. Serve with Sauce Verte (page 181) and toast.

Little Hot Mousses of Salmon in a Leek Case

This is exactly the same recipe as the one for pheasant on page 87, but I have made it with
equal success with salmon (and cod, for that matter!). It always elicits a request for the recipe,
so here it is.
Serves 8

5oz/150g salmon fillet (tail will do)
2 clean leeks
1 teaspoon butter
1 egg, plus 1 yolk
7fl oz/200ml milk

¼pt/150ml double cream
salt and freshly ground pepper
4 sprigs chervil (optional)
1 teaspoon butter

Take 8 ramekins and grease with butter. Set to one side to keep cool. Boil a large pan of salted water. Trim
the tops of the leeks, peel away any tough outer layers and trim off the rest. Separate the leaves, slicing any fat
ones lengthways to make ribbons about ½ inch/1cm wide. Plunge into the boiling water and blanch for one
minute. Remove from the pan with a slotted spoon and plunge the leek ribbons immediately into ice cold
water, then drain and dry with kitchen paper. Take the ramekins and line them with the leek ribbons, laying
four or five across each other to form a star and leaving the ends hanging over the edge of the ramekins. Make
sure that you have used green as well as white in each arrangement as this will give the overall effect at the
end. Cover each ramekin with clingwrap and refrigerate. This can be done half a day ahead. Dice the salmon
fillet and place in a food processor with the chervil, egg and egg yolk, milk, a good teaspoon of salt and a
generous sprinkling of white pepper. Whizz till you achieve a fine purée and add the cream. Adjust the
seasoning if necessary. Spoon the mixture into the ramekins, fold the overhanging edges of the leeks over to
enclose the mousses and place the ramekins in a *bain-marie* reaching two thirds of the way up the ramekin
dishes. Place in a pre-heated oven (170C/320F/Gas Mark 3) and cook for 20-25 minutes until firm to the
touch. Turn out on individual plates and carefully pour round some hot Lemon, Cream and Butter Sauce (page
176) or Tomato Butter (page 178) to surround the base of each mousse. Garnish with chervil or dill leaves and
serve with thin crispy Melba toast.

Roast Salmon

Roasting has become a popular alternative to baking for salmon recently and it certainly saves
all the wrapping and unwrapping of foil involved in baking. And as long as you time the
cooking carefully the results are just as moist and succulent as in baking or poaching. I also
rather like the look of the shiny crackly skin on the fish as it is served.

1 whole salmon
4 tablespoons butter
1 whole lemon, cut into six wedges

sprigs of fresh dill and parsley, or any other
fresh herbs to taste
1 teaspoon salt

Gut the salmon, leaving the head and tail. Sprinkle the salt along the length of the spine and then fill the fish
with two tablespoons butter and stuff with the fresh herbs and lemon wedges. Melt the other two tablespoons
butter and paint all over the skin. Measure the salmon across the middle at its widest point and then roast in a
high oven (230C/450F/Gas Mark 8) for ten minutes to the inch. Remove and serve immediately with
traditional Hollandaise Sauce (page 175), new potatoes and green peas.

Salmon and Sole Shoals

My brother-in-law, Derek Johns, is an art dealer who is constantly whizzing around Europe. When he isn't travelling he devotes his ceaseless energies to two other passions, gardening and cooking. This recipe is one he tried out on us before going in for the South of England heats for Masterchef. He won, and went on to become Masterchef 1993. The recipe is his, the name mine...

Serves 4

4 salmon fillets, 2in x 4-5in
4 sole fillets, 2in x 4-5in
1 very large sorrel leaf, shredded into 4 bits
16 leaves fresh tarragon
8 sheets filo pastry
about 2 tablespoons melted butter
4 black grapes

For the sauce *(makes 1-1½ pints)*
7fl oz/200ml fish stock
1 teaspoon tomato purée
3fl oz/100ml Noilly Prat
2fl oz/75ml white burgundy
4oz/100g shallots, very finely chopped
4oz/100g leeks, very finely chopped
¾pt/450ml double cream
2fl oz/50ml Sauternes
2 tablespoons chopped chives or tarragon or both
2oz/50g butter
salt and pepper to taste

Unravel one sheet of filo pastry and paint it, uppersidemost, thinly with butter. In the middle, at one end place the sole fillet. On top of that arrange 4 tarragon leaves diagonally across the strip. Place the salmon fillet on top, and cover that with a piece of sorrel. Sprinkle some salt and pepper over it and then trim off excess filo pastry down each side to leave about 2 inches protruding either side of the fish. Now roll the fish in the strip, over and over till the end. Tuck the protruding side neatly in. Take another piece of filo pastry, trim as before, paint again with butter and roll up round the first parcel. This time turn the protruding end in at one end to make a pointed shape like a fish's head. At the other end, keep it flat but pinch it in where the fish stops so that it fans out to form a tail. Make an indent in the 'head' bit enough to take a single black grape and insert the grape. Repeat with the other fish till you have your 'shoal' ready to place on a baking tray. Paint the tops again quickly and lightly with butter and pop into a hot oven (200C/400F/Gas Mark 6) for 10-15 minutes till golden brown. Remove and arrange on individual plates, lying diagonally side by side. Remove the grape from each eye to leave a darkened indent.

To make the sauce, reduce the fish stock, *Noilly Prat*, Burgundy and shallots over a low heat to 4 tablespoons of liquid. Simmer the leeks in ¼pt/150ml water till it is reduced to 2 tablespoons of liquid. Work this through a fine nylon sieve and add to the reduced stock. Add the cream, Sauternes, tomato purée and chives and bring to the boil. Beat in the butter bit by bit and whisk to make the sauce slightly fluffy.

Salmon Quenelles

People tend to think that quenelles are extraordinarily difficult to make – restaurant food only. But they are not, and salmon quenelles are really special. The mousseline mixture itself is very easy (especially in the day of the food processor) and versatile – you can use it for a cold terrine or hot, enveloped in pastry as a starter. Once you have made the base, it can be kept for a day or two in the fridge before it is used. Equally, once the quenelles have been poached they can be kept chilled in the fridge for a couple of days and revamped with a variety of sauces (see page 172 onwards), or even frozen and revamped for an instant last-minute supper party.

Serves 6

1lb/500g filleted salmon
6fl oz/175ml double cream
2 egg whites
freshly ground sea salt and pepper

pinch of freshly grated nutmeg
Hollandaise or Saffron Sauce (page 175 and 180)

Check the fish is clean and entirely free of bones, chop into chunks and place in the bowl of a food processor and whizz the electric blade for about 20 seconds. Add the cream, egg whites and season and whizz for another 30 to 40 seconds until the mixture is completely smooth. Chill in the fridge for at least half an hour.

For the poaching, heat a large *shallow* pan of water to just below simmering. Prepare nearby a bowl of chilled water and two dessertspoons. Use the spoons to make oval shapes of the mixture and then slide each gently into the simmering water. Dip the spoons into the chilled water (keep lumps of ice floating in the bowl) before making each new quenelle. Repeat the process until you have filled the pan. After a minute or two the quenelles will flip themselves over, and then let them cook on this side for a further two minutes. Remove from the water with a slotted spoon, drain, pat dry with kitchen paper if necessary and keep warm on a shallow ovenproof dish. Continue until all the mixture is finished, and then gently pour the hot sauce straight over (for Shellfish Sauce, see page 177). If you are serving the *quenelles* with Hollandaise Sauce, garnish the *quenelles* with sprigs of parsley, or sprinkle finely chopped parsley all over, and serve the Hollandaise separately.

Prawn Mousse in Smoked Salmon

The sweetness of the prawn mousse counterbalances the saltiness of the smoked salmon well, but this is a rich combination as well. Depending on your stomach, therefore, you can vary the size of your parcels. I tend to make them smaller rather than larger on the basis that I don't like having to plough my way through a large helping of something very rich when I'm a guest myself.

Serves 4-6

½lb/225g peeled prawns
½pt/300ml double cream
finely chopped chives

1 dessertspoon brandy
pinch of cayenne pepper
12 slices smoked salmon

Whizz prawns very quickly in the food processor till shredded. Be *very* careful not to over-whizz as you will lose the body and the flavour. Whip double cream till it stands and then fold in prawns, brandy, cayenne and chives. Stir together well. Wrap dessertspoons of the mixture in half slices of smoked salmon – or if the appetites are stronger use one large tablespoon of the mixture per slice of smoked salmon. Serve with crisp brown toast and slices of lemon.

Poached Salmon Steaks with Tarragon Sauce

Tarragon goes very well with salmon and it is really worth the effort to make a proper court bouillon (see page 174) for this cold fragrant dish.

Serves 4

4 thick salmon steaks
2¹/₂pts/1.5 litres court bouillon
2 cucumbers peeled, de-seeded and cut into
  juliennes
¹/₂ teaspoon salt
1 teaspoon sugar

2 tablespoons white wine vinegar
7oz/200g mayonnaise (page 176) made with
  tarragon vinegar
7oz/200g Greek yoghurt
1 tablespoon finely chopped fresh tarragon, with
  a few sprigs for garnish

Wash the salmon steaks and dry with kitchen paper. Place in the warm *court bouillon* and bring gently to simmering point. Let the liquid bubble for a few seconds, then remove the pan from the heat and allow to cool turning the steaks every so often in the liquid until they are completely cold. Remove from the liquid and set aside on a plate. Keep the poaching liquid. Next beat together the mayonnaise and yoghurt, fold in the chopped tarragon and slowly add about 4 tablespoons of the poaching liquid until the mixture is of a coating consistency. Place each steak on a large plate, coat with the mixture and decorate with a sprig of tarragon. Serve with salad and tiny, scraped new potatoes soused in melted butter and chopped mint.

Terrine de Saumon a la Mousse d'Epinards

My great-aunts embodied all the traditions of Edwardian cuisine, and mousse was a *sine qua non* at their table. My indifference to the mousse – a combination of mushed-up meat or fish in cold *béchamel* – probably goes back to these childhood tastes of it, which is why I haven't included the traditional salmon mousse in this collection. But I do love a terrine, partly because the fish is less adulterated, and partly because a slice of it can look so pretty on a plate.

Serves 8-10

14oz/400g salmon fillet, diced
4 tablespoons double cream or crème frâiche
6 eggs

¹/₂ teaspoon paprika
1lb/450g puréed fresh spinach
salt and pepper

Place the salmon with the 2 tablespoons cream, three eggs, paprika, salt and pepper in a food processor and whizz till it is fine. Remove to a bowl. Place the spinach in the food processor with the remaining three eggs, cream, salt and pepper and whizz to a fine purée. Grease a terrine or loaf tin, line with clingfilm and fill with half the salmon mixture. Cover with the spinach purée and finish with the rest of the salmon. Fold the overlapping clingfilm over the top of the mixture, cover with foil, place the terrine in a *bain marie* and bake in a pre-heated oven (180C/350F/Gas Mark 4) for one hour. Remove and leave to cool. Turn out of the terrine, remove the clingwrap and slice to serve. Serve with Tomato Sauce Provençale (page 180) or Salsa Verde (page 181) or Mayonnaise (page 176). You can vary the spinach filling with red peppers (blanched and puréed) or peas.

Salmon Cakes

Always a hit – and at any time, breakfast, lunch or supper. These freeze very well too and are an easy way of using up any leftover poached salmon (see page 138).

Serves 4

1lb/450g potatoes
4 tablespoons butter
1 tablespoon finely chopped onions
8oz/225g cold poached salmon, flaked
1 teaspoon grated lemon rind

freshly ground salt and mixed black and white
*   peppercorns*
1oz/25g flour
1 egg, beaten
1oz/25g toasted breadcrumbs
oil or butter for frying, or a combination

Fry chopped onions in a little oil till translucent and set to one side. Boil potatoes till very soft and mash finely. Combine with 4 tablespoons butter and the fried chopped onions and the salmon. Season with the lemon rind and salt and pepper and form into 8 small cakes. Dip in flour, then egg and then breadcrumbs. If freezing, wrap individually at this stage and freeze. If eating straight away, fry in the oil or butter till golden brown. Serve with Sauce Tartare (page 179) or – delicious heresy – ketchup!

Salmon Timbales

Many recipes for salmon and sea trout are interchangeable and this is no exception. It is a wonderful standby either as a starter (one each) or as a main course for supper (two each!). And it is virtually foolproof.

Makes 4

1lb/450g boned and very finely chopped or
*   shredded salmon*
¹/₂ teaspoon salt
pinch paprika

¹/₂ teaspoon grated lemon rind
2 teaspoons lemon juice
4fl oz/125ml double cream
3 egg whites

Combine the salmon, salt, paprika, lemon rind and lemon juice. Whip the cream till it holds stiff peaks and fold into mixture. Whisk egg whites till they are stiff and fold gently into the mixture. Spoon into greased ramekin dishes and set in a bain marie of hot water which reaches halfway up the moulds. Bake in a moderate oven (180C/350F/Gas Mark 4) for 30-40 minutes depending on depth of the dishes. Test with a thin-bladed knife inserted in the centre – it should come out clean when they are ready. Remove from *bain marie*, slide knife around the sides and tip out onto individual plates. Serve with a spinach sauce – a little spinach purée combined with cream and seasoned with salt and pepper.

Gravad Lax with Mustard and Dill Sauce

This is the classic Scandinavian way of treating salmon – a rather more subtle and gentle form of curing than smoking. It is very easy to do at home and also freezes extremely successfully, so it is worth doing a whole side at a time. Dried dill really is not as successful as fresh in this recipe, so it is worth making the effort to buy the fresh stuff if you don't grow it in your garden yourself. Freeze-dried dill makes a better substitute for the fresh. Careful chopping of the dill also releases the aromatic flavour, and again it is worth making the effort to do it properly rather than just laying the sprigs onto the fish. You can use the tail end of the fish if you are making Gravad Lax for a small number of people, and this keeps the price down. A whole salmon is much more expensive, obviously, but still much cheaper, if you are catering for large numbers at a party for example, than the rather tasteless, plastic vacuum-packed varieties of Gravad Lax you find in supermarkets. The taste does not compare!

Serves 4-6

2lb/900g tail piece or middle cut salmon,
*   descaled and filleted, but with skin left on*
2 tablespoons rough sea salt
2 tablespoons caster sugar
2 tablespoons black peppercorns, roughly
*   crushed*
4 tablespoons freshly chopped dill
2 tablespoons brandy (optional)

Mustard and Dill Sauce
2 tablespoons Dijon mustard
1 tablespoon of brown soft sugar
lemon juice or white wine vinegar to taste
5fl oz/150ml vegetable oil
2 tablespoons finely chopped fresh dill
salt (optional)

Check that all the bones have been removed, using tweezers to ease out any malingerers. Wipe the fish clean and dry thoroughly. In a bowl mix together the sugar, salt, pepper, dill and brandy. Spread a thin layer of the mixture on the bottom of a large glass, china, plastic or enamel (*not* metal) deep container and lay on side, skin down, on top of this. Cover the upper side with nearly all the rest of the mixture. Place the other side of salmon on top, skin side uppermost and press down. Cover with the remaining sugar and salt mixture. Cover the whole 'sandwich' with foil and place heavy weights on top. Leave to marinate in a fridge or cool place for 2-5 days, turning the whole sandwich every 12 hours to ensure that it is evenly cured. During this time the flesh will darken to a deeper pink, like smoked salmon, and the fish will also release a lot of oils and juices which is why a deep enough container is essential.

The Mustard and Dill Sauce can be made ahead of use as it keeps very well. Put the mustard into a small bowl and stir in the sugar. Add the oil slowly, drop by drop as in mayonnaise. Stir in the chopped dill, and lemon or vinegar to taste. Some people like a hint of salt as well, but it is entirely optional.

To serve the Gravad Lax, scrape all the curing mixture off the fish and carve in very thin slices like smoked salmon. Serve with fresh brown bread and butter and Mustard and Dill Sauce.

Raw Salmon Marinated with Lime and Fresh Coriander

This is a recipe of Jenny Hughes-Gibbs, a friend and brilliant professional cook who spent 8 years as head chef at Cybele Lodge in the Transvaal, the only *Relais et Château* hotel in South Africa. We ask her for it every time she cooks for our European guests. Many people have versions of this sort of recipe, sometimes mistakenly dubbed seviche (real seviche should be made with marinated white fish with a combination of peppers, avocados and onions). This recipe omits the onions – their flavour is so strong they detract from the delicate combination of the salmon and coriander. Many recipes also advise the marinating to be done for anything from 1-24 hours. This can 'burn' the fish, especially if the marinade is made with limes rather than lemons. The secret to the success of this is very short marinating – between 10 minutes and 20 minutes at the absolute maximum. You can use frozen salmon for this, but it really is another world made with fresh.

Serves 6

2lb/1kg fresh salmon tail, filleted and D-sliced
  (as in Gravad Lax)
3-4 limes
1 teaspoon chives, finely chopped

1 good tablespoon olive oil
1 dessertspoon caster sugar
1 tablespoon chopped coriander
salt and freshly ground black pepper

Slice the tail finely through the D shape and arrange three slices per person on individual plates. In a small bowl mix thoroughly together the sugar, lime juice, herbs and olive oil, making sure that the sugar is completely dissolved. Sprinkle the salmon slices with salt and pepper (they can take a surprising amount of salt). Ten minutes before serving spoon the marinade evenly over the slices on each plate. Garnish with coriander sprigs and serve with walnut bread.

Salmon Kebabs

These are a favourite with my sons, and can be done as successfully in a hot oven as over a barbecue. They are so easy and light and can be varied by any number of accompanying sauces – pesto, tomato, sweet/sour/*Salsa verde*, Hollandaise (see Sauces, page 172). Many people find peppers indigestible so I usually make the kebabs with just mushrooms and onions, leaving the sauce and salad to add the colour.

Serves 4

2lb/1kg salmon fillet, skinned and boned
8 slices bacon, diced
about 24 button mushrooms

freshly ground salt and pepper
1 dessertspoon butter

Melt the butter in a frying pan and gently cook the mushrooms so that they are half-cooked and still firm to the touch. Remove from the heat and set to one side. Cut the salmon into inch sized (2cm) cubes and thread onto skewers already oiled to prevent the fish sticking to them. Alternate a cube of salmon, bacon and mushroom along the skewer, allowing two skewers per person. Heat the grill until very hot and oil the grill rack. Cook the skewers under the grill for about 4 minutes, turning occasionally. If you like you can marinate the kebabs in a mixture of oil and lemon juice (1 lemon to 4 tablespoons olive oil) and use the mixture for basting, but since salmon is a naturally oily fish I prefer to sprinkle the kebabs just simply with salt and pepper and then serve with one of several sauces. If you prefer to cook the kebabs in the oven, turn the heat high (230C/450F/Gas Mark 8) and roast for about 5 minutes.

Puff Pastry Case with a Râgout of Salmon in a Saffron and Lime Sauce

This is very easy once you've got the hang of making the puff pastry cases. It is also a very pretty way of doing salmon for a dinner party.

Serves 2

2 puff pastry cases, pre-baked or frozen
 or
3oz/75g puff pastry (and a little flour for dusting)
1 tablespoon vegetable oil

7oz/200g fillet of salmon (no skin) cut into
 ¹/₂ inch/1¹/₂cm cubes
salt, freshly ground white pepper
1 sprig dill

If you aren't using ready-made pastry cases, make your own as follows. Dust the puff pastry with flour. Roll out till it is 3mm thick. Cut into two rectangles, 3¹/₂in/9cm x 2¹/₂in/6cm. Chill in fridge for 30 minutes. Mark out a line with a sharp knife without cutting all the way through the pastry, leaving a small border all the way round the edge of the case. Place on a baking tray and cook for about 15 minutes in a moderate oven. (350F/180C/Gas Mark 4) until golden brown. Cut out the premarked lid. Remove and keep aside in a warm place.

Sauce
7fl oz/200ml dry white wine
4fl oz/100ml fish or vegetable stock
4fl oz/100ml single cream
2 teaspoons butter or margarine

2 teaspoons flour
salt, freshly ground white pepper
2 tablespoons herbs chopped, e.g. dill, parsley,
 chives

Mix butter or margarine with the flour until you have a smooth paste. Bring white wine and stock to the boil and reduce to half the quantity. Add the cream and bring to the boil again. Add flour and butter mixture (kneaded butter), stirring constantly. Boil for 4-5 minutes till a creamy consistency is obtained. Season with salt and white pepper. Add chopped herbs, a pinch of saffron powder and lime juice to taste. Keep aside.

To finish off, season the salmon cubes with salt and pepper. Heat the oil in a non-stick pan and lightly toss the salmon until very lightly cooked through. Remove and drain on kitchen towel. Place the puff pastry cases on a dish and fill with the cooked salmon cubes. Pour the sauce carefully over the fish and garnish with the lid and a sprig of dill.

Hot Smoked Salmon on Ginger and Cucumber with *Beurre Blanc*

This is another of Matthew Fort's inspirations. Some might consider it a sin to eat smoked salmon hot, but we all know sinful things are the best! This requires not slices of smoked salmon, but smoked salmon steaks, and since first being introduced to this concept a few years ago I have seen smoked salmon steaks now available on the shelves in Marks & Spencer. So you don't need to buy a whole side of smoked salmon to do this.

Serves 8

1¹/₂ large cucumbers
¹/₂ ginger root
beurre blanc *(see page 185)*

8 smoked salmon steaks, cut vertically through
 the thick end of a side of smoked salmon
parsley for garnish

Peel the cucumbers and cut the flesh into very fine *juliennes* about two inches long. Peel the root ginger and cut more *juliennes*. Make the *beurre blanc* and keep warm to one side. Take 8 plates and scatter the ginger and cucumber *juliennes* over them. Place the steaks on a tray and bake in a preheated very hot oven (230C/450F/Gas Mark 8) for 5 minutes until the outside is slightly hard and an even brown. Place each steak on the bed of *juliennes,* pour the sauce around the salmon and garnish with parsley.

Marinated and Grilled Salmon with Warm Walnut Oil and Tarragon Dressing

Altough an oily fish, salmon is all too often presented dried up through overcooking. This method keeps it moist and succulent. The citrus juices 'cook' the flesh slightly before it is grilled (see raw salmon slices marinated in lime and coriander, page 148).

Serves 4

4 x 6oz/175g salmon fillets with skin left on
4 tablespoons lemon juice
3 tablespoons orange juice
3 tablespoons olive oil
sprig of thyme
black pepper

Dressing
1 teaspoon dry mustard
2 tablespoons sherry vinegar
1 tablespoon finely chopped onion
5 tablespoons walnut oil
freshly ground salt, black pepper
pinch sugar
2 tablespoons finely chopped tarragon

Trim each fillet of bones, and remove any scales from the skin. Place the fillets, skin side up, in a shallow dish. Marinate in the citrus juices, oil, pepper, thyme for one hour, turn the fish once or twice. Cover a grill rack with foil and turn the grill on high. Take the salmon out of the marinade and pat dry with kitchen paper. Lightly salt the flesh side, then place, skin side up, on the rack and position fairly close to the grill. When the skin browns, turn the heat down and lower the grill pan. Depending on thickness, five minutes' exposure to the heat should be enough to cook the salmon through without turning. If it is too underdone for your taste, transfer to heated plates and put in a low oven for one or two minutes. The flesh should be just opaque. Combine the vinegar with the mustard and onion and whisk in the oil. Season to taste with salt, pepper and sugar. Heat gently – do not allow to boil. Stir in the tarragon and spoon the sauce onto each plate over each fillet.

Game Fish Pie

This can be made, like any fish pie, with any of the game fish – salmon, sea trout or trout, a mixture of any of them, mixed with white fish, or mixed with smoked trout. I find I usually make fish pie with leftovers rather than from scratch – it seems such a waste not to savour the delicate flavours first time round on their own.

Serves 4-6

2lb/1kg flaked cooked salmon, sea trout, or trout
*   or smoked trout   or a mixture of any*
8oz/225g mushrooms, sliced
2oz/60g butter
4 hard boiled eggs
1 large bunch parsley, finely chopped
1 pint/600ml Béchamel or Velouté Sauce
*   (page 184)*

2 tablespoons cream
2 tablespoons dry white wine
pinch of sugar
tablespoon chopped chives
salt and pepper

Melt the butter in a saucepan, and sauté the mushrooms till they are soft. Remove from the pan with a slotted spoon and place in a bowl with the flaked fish. With these mix in the chopped chives and parsley and arrange in a pie dish. Warm the *Béchamel* or *Velouté* Sauce, add white wine and cream, a pinch of sugar and seasoning to taste and pour over the fish. Brown in a medium oven (180C/350F/Gas Mark 4) for 45 minutes. If desired, add a topping of mashed potatoes or pastry and brown similarly. Serve with peas.

Steamed Salmon with Sorrel and Spinach Sauce

Lososina s Sousom iz Shchavelya i Shpinata

Sorrel grows in great abundance in Russia and has always been a staple diet in the peasant kitchens, but somehow never made it into Russian haute cuisine. However, it is now making its mark on menus all over the place and you can even find it in some specialist shops. If you don't have any of those at hand (as I don't) you can either grow your own or pick it in the hedgerows and verges and fields. It is absolutely delicious and worth making the effort for.

Serves 4

4 salmon steaks (about 6oz/175g each)
freshly ground sea salt and black pepper
¼pt/150ml vegetable oil
3 tablespoons lemon juice

2 teaspoon capers, drained
sorrel and spinach sauce (see below)
sorrel leaves and lemon for garnish

Skin and bone the salmon steaks, then rub with salt and pepper. Mix the oil, lemon juice and capers in a shallow bowl and add the steaks, turning them to make sure they are well coated with the marinade, then arrange in a steamer over simmering water. Cover and steam for 6-7 minutes until opaque. To serve, divide the sauce on to four plates and arrange the salmon steak to one side, or on top. Garnish with a fan of half slices of lemon and a sorrel leaf.

Sorrel and spinach sauce
8oz/225g rinsed, drained and chopped sorrel
4oz/100g rinsed, drained and chopped fresh
  spinach
¾pt/450ml double cream

¼pt/150ml dry white wine
2 tablespoons butter, cut into small pieces
freshly ground sea salt and black peppercorns to
  taste
fresh lemon juice to taste (optional)

Scald the sorrel and spinach in boiling salted water for 2 minutes. Rinse under cold running water, drain and squeeze completely dry. Purée the spinach and sorrel and a quarter of the cream in a liquidiser or food processor. Pour the rest of the cream and the wine into a saucepan, bring to the boil over a high heat and continue boiling till reduced to half (about 7 minutes). Add the sorrel and spinach and cook for 2 more minutes, stirring. Take off the heat and stir in the butter, bit by bit, until completely amalgamated. Season the sauce with salt and pepper to taste, and lemon juice if a tarter flavour is preferred.

Salmon Koulibiaka

Koulibiaka, which simply means a long pie made of rolled pastry, is popular throughout Russia. But the fame of this dish first spread to France in the 18th century when Parisian chefs employed by the Russian nobility took the recipe home with them. The Russians usually made it with salmon, and sometimes with sturgeon from the Caspian Sea. But it can actually be made with any sort of fish or meat. The traditional recipe is made without raisins but I like the touch of sweetness they provide.

Serves 6

1lb/500g fresh salmon, skinned
2 onions, peeled and chopped
6 black peppercorns
slice of lemon
salt
2oz/50g long-grain rice
1oz/25g butter
6oz/175g button mushrooms, sliced
2oz/50g raisins
1 tablespoon lemon juice

6fl oz/175ml single cream
pinch of ground nutmeg
freshly ground sea salt and mixed white and
   black peppercorns
1 tablespoon cornflour
2 tablespoons water
2 tablespoons chopped fresh parsley
1 x 13oz/375g frozen puff pastry
2 eggs, beaten

Put the salmon into a pan with the onions, peppercorns, slice of lemon and salt and cover with water. Bring slowly to the boil then remove instantly and leave to one side for 10 minutes. Strain and reserve the liquid. Skin, bone and flake the fish. Cook the rice in the fish stock, drain and allow to cool. Melt the butter in a saucepan and gently fry the mushrooms till soft. Stir in the lemon juice, cream, nutmeg, raisins, salt and pepper. Cook till well amalgamated – a few minutes. Mix the cornflour with the water and stir into the sauce. Simmer for 2-3 minutes, then stir in the chopped parsley and allow to cool.

Roll out the pastry to a 14inch/18cm square. Spread half the rice over the pastry to form a 7inch/18cm square in the middle. Cover the rice with half the mushroom mixture, then all of the flaked salmon. Spread the rest of the mixture over the fish and top with the rest of the rice. Draw up two sides of the pastry to overlap by 1 inch/25cm and seal with beaten egg. Trim away the pastry from each end to within 1 inch of the filling. Crimp the edges together and seal with beaten egg. Cut a 2inch/5cm wide strip of pastry from the trimmings, and place over the join, brushing with beaten egg to seal. Make pastry leaves from the remaining trimmings, and use to make a pattern down the sealing pastry strip. Brush with beaten egg to glaze and bake in a moderate oven (350F/180C/Gas Mark 4) for 45 minutes. Serve, sliced, with Hollandaise Sauce (page 175).

Hot Sea Trout Mousse in a Puff Pastry Case

I usually make this in one big case to look rather like a cake which you slice into. It could be made as well into little individual 'cakes' as a starter. The whole 'cake' works either as a starter or as a main course. It is very good looking and melts in the mouth (especially with lots of fattening Hollandaise!)

Serves 8

1lb/450g raw filleted sea trout (or salmon)
3 egg whites
1pt/600ml double cream
½ teaspoon ground mace

generous pinch of salt and white pepper
1lb/450g puff pastry (frozen is fine)
1 egg yolk, beaten

Dice the sea trout, place it in the food processor with the salt, white pepper, mace, egg whites and whizz to a fine purée. Chill for half an hour. Return to the food processor, blend in the cream and chill again until it is needed. Divide the pastry roughly into one lump of one third and another lump of two thirds. Roll out the one third into a neat circle. Roll out the two thirds into a much larger neat circle. Place the mixture in the middle of the large circle and cover with the small circle of pastry. Fold the overlapping edges of the large circle of pastry over the small circle, binding with some milk or beaten egg painted on. Turn the whole 'cake' carefully over and place, small circle side down, on a round ovenproof plate or baking tray. Decorate with a small fish made out of the leftover scraps of pastry. Brush with beaten egg yolk and bake in a moderate oven (180C/350F/Gas Mark 4) for 30 minutes. Serve with lavish quantities of Sauce Hollandaise (see page 175).

WINES

SALMON & SEA TROUT

When the king of fish is served fresh on a great occasion, or just when you feel like having the very best, there is no need to look further than the magnificent classic white wines of Burgundy's Côte de Beaune, including the famous names of Montrachet, Corton and Meursault. The buttery fullness of these is the best possible complement for the soft richness of fresh salmon. Also magnificent with salmon are the rich white wines of areas of the Rhone like Hermitage and Chateauneuf-du-Pape, which we tend to associate more with their massive reds.

Good quality rosés like Tavel are also a good choice, both with fresh and smoked salmon, and good quality German and Austrian Rieslings, especially *spätleses* and *ausleses,* are also highly recommended. Gewurztraminer goes well with fresh salmon and sea trout, and is also a good complement to them when they have been smoked. Champagne, especially in the old-fashioned style with a distinct hint of apples in the flavour, is a traditional accompaniment to smoked salmon and sea trout, and is always appropriate. So too are some of the New World sparkling white wines, and also the best Australian and New Zealand sparkling rosés. Disregard the misleading adage that fish always means white wine. Some light reds are excellent with fish, especially salmon and sea trout, and it is well worth looking closely at some of the deliciously fruity light red wines of Germany, Alsace and the upper Loire. Light Beaujolais is also excellent.

TROUT: *Salmonidae salmoniformes*

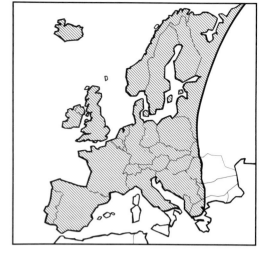

Habitat:	freshwater rivers and ponds
Length:	10-18ins (20-36cm)
Weight:	1-3lb (500g-1½kg)
Season:	February – September (brown trout)
	all year (rainbow trout)
Best time for eating:	as season

French: *la truite*   Serbo-Croat: *pastárva*   Dutch: *forel*
German: *die Forelle*   Romanian: *pastrav*   Flemish: *de forel*
Italian: *la trota*   Bulgarian: *pastárva*   Norwegian: *en ørret*
Spanish: *la trucha*   Russian: *pastárva*   Danish: *ørred*
Greek: *i péstrofa*   Czech: *pstruh obecny*   Swedish: *forell*
Portuguese: *truta*   Polish: *pstrag*   Hungarian: *pisztráng*

There are basically two kinds of trout: the brown trout which live wild in rivers and ponds, and the rainbow which can be wild but nowadays is very often farmed. Their flesh is pink and delicate and not as oily as salmon; they make for good healthy eating! They are at their best eaten straight out of the water and cooked very simply – poached or baked in foil. If they are cooked in the traditional manner *en bleu* do not wash off the slime around the fish before cooking as this is what turns the fish blue (in an ideal world the fish should be stunned and popped alive into the boiling water). Trout are the perfect size for an individual helping, but any leftovers can, as those of salmon and sea trout, be magicked into any number of treats. Our favourite is trout soufflé. Trout are also excellent smoked and eaten with horseradish sauce or combined in fish pies and pâtés.

Trout with Tarragon and Pomegranate.

Truite au Bleu

The classic recipe for trout. If they aren't actually alive when you drop them into the water (only for the strong-hearted I suspect), then they should be very fresh and properly gutted. You can serve with any number of sauces, but personally I think a simple melted butter with a squeeze of lemon juice, a good screw of black pepper and a pinch of salt is the best.

Serves 4

4 trout
1 large pan of simple court bouillon *(3 parts water, 1 part white wine vinegar, pinch salt)*

8oz/225g butter
juice of ½-1 lemon
salt and pepper

Bring a large pan of water, vinegar and salt to the boil. Let it die down and when it is just simmering drop the fish into the water and poach till cooked through – about five minutes, depending on the size of the fish. The trout will curl once they are in the water. Serve with the melted butter and lemon juice, and plain boiled potatoes sprinkled with parsley, and green salad.

Trout in Foil
Psari sto harti

Oregano grows wild all over Greece and the Greeks use it in all their cooking. It goes very well in this Greek version of trout in foil – at its best eaten outside on a hot sunny day!

Serves 4

4 trout, gutted and cleaned
4 onions, finely chopped
1 celery branch finely chopped
1 teaspoon chopped parsley
6 medium mushrooms finely chopped
olive oil

oregano
¼pt/150ml white wine
salt and pepper
lemons
butter

Sauté the onions, celery, parsley and mushrooms in 3 tablespoons butter; season with salt, pepper and a pinch of oregano; add wine and simmer for 10 minutes. Meanwhile wash and dry the trout and then stuff each with the sautéed mushroom mixture. Secure with a skewer and place on individual double sheets of foil. Sprinkle each trout with salt, pepper and oregano; squeeze the juice of half lemon on each and sprinkle with olive oil. Seal and bake for about 20 minutes in a moderate oven. Take the trout out of the foil and serve with Greek garlic sauce (below).

Garlic Sauce
Skordalia

6 cloves garlic, minced
2 cups mashed potatoes
½ teaspoon salt

½pt/300ml olive oil
¼pt/150ml vinegar

Place the minced garlic, potatoes and salt in a blender and blend at high speed till smooth. Slowly add olive oil, alternating with vinegar and blend till smooth. If the sauce is too thick, then thin it with several tablespoons water. Chill in covered jar for several hours before serving.

Forel s Estragonom

The Russians use pomegranate seeds with game and also with fish. Trout abound in the rivers
of the Caucasus and the lakes of Armenia. This is how they like to grill or barbecue them there.
Serves 4

4 trout
¹/₄pt/150ml extra virgin olive oil
2fl oz/75ml lemon juice
2 cloves garlic, crushed
¹/₂ teaspoon sea salt

6-8 crushed sprigs fresh tarragon, leaves and
 stem
freshly ground black pepper
tarragon twigs for garnish
promegranate seeds for garnish

Crush the garlic and salt together in a bowl and add the oil, lemon juice, chopped tarragon and pepper. Mix
all together. Add the fish to the marinade, turning them over to make sure they are completely coated. Chill
for 30 minutes. Heat the grill so that it is hot rather than very hot, and oil the rack. Make several criss-cross
incisions in the skin of the trout to prevent it from splitting during cooking. Basting every so often with the
remains of the marinade, place the fish 2-3 inches from the grill and grill for 5 minutes each side. Serve
garnished with pomegranate seeds and extra tarragon twigs.

Hot Trout Soufflé

Perfect for a light lunch or supper, or even as in individual ramekins as a starter for dinner, this
is my favourite way of dealing with leftovers. There is no mystique to soufflé making,
but it does help to use older rather than fresher eggs (the whites whip up better) and also
to use extra egg whites.
Serves 4

8-12oz/225-350g trout
1¹/₂oz/45g butter
¹/₂pt/300ml milk
1¹/₂oz/45g cornflour

5 eggs, separated
2 extra egg whites
salt and pepper

Make sure that the oven has reached a stable temperature by the time you put your soufflé mixture in, and
cook at a medium heat (200C/400F/Gas Mark 6). Most recipes tell you to grease your soufflé dish, but I never
do – on no scientific basis I think that clinging to the side helps it to rise (which it always does) but it does
make washing up hard work! Prepare a 3-3¹/₂pt (1.7-2 litre) soufflé dish, greased or ungreased according to
preference. If you are using fresh trout skin and fillet it and lightly poach the flesh in the milk so that it is *just*
cooked. If using leftovers, flake the flesh. Keep the milk you have poached the sauce in for the soufflé
mixture. Melt the butter in a non-stick pan, stir in the flour till it is all absorbed and slowly add enough milk to
make the consistency of creamy custard. Season quite strongly and remove from the heat while you stir in the
egg yolks. The mixture will become more liquid. Carefully stir in the flaked fish and keep to one side. Whisk
up the egg whites till they form peaks (a pinch of salt helps to make them stiffer) and then carefully *fold* the
mixture (never, ever stir it) into the egg whites. Fill the soufflé dish four-fifths of the way up to allow room to
rise but not spill over. Cook in the middle of the oven for 25-30 minutes and serve immediately or it will sink
with the change in temperature. Serve with a Tomato (page 180) or fresh Spinach and Sorrel Sauce (see
page 180).

Can also be made with salmon or sea trout.

Hot Smoked Trout Fillets wrapped in Spinach Leaves

If you want to serve smoked trout as a starter, but don't want to look as if you've 'copped out' then this makes for a first course with a difference. If fresh spinach leaves are hard to come by, you could vary this by using cabbage (Savoy is best) or lettuce (Cox, Webbs Wonder or ordinary soft lettuce, not Iceberg).

Serves 4

2 smoked trout, skinned and filleted　　　　　　*butter*
16 large spinach leaves　　　　　　　　　　*freshly ground black and white peppercorns*

Skin and fillet each smoked trout and divide each side into two. Put neatly to one side. Bring a large pan of salted water to the boil and blanch the spinach leaves for 1-2 minutes. Drain and plunge immediately into ice cold water to refresh and retain their colour. Drain again and pat dry with kitchen paper. Wrap each slim fillet carefully in 2 spinach leaves making sure that it is completely enveloped in the spinach. Tear off 8 squares of foil large enough to wrap round each fillet, and lightly grease with oil to ensure the spinach doesn't stick and sprinkle with pepper. Place each enveloped fillet with a knob of butter on the foil and wrap up firmly. Place on a baking tray and warm in a moderate oven (180C/350F/Gas Mark 4) for 7-10 minutes. Remove from the oven, unwrap and place two fillets on individual, pre-heated plates. Carefully pour Lemon, Cream and Butter Sauce (page 176) onto each plate.

WINES

TROUT *(brown trout & rainbow trout)*

Freshwater trout lack the fatty richness of their seagoing migrant cousins, and when cooked fresh have a more austerely delicate flavour. Smoked trout comes much closer to the richness of salmon and sea trout, and goes well with the fuller bodied white wines and also the light reds. Most freshly cooked trout is best accompanied by a white wine, or a rosé. The crisp and fruity white wines of Gascony are excellent, and also the Rieslings of Germany, Austria and Alsace. Young white Burgundy is delicious with trout, as are the cheaper alternatives of white Rioja and Dão, and the white wines of northern Italy.

For cold trout dishes including salads Muscadet and Gros Plant are ideal, and there is a wide choice of sparkling wines from Champagne, from other regions of France, and from the increasingly comprehensive range of fine New World sparkling white wines.

Trout Cooked in Spinach.

PIKE and CARP

Very popular throughout Eastern Europe, pike, perch and carp are eaten less here in Britain. But in Poland and Czechoslovakia they are highly prized and are traditional fare on Christmas Eve when dinner is supposed to be without meat and even fats are avoided in cooking. Yugoslavia and Romania also have large lakes which abound with these large fish. Many people find carp are muddy in taste and it is not unusual to soak the cleaned fish for anything up to two days in fresh water (changing it every so often) to get rid of the muddy flavour. Polish/Jewish recipes for carp often include sweet elements – raisins, ginger, sugar, vinegar, nuts – to disguise this characteristic. The famous Jewish *gefillte* fish, which originated from Lithuania and could be made of pike and carp and perch combined, or each separately, gets over the problem of the multitudinous bones as well as the flavours.

Serves 6

One 2 to 2½lb/1kg pike or carp
salt
3 large onions
2 tablespoons fresh white breadcrumbs
pinch of sugar
1 tablespoon grated horseradish (or good ready-
*   made sauce like Elsenhams)*
1 egg white
2 bay leaves
pinch ground white pepper

For the stock
1 onion
1 stick celery, diced
1 large carrot, sliced
1 parsnip, sliced
1 celeriac, cubed
1 bouquet garni
pinch salt and pepper
3½pt/2 litres water

Using a very sharp knife remove the head and tail from the fish and then divide the body into six equal slices about 2inches (5cm) thick. Take each cutlet and carefully cut inside the skin to remove all the flesh and bones, leaving the skin intact. Put the skin carefully on a plate, sprinkle with a little salt and keep cool in the fridge. Throw away the small bones but reserve the main bones, head and tail for the stock. Make the stock by putting the fish bones in a large saucepan with all the vegetables. Cover with the water and simmer for an hour. While this is simmering put the fish with 2 onions, chopped fairly finely into a food processor and whizz till they have formed a smooth mixture. Then add the egg white, horseradish, sugar, breadcrumbs and salt and pepper and whizz again for as short a time as possible till completely mixed. If necessary add up to 2 tablespoons of water to make a light soft consistency. Form the mixture into 6 oval shapes that will fit into the skin and arrange inside the skin, securing with a toothpick if needed. Arrange the portions side by side to reform the shape of the original fish, placing the head and tail at each end and lay carefully in the bottom of a fish kettle. Add the two remaining onions, sliced, around the fish and gently ladle the stock all over to cover. Simmer very gently for one hour, remove from the heat and allow to cool in the pan. Once it is cold, reassemble the whole fish in a separate deepish dish, cover with clingfilm and refrigerate until you have made the jelly to cover. To do this measure the amount of fish stock and for every pint (600ml) of liquid you will need one packet (0.4oz/11g) gelatine. Dissolve the gelatine by sprinkling on to a little of the hot fish stock and stirring until completely dissolved. Add to the rest of the stock and when it is cool but not yet set pour over the fish to form a clear glaze over and around it. Place in the fridge to set and serve garnished with parsley. You can, of course, eat this warm straight from the pot, but traditionally it is eaten cold with other fish dishes on Christmas Eve.

Quenelles de Brochet

Underestimated on the whole in Britain, pike is eaten nearly everywhere else in Europe and *quenelles de brochet* are almost a *sine qua non* on the menus of any self-respecting lakeside restaurant, especially in France and Switzerland.

Serves 4

¾lb/350g pike
3 slices day old bread, without the crusts
* (preferably not 'instant sliced')*
4 tablespoons single cream

5oz/150g butter
2 eggs and 1 extra white
pinch nutmeg
salt and white pepper

Skin and bone the fish and cut it into small bits. Soak the bread in the cream and then squeeze out most of the liquid. Crumble it into a small saucepan, add a nut of butter and stir over a low heat until it forms a smooth mixture which leaves the sides of the pan. Remove from the heat and cool. Put this together with the fish and eggs into a food processor and whizz for a few seconds till it makes a very smooth paste. Melt the rest of the butter and add in a thin stream to the food processor until you have a soft white purée. Remove the mixture to a bowl, season with salt and pepper and nutmeg and chill in the fridge for at least an hour before using. To make the *quenelles* have ready a bowl of iced water and two dessert spoons. Use both spoons to shape the mixture into smooth, soft little lozenge shapes. Put these onto a lightly floured plate and chill again to get them firm again. Meanwhile bring a very large heavy-bottomed frying pan of salted water to the boil, reduce the heat till the water is just moving and gently drop the *quenelles* into this one by one. They will need about 2 minutes each side till they are done. Remove carefully with a slotted spoon and arrange in an ovenproof dish. Cover with a Velouté Sauce (page 184) or Shellfish Sauce (page 177), and bake in a preheated oven (190C/375F/Gas Mark 5) until lightly browned. If you need quicker results pass the dish quickly under the grill to brown lightly.

WINES

PIKE

Despite its unprepossessing appearance and predatory habits, pike combine delicacy and surprising richness, and deserve the fullness of a white Burgundy, a Rhone or a Rioja. The fuller style Riesling wines of Germany and Alsace are also favourites with pike, and Gewurztraminer for some of the richer recipes involving creamy sauces. Tavel and Alsace rosés are also very suitable, and also some of the light red wines of Germany, the Loire and northern Italy.

Karp w Sosie Ikrowym

Carp, like pike, is the Christmas Eve dish of many families in northern Europe from Poland to Germany. It has been bred since the 13th century and is held in high esteem. But it can have a muddy taste and may need to be rinsed (live) in a bucket of water for a day or so, changing the water several times. The Serbs and Hungarians like to cook their carp with sour cream, and it is also popular *au bleu* with horseradish sauce, and again, like pike, it features in Jewish cookery quite strongly. But of all the East European recipes, this Polish poached carp with roe sauce is probably the most traditional. It is said, incidentally, that if you save a scale off your Christmas Eve carp it will bring you luck for the following year.

Serves 8

1 carp, cleaned and scaled, with its roe
salt
1oz/25g butter
1 bay leaf
5 black peppercorns
4 juniper berries
1pt/500ml dry white wine
1 tablespoon white wine vinegar
7oz/200g mushrooms, finely sliced
2oz/60g butter
1 tablespoon flour

2 tablespoons sour cream
1 egg yolk
pinch paprika
For the stock
2 onions, sliced
2 leeks, sliced (white part only)
3 stalks of celery, chopped
1 whole clove
1 bouquet garni
salt and pepper
1¹/₂pt/1 litre water

Put all the ingredients for the stock into a large pan, bring to the boil and simmer for half an hour. Meanwhile, rinse the carp, remove and reserve the roe, and sprinkle the fish with salt. Leave to stand for half an hour, then rinse well and place in a fish kettle. Pour in the vegetable stock and add the 1oz (25g) butter, bay leaf, peppercorns, juniper berries and wine. Cover the pan and simmer for 20-25 minutes, basting often. Remove the fish carefully and keep warm in a shallow ovenproof dish. Reserve the stock. Put the roe into a saucepan and onto it pour ¹/₄pt (150ml) boiling water with 1 tablespoon vinegar added to it. Bring to the boil and simmer for a few minutes until the roe is cooked through. Remove the roe, cut into neat slivers or cubes and cook with the sliced mushrooms in a saucepan with half (1oz/30g) of the butter. Melt the rest of the butter in another saucepan and stir in the flour till it is all absorbed. Gradually add enough strained stock from the fish to make a smooth thin sauce the consistency of single cream and then whisk in the sour cream, egg yolk and paprika. Finally, carefully stir in the mushrooms and roe, and pour some of the sauce over the carp. Garnish with lemon wedges and serve the rest of the sauce separately.

Game Fish and Mussel Soup

This is rich and warming and absolutely delicious. You can make it with any of the white game fish – pike, carp, perch, eels etc – and, of course, if those aren't available you can resort to good old haddock or whiting.

Serves 6

12oz/350g fresh pike or carp or perch or eel (or any combination)
1 onion, finely chopped
1 clove of garlic, crushed
1 tin smoked mussels
1 tin mussels in brine
4-6 fresh tomatoes, skinned and chopped

1 dessertspoon tomato purée
1-2 teaspoons ground fenugreek, chervil, parsley
1 tablespoon olive oil
1 pint/600ml fish stock and/or water (for fish stock see page 174)
salt and freshly ground pepper

Heat the oil in a large, deep heavy-bottomed frying pan and in it cook the chopped onion and crushed garlic till they are softened. Add the chopped tomatoes, tomato purée, skinned and chopped fish, both lots of mussels with their juices and 1-2 teaspoons of the mixed herbs, according to taste.

Cover with stock and/or water, season well and cook gently for about 20 minutes. Remove from the heat, strain the soup and liquidise the fish and return to the juice. If it is too thick add more stock or water, check the seasoning, return to the heat and add more herbs if necessary. Serve with floating croûtons of French bread (sliced French bread, baked in a medium oven for about 20 minutes till dry and golden) each with a good dollop of *Salsa all'aglio* or *Aioli* Sauce (see page 183) or *Rouille* (see page 182).

Anguilla alla Tartara

When eel is really fresh, straight out of the pond, this is a lovely clean, simple way to eat it. If the fish is fresh you will notice the striped back, the brown shading to green at the sides and going to silver underneath. If the back is black and the underside yellow this is usually a sign that it has been living in stagnant, muddy water. So avoid!

Serves 6

2lb/900g eel
1pt/600ml court bouillon (see page 174)
4oz/100g seasoned flour
1 egg, beaten
6oz/175g fresh white breadcrumbs

4oz/100g butter
4oz/100g sliced gherkins
salt and freshly ground pepper
Sauce Tartare

Skin the eels by making an incision, skin deep, around the circumference of the head. Hold the head with your left hand making sure it is wrapped in a cloth to prevent it slipping and with your right hand turn back the skin at the incision. Pull it off, rather like a pair of tights, all the way down to the tail. Cut off the head and it is then ready for cooking – either whole, or more commonly sliced into chunks. Make sure the eel is clean then slice into 3-inch pieces. Put them in a large heavy saucepan, cover with the *court bouillon* and bring to the boil. Reduce the heat and simmer for 8 minutes. Drain the eel pieces and while they are draining completely dry, gently melt the butter in a large saucepan (if you haven't got one large enough to hold all the pieces evenly at one time, use two frying pans simultaneously). Lightly dust each piece in flour, then dip into the beaten egg and then into the breadcrumbs. Turn the heat up under the frying pan to medium-high and add the bits of eel, cooking and turning till they are golden brown all over. Remove from the pan, arrange on a large platter, sprinkle lightly with salt and pepper, garnish with the sliced gherkins and serve with Sauce Tartare (see page 179).

Anguilla al Vino Rosso

The Italians are great with fish, and here is one of their rich ways of dealing with eel.

Serves 6

2lb/900g fresh eels
18 small shallots for glazing
¼pt/150ml white stock
1 bouquet garni
3 sprigs parsley
½ teaspoon dried thyme
1 bay leaf
3 tablespoons butter
salt and pepper
1 teaspoon sugar
2 tablespoons oil
2 tablespoons butter

1 large onion, finely chopped
pinch nutmeg
1¼pt/750ml red wine with ¼pt/150ml water
1 bay leaf
12 thin slices Italian or French bread, fried in
  butter till golden
3oz/75g unsalted butter
2½oz/65g anchovy fillets, rinsed and chopped
juice of ½ lemon
2 tablespoons chopped parsley
salt and freshly ground pepper

First prepare the glazed onions. Peel the shallots and place them in a large frying pan and sauté till golden. Transfer to a shallow flame-proof casserole with the butter, stock and bouquet garni. Season with a little salt and pepper, bring to the boil over a medium heat, cover tightly, reduce the heat to a very low flame and cook for about 30 minutes or until the onions are tender, shaking the pan every so often to ensure even cooking. Remove the cover, sprinkle with a teaspoon of sugar, raise the heat and shake the casserole till the liquid has evaporated and the onions have become slightly caramelised and glazed. Remove to one side and keep warm. Now heat the 2 tablespoons of butter and of oil in a large, heavy saucepan over a medium heat and add the chopped onion and sauté until golden. Add the pieces of eel, sprinkle very lightly with salt, pepper and nutmeg and turn in the butter for 3 minutes. Add the wine and water mixture and the bay leaf. Bring to the boil, reduce the heat and simmer for 8 minutes. Remove the eel pieces and keep hot. Replace the casserole over a high flame and boil rapidly to reduce the liquid by half. While it is reducing, brown the slices of bread in butter and keep warm separately. Also mix the unsalted butter and anchovy fillets well together to form a smooth paste. Remove the reduced sauce from the heat, stir in the anchovy butter and lemon juice. Taste and adjust the seasoning. Arrange the eel in the centre of a large serving dish, pour the sauce over them, and arrange the fried bread and glazed onions around the edge. Sprinkle all over with chopped parsley and serve.

Elvers

After their awesome journey, from their spawning grounds in the Sargasso Sea, I feel it's almost unfair to eat any elvers who actually make the journey into Europe. But they are so delicious. Millions of eels set off every year not in shoals but in great long ribbons, miles long and very dense, called 'eel-fares' – hence the term elver (young eel). Only those caught in the Gulf Stream ever make it to Europe. Probably the best-known area for them in Britain is round about the Severn. But they are much more commonly eaten in Spain where you have them sizzling hot in lots of oil and garlic. And eel which used to be so commonly eaten round Britain in the past (jellied eels, eel pie) is not at all common now – except, perhaps, in its smoked guise which you will find in the better fish shops and groceries. But it is an excellent fish and all the better for being cooked simply.

Angulas

You will find angulas (elvers) served in restaurants from Bilbao to Malaga and they are irresistible. If you are buying, try to insist on getting them fresh, but you may find (both here and on the Continent) that they have been given a quick initial cooking to keep them from spoiling.

Serves 4

1lb/450g elvers	*3 garlic cloves*
4 tablespoons olive oil	*salt to taste*

In a large heavy-bottomed frying pan, heat up the oil, add the garlic and let it cook till it is golden. Remove the garlic, and very quickly fry in elvers in the garlicky oil over a high heat for a minute or so till cooked through. Add salt and serve piping hot.

Gloucestershire Elvers

Frampton-on-Severn is famous not only because it is a very pretty village and the subject of Richard Mabey's *The Frampton Flora*, but also because of its annual elver-eating competition. This is how elver-addicts round about like to cook their elver.

Serves 4

1lb/450g elvers	*3 large eggs, beaten*
2 tablespoons fat (lard or vegetable oil)	*salt and pepper*
8 rashers rindless streaky bacon	*chopped parsley*

Rinse the elvers several times till they are completely clean and then drain and dry. Melt the fat in a large heavy-bottomed frying pan and fry until crisp. Remove with a slotted spoon and arrange around a warm dish. Fry the elvers in the bacon fat and when they have turned white (it only takes seconds) add the beaten, seasoned eggs. Stir all together and cook until just set to make a sort of scrambled-eggs-omelette. Arrange in the middle of the bacon and serve instantly sprinkled with parsley.

PIES, SAUCES & STUFFINGS

TERRINES, PIES, LEFTOVERS

Fricot de Volaille

These lovely light game fritters are a delicious way of using up almost any game leftovers.

Any leftover game
Nutmeg
Salt and pepper
Fresh chopped herbs
Lemon juice
Oil

Batter
4oz/100g plain flour
1 teaspoon baking powder
½ teaspoon salt
1oz/25g melted butter
6fl oz/175ml milk
1 egg white, whisked until stiff

Chop the leftover meat very very small, add the seasonings, herbs, lemon juice and a little oil and moisten and bind. Leave for 1 hour. Mix the batter (vary quantities according to amount of leftover meat) and stir into the meat mixture. Meanwhile heat a pan of oil to smoking point and drop spoonfuls of the mixture into it till they turn crisp and pale brown. Serve with fresh tomato sauce or sauce tartare.

Alheiras

This is a game sausage from Portugal, sometimes known as the Jewish sausage. Alheiras were invented in the 16th/17th centuries in North East Portugal by the so-called 'New Christians' (i.e. Jews) who wanted their neighbours to be sure that they were eating pork. In fact they used game and therefore didn't have to betray their religeous beliefs. The region still abounds in game today but modern alheiras contain more pork than any other meat. Alheiras are made by the dozen, so it is advisable to start work in the morning!

For every 10lb/5 kilos of any of the following
meat mixture on the bone: rabbit, partridge,
hare, turkey, duck, chicken, pork belly and
other fatty pork parts Use:
10lb/5 kilos of 2-day old compact bread
1 head of garlic and three cloves of garlic for
broth
1 teaspoon black peppercorns

freshly ground pepper
salt
piripiri (hot melagneta pepper)
1 red pepper
2 onions
1¼pt/750ml olive oil
sausage casing (from the butcher)

Bring a very large flame-proof casserole of water to the boil and add all the various meats with their bones, 3 cloves of garlic, the peppercorns, onions and salt. Cook until they are all tender (40 minutes to 1 hour or more depending on which meats you have used). Remove the meat from the stock and carefully take off the bone. Chop the meats into smallish pieces. Remove the onions and peppercorns from the stock, and adjust seasoning adding more salt if necessary. Cover the broken up bread with the strained stock so that it is thoroughly wetted. Using a wooden spoon add the meats, the ground pepper, the piripiri and finely chopped red pepper to the bread and stir well together. Next take each clove of garlic from the head, peel, cut and put each clove through a garlic press and add to the mixture. Heat the olive oil in a saucepan and when it boils add to the mixture. Mix well with a wooden spoon and then fill the casings. Leave in a cool place for 3-4 days to settle. Alheiras are usually served fried in olive oil or roasted in the oven, and accompanied by boiled or fried potatoes and turnips.

Game Pasties

Venison pasties were a traditional old-fashioned favourite that are now resurfacing with the wider availability of venison. The same basis can be applied for other game meat, red or white. These are very good served hot for buffet parties, making a change from the inevitable quiches and getting over problems with knives and forks.

Serves 6

*1lb/450g game, white or red, preferably the
    better cuts: diced very finely*
1-2 red onions, finely chopped
*1pt/600ml game stock or chicken or beef cubes if
    proper stock not available*
4oz/100g button mushrooms, chopped very finely
1 tablespoon butter/margarine
1 level teaspoon cornflour

salt and pepper
1 teaspoon mixed herbs
1 bouquet garni
2 tablespoons redcurrant jelly for red meat only
*12oz/350g shortcrust or flaky pastry (I use
    Saxby's when I'm making a lot)*
1 beaten egg

Melt the butter in a non-stick saucepan and gently cook the mushrooms and onions till they are softened. Add the meat, diced very small, seasoning, herbs and stock and bring to the boil. Cover and simmer until the meat is tender 30-45 minutes, depending on the type. Strain off the stock and pour into another pan and boil rapidly until it is reduced to about 1/4pt/200ml. Mix the cornflour with one tablespoon cold water to make a smooth paste, add to the stock, stirring till it is all evenly mixed in, then bring back to the boil to thicken. Stir in the meat and adjust seasoning again. Roll out the pastry and cut into six 7in/18cm circles. Place a small mound of the mixture on one half of the pastry. Paint round the edge with beaten egg, fold over the other half of the circle and crimp the edge together. Paint the top side of each pastie with beaten egg, place on a greased baking tray, make a small slit in each to allow the steam to escape, and bake in a hottish oven (200C/400F/Gas Mark 6) for about 30 minutes. Serve hot or cold.

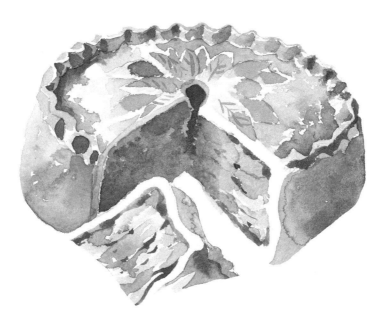

Game Pie

This is easy and delicious. If you want to use it for a dinner party but feel a pie isn't smart enough, just invert the use of the pastry by making individual tartlet cases and filling them with the mixed game in its rich gravy. Alternatively, you can make little individual puff pastry cases, top with a little cap and put a long thin triangle of pastry to one side so that the whole looks like a mini saucepan of the 'stew'. I have also made it served on little rectangular cases, made of chunks of white loaf scooped out in the centre, garnished with melted butter and then baked till golden.
Serves 6-8

2lb/900g mixed assorted game (pheasant, rabbit, venison, any of the small game birds) cut into cubes
4 tablespoons seasoned flour
8oz/225g smoked bacon, diced
1 large onion, finely chopped
stock made from the bones and giblets (see page 165)

¹/₂pt/300ml red wine
8oz/225g mushrooms, finely sliced
4-6 crushed juniper berries
3oz/75g butter
12oz/350g shortcrust pastry (see page 174)
freshly ground sea salt and mixed white and black peppercorns

Melt the butter in a flameproof casserole or a heavy bottomed frying pan. Toss the cubed game in the seasoned flour. Brown the bacon, mushrooms and onion lightly in the butter and remove. Next brown the game, adding more butter if necessary. Put everything into an ovenproof casserole, cover with the wine and stock, and more salt and pepper to taste. Place in a moderate oven (350F/180C/Gas Mark 5) and cook for 1-1¹/₂ hours. Check every now and then and add more stock if necessary. Pour into a pie dish with a funnel. Cut a strip of pastry to fit onto the lip of the dish and then cut out the lid to fit. Damp the pastry strip at the lip and press the lid to it, crimping the edges firmly. Decorate with leaves, and cook for another half hour or till golden.

Terrine of Rabbit

Ideal for picnics or salady lunches, this can also be made with any of the other white-meated game birds.
Serves 6-8

6 rashers streaky bacon
1¹/₂lb/675g rabbit
1¹/₂lb/675g fat pork, finely minced
2 tablespoons brandy
2 garlic cloves, crushed

1 teaspoon dried thyme/2 teaspoons fresh thyme leaves, chopped
freshly ground sea salt and mixed black and white peppercorns
a pinch of sugar, dash of Worcester sauce

Using the flat of a knife blade, thin and stretch the bacon rashers and then line a 1lb/500g loaf tin or earthenware rectangular casserole. Mince the rabbit very finely (if necessary ask the butcher); do *not* use the metal blade of the food processor. Mix together with the minced pork and stir in all the other ingredients. Add salt and pepper to taste. Spread the mixture in the terrine, fold over any overhanging bits of bacon, cover with foil and cook in a *bain marie*, in a pre-heated oven 350F/180C/Gas Mark 4 for 1¹/₂ hours. Remove from oven, allow to cool off for ¹/₂ hour, then cover with weights and leave to cool completely. Decorate with parsley or sprigs of thyme and serve either straight from the terrine or turned out and sliced.

Raised Game Pie

A perfect solution of picnics and lunch outside. Making the hot-water crust pastry is not as daunting as many people think it is, and it is worth persevering with. Once perfected, you will find this an invaluable way of using up all sorts of bits of game – any combination of the game birds will work, though I find with children it usually goes down better mixed with chicken.

Serves 6

Pastry
1¼lb/550g plain flour
5oz/150g lard
¼pt/150ml milk
¼pt/150ml water
beaten egg to glaze

Filling
12oz/350g mixed chopped game (pigeon,
   pheasant, duck, partridge etc)
12oz/350g chopped chicken meat
12oz/350g chopped fat pork
3-4 tablespoons brandy

1 teaspoon dried mixed herbs
freshly ground sea salt and mixed black and
   white peppercorns
6 streaky bacon rashers, roughly chopped
½pt jellied chicken or veal and pork bone stock

Stock
1lb/450g veal and pork bones, or chicken
   carcase
8oz/225g mixed chopped vegetables (carrot,
   celery, onion, leek)
1 bay leaf
salt and freshly ground black pepper

First make the stock. Put the bones and vegetables in a large pan with the vegetables, bay leaf, salt and pepper, cover with water, bring to the boil and simmer for 1¾ hours. Strain and return to the pan. Boil until reduced to ½pt/300ml. Cool and chill until set and jellied.

Meanwhile make the pastry. Sift the flour and salt into a bowl. Heat the lard, milk and water in a saucepan over a low heat until the lard has melted; do *not* boil. Add this mixture to the flour and mix well. Roll out two-thirds of the dough and use to line a 7-inch (18cm) loose-bottomed cake tin, leaving the dough overlapping the tin edge. Chill in fridge.

Now for the filling! Mix together the game, chicken, fat pork and bacon. Stir in the brandy, mixed herbs and salt and pepper to taste. Spoon this mixture into the lined tin. Roll out the remaining dough to a circle, dampen the edges at the lip of the tin and cover the pie, crimping the edges well together. Decorate with pastry trimmings. Make a hole in the centre of the pie. Brush with beaten egg to glaze. Bake in the centre of a hottish oven (400F/200C/Gas Mark 6) for 30 minutes, then reduce the heat to moderate (350F/180C/Gas Mark 4), cover with foil and cook for a further 2 hours. Leave to cool. Bring the jellied stock to just below boiling point and allow to cool. Pour through the hole in the lid of the pie, using a funnel, and leave to set. If you prefer to see the different types of meat you are using, you can par-cook the birds on the bone, cool and take the meat off the carcase carefully. Then arrange these carefully in slices in the pie.

Mixed Game in Cabbage Parcels

This is a good way of using up any type of game, or a mixture of any variety, especially if you have any doubts at all about its tenderness. The correct mincing is important; do not use your food processor, wonderful as it is, as it just does not give the right texture when it comes to mincing meat. Either take your meat to a butcher to put through his mincer, or use the electric mincer attachment to a food processor, or even the good old-fashioned hand mincer which clamps on to your work surface. Now you can go ahead with a very flexible idea for lunch or supper.

Serves 4-6

2 tablespoons bacon fat, oil or garlic oil
1lb/450g minced game
4oz/100g onion, finely chopped
4 level tablespoons finely chopped fresh parsley
freshly ground sea salt and mixed black and
  white peppercorns

2 level teaspoons ground coriander
¹/₄pt/150ml red wine
12 leaves spring cabbage
4oz/100g mushrooms, finely chopped

Heat the fat or oil in a heavy bottomed frying pan. Add the minced game, mushrooms, onion, parsley, salt, pepper, ground coriander and red wine. Cook over a medium heat for 45 minutes, stirring from time to time. Drain off the liquid, but do not discard. Meanwhile, separate the leaves of the cabbage, trimming out the thick stalk and blanch in boiling unsalted water for 2-3 minutes. Drain and rinse immediately under cold running water. Pat dry and leave flat. Divide the mince mixture between the cold leaves and fold each one into a neat rectangular parcel. Arrange in an ovenproof shallow dish, with enough of the liquid to just cover the bottom. Reserve the rest of the liquid, heat up and serve separately in a sauceboat. Heat the parcels through in a moderate oven (350F/180C/Gas Mark 4) for 15-20 minutes and serve. Alternatively, serve with a rich Tomato Sauce (page 180 or 184).

Hot Game Liver Timbales with Tomato Sauce

These are hot little mousses of game livers, turned out from their moulds onto a neat little circle of cold tomato sauce. The contrasts between the hot and cold, the creamy richness of the liver with the tart freshness of the tomato work brilliantly. You can, of course, use any game livers for this, or a combination of any, or any combined with chicken liver, or even just chicken liver on its own! It is excellent as a first course or as a main course for lunch, served with French bread and green salad.

Serves 5 (makes up into 5 ramekins)

1 small onion, finely chopped	*6fl oz/150ml* crème frâiche *or cream*
1oz/25g butter	*pinch of nutmeg*
1 teaspoon chopped parsley	*salt and freshly ground pepper*
1 clove garlic, crushed	*oil or butter to grease the ramekins with*
1lb/450g game livers, rinsed and cleaned	*2 large tomatoes (sweet, beef if possible)*
2 slices white bread	*1 dessertspoon* crème frâiche/*or cream*
3 eggs	*10 large basil leaves*
8oz/225g bacon fat, finely diced and then minced	*pinch sugar*

If you are not sure of the age of the livers, soak them for 2-3 hours in a bowl of milk to get rid of any possible taint or taste of bitterness.

Melt the butter in a small frying pan and gently cook the onion and garlic till they are softened and translucent. Soak the white bread in water and then squeeze the liquid out. Put the bread, the onion and garlic, the fresh chopped parsley, the liver, eggs, bacon fat and *crème frâiche*/cream into a food processor and whizz until it forms a very smooth fine purée. Season with salt, pepper and nutmeg and quickly whizz again to mix in properly. Grease 5 ramekins, fill with the mixture, cover each with tin foil and cook in a *bain marie* for half an hour at a temperature of 160C/325F/Gas Mark 3. Meanwhile make the Tomato Sauce. Skin and deseed the tomatoes and liquidise the flesh with the dessertspoon of *crème frâiche*/cream, a pinch of sugar, salt and pepper and five basil leaves. Arrange smooth even circles of the Tomato Sauce on individual plates and when the liver mousses are ready, turn them out onto the middle of each tomato circle. Garnish each little mousse with a single basil leaf and serve immediately.

SAUCES

Gravy

Most game needs gravy or a sauce with it, especially if it is simply roasted. The best gravy is made from the pan juices and it helps to have some stock of the particular bird to hand – grouse, pheasant, duck etc – but if not, chicken stock will probably do almost as well. It is worth making the effort when there is time to make some varieties of reduced game stock (see page 181) to add richness to the gravy as there is usually very little to scrape off the bottom of the pan after roasting game. Otherwise, as a general principle, the way to make gravy for most game is to pour off the fat from the roasting pan and add some boiling stock (water will do if you haven't any stock) to the juices or scrapings in the bottom. Add a good pinch of salt and a generous screw of pepper, with a teaspoon of grated orange or lemon rind to sharpen the flavour. You can also add a dash of port or wine, or a teaspoon of redcurrant jelly as well, depending on preference. Return to the pan and boil rapidly to reduce a little and deepen the taste.

Instant Gravy

This is a method I devised out of desperation and self-defence at the beginning of our marriage to allay my husband's impatience while he hovered with the carving knife, and I was still busy stirring the pan juices! You can prepare the base two or three days before and then all you have to do at the time of serving is to add the juices from the pan – gravy in two seconds flat. To every ounce (25 grammes) of butter add one ounce (25 grammes) of flour, and half a pint (300ml) liquid, preferably stock. Multiply the quantities according to the amount needed. Put the butter in a non-stick pan and allow it to burn slightly. Stir in the flour until it is absorbed and add a stock cube (chicken or beef, depending on whether it is red or white meat). Allow to cook for 30 seconds and then gradually add the liquid – stock, water or wine, or a combination of the three, depending on what is available. Season to taste with salt and pepper, add a dash of Soya sauce or Worcestershire sauce for extra zest if desired. Later, add some wine or water to the roasting pan to add to this base. This evaporates a little during cooking, but also mixes with the natural juices and can be added to the reheated base just before serving.

Cumberland Sauce

This very English sauce is said to be called after Queen Victoria's uncle, the Duke of Cumberland, and is a favourite accompaniment to game and ham, and has been adopted all round Europe. In fact by the last year of Queen Victoria's reign it was almost *de rigeur* to serve this with game. As with anything popular, there are many variations. Here is a traditional recipe from England, followed by another version from Poland. Many English recipes include arrowroot, but personally I don't like the glutinous effect this gives – especially if you want to have it later cold with game. I prefer to get depth by reduction.

Serves 8-10

1lb/450g redcurrant jelly	*1 teaspoon Dijon mustard*
½ bottle port	*pinch ground ginger*
juice of 1 lemon, and rind cut into thin juliennes	*dash of Worcestershire sauce*
juice of 1 orange, and rind cut into thin juliennes	*pinch of salt and pepper (optional)*

Peel the skin off the orange and lemon as thinly as possible and cut into very fine *juliennes* (strips). You can use an orange zester for this if you prefer. Plunge into a small saucepan of boiling water and boil for 3-5 minutes to take the bitterness out and to soften them. Rinse off immediately in very cold water and leave to drain. Now spoon the redcurrant jelly into a saucepan (preferably non-stick), add the port and bring to the boil, stirring constantly to dissolve the lumps of jelly. Simmer over a gentle heat until the liquid is dissolved by about a third, and is just runny. Add all the spices and seasonings, and stir well until the sauce is completely smooth. Add the *juliennes* and serve immediately, or leave to cool, and serve cold.

Polish Cumberland Sauce

Here the orange rind is fried, which increases the spiciness. It makes about ¹/₂ pint/300ml.

2 tablespoons redcurrant jelly
1-2 tablespoons horseradish sauce
rind of 1 orange, very finely chopped

1 tablespoon lemon juice
1oz/25g butter
pinch of salt

Mix together in a bowl the horseradish (I think Elsenham's is the best of the ready-made), redcurrant jelly, and lemon juice. Warm up in a saucepan and stir well until all is dissolved and well amalgamated. Leave aside to cool. Melt the butter in a small frying pan and lightly fry the orange rind. Mix into the sauce and serve cold with game pâtés and terrines.

Bread Sauce

A Frenchman who was once served some bread sauce to accompany his roast pheasant is rumoured to have said 'Am I supposed to eat zees, or 'as someone already done so?'. A lot of people feel like that about bread sauce, my own sons included (in fact they quote the mythical Frenchman every time it is put in front of them), but it can be simply delicious. The secret is to get the consistency right – not too sloppy and not too stodgy. This is a completely British, totally un-European accompaniment to game! I include two recipes for it, one traditional method, and my own short-cut way to make when one is rushed (when isn't one?!)
Serves 6 enthusiastic Britons!

8oz/225g stale white breadcrumbs, made from
  good white (not 'instant' sliced) bread
1¹/₄pt/750ml milk
1 large onion stuck with cloves
1 bay leaf
a pinch of mace

a pinch of nutmeg
2oz/50g butter
a dash of cream
salt and pepper
extra breadcrumbs – in case

Pour the milk into a large saucepan and to it add the onion stuck with the cloves, the nutmeg, mace and bay leaf. Cover and put over a very low heat to infuse for 10 to 20 minutes, or until the milk is really well flavoured. You can remove from the heat and leave it for up to an hour to infuse. Then remove the onion and bay leaf, stir the breadcrumbs in carefully and simmer, watching carefully and stirring, until the mixture is thick and creamy. Then add the butter, seasoning and a dash of cream and serve immediately.

For the short-cut method use the same ingredients, but substitute a pinch of ground cloves for the whole cloves. Put the milk into a saucepan with all the spices and the onion cut into chunky slices. Bring to the boil and simmer for a minute or two till the onion has all softened. Transfer to a liquidiser and whizz everything up together till the onion has disappeared. Transfer back into the saucepan, stir in the breadcrumbs and simmer very gently, stirring till the sauce is thick and creamy. Then add the butter, seasoning and a dash of cream to taste. Serve immediately.

Keep extra breadcrumbs at the ready to add if the sauce seems too sloppy. If it is too thick, adjust with extra cream or milk.

Court Bouillon

This simple base will do for poaching all fish in. It is particularly useful for adding to any sauces accompanying the fish, and really worth the little bit of extra trouble. Once the fish has been removed from the court bouillon after poaching, it can be reduced by boiling down hard to half or one third the original quantity which concentrates the flavour and thickens the stock.
Makes about 2¹/₂pints/1.5 litres

2 pints/1 litre water
8oz/225g chopped carrots
2 medium onions, sliced and quartered
1-2 sticks celery

1 bouquet garni
pinch of salt
10fl oz/300ml white wine or cider
6 black peppercorns, crushed

Put everything except the peppercorns into a large saucepan. Simmer for 40 minutes, add the crushed peppercorns for the last 15 minutes. Strain and cool.

Fish Stock

This is important as a base for any of the sauces you might want to make to accompany your fish dish. You only need the head, tail and bones to make a good stock, and if you can't take them off a whole fish then your fishmonger ought to be able to provide enough for your needs. Ask him for 'frames', which are the whole fish minus the fillets. Avoid any of the oily fish such as mackerel or herring for stock. Once you have made this basic fish stock, you can reduce it to half, and reduce again even further and then combine with whatever flavour you want – tomato, lemon, herbs – to make the most sublime sauces.
Makes about 2 pints/1.2 litres.

1¹/₂lb/675g fish trimmings
1¹/₂pt/900ml water
1 onion, sliced
1 carrot, sliced
1 leek, sliced

¹/₂pt/300ml white wine or cider
pinch salt
bunch of parsley or bouquet garni
6 black peppercorns, crushed or bruised

Put everything except the peppercorns into a large saucepan, bring to the boil and simmer for no longer than 30 minutes. Fish stock gets a horrible boney taste if you cook it too long. Add the peppercorns 10 minutes before the end.

Hollandaise

This is the perfect accompaniment to fish, so fattening and full of cholesterol and utterly irresistible. I always make this by hand and also make it in advance, keeping it warm throughout the afternoon in a bowl of (topped up) warm water until I need it at night. But others prefer to make theirs at the last minute in the food processor. I don't think my nerves are up to any last-minute crisis which is why I prefer to make this slightly temperamental sauce earlier in the day.

Enough for 6

8oz/225g softened butter
4 large egg yolks at room temperature
1 tablespoon cold water

salt and freshly ground black and white
peppercorns
juice of ½ lemon

Divide the butter into small cubes, or leave to get very soft, even melted, and set to one side. Take a small heavy saucepan and half fill with warm water. Take a small Pyrex bowl or pudding bowl, put the egg yolks into it, add 1 tablespoon of cold water and whisk together. Place the bowl in a warm *bain-marie* and set over a low heat so that the water eventually simmers very gently. Add the butter, drop by drop, to the eggs, stirring all the time so that it gets carefully emulsified and slowly thickens. Do *not* let it get too hot or it will curdle. When all the butter has been added, add the lemon juice and seasoning to taste. Keep the heat constant so that the sauce never heats up rapidly. If it does curdle, start again with one yolk in a bowl, to which you add the curdled Hollandaise very slowly, drop by drop. You should regain a perfect sauce without any problems.

Blender Hollandaise

Using the same ingredients as above, put the egg yolks, lemon juice, water, salt and pepper into a food processor and whizz. Heat the butter almost to boiling point and quickly pour into the egg mixture, whizzing all the time. The mixture 'takes' very quickly so don't overwhizz. You will get a lighter, frothier consistency than with the handmade version.

Sauce Mousseline

Although this is actually richer than pure Hollandaise, it doesn't seem so as it is a less dense sauce. But it is just as deadly, and quite irresistible! You just add one part whipped cream to three parts Hollandaise before serving. Taste and adjust seasoning if necessary.

Mustard Sauce

Particularly good with cold meats this is also served in Eastern Europe with roast eel.
Makes about ¼pt/150ml

4 hard boiled egg yolks
1 tablespoon Dijon mustard
¼pt/150ml vegetable oil

pinch of salt
pinch of sugar

Mash the egg yolks to form a smooth paste and add the mustard. Mix together till they are smooth and then pour the oil in a slow, steady stream, stirring all the time. Add salt and sugar to taste.

Quick Butter, Lemon and Cream Sauce

Necessity is the mother of invention they say. This was an experiment once when I was in too much of a hurry to make proper Hollandaise. It worked and I now use it a lot. It goes very well with asparagus and artichokes as well as fish. I also use it with the hot pheasant and/or salmon mousses (see page 87 and 142).

Makes ½pt/300ml

4oz/100g butter
juice of ½ lemon

¼pt/150ml double cream
salt and freshly ground black pepper

Melt the butter in a small saucepan, bring it to bubbling point and add the lemon juice. Stir well together, heat up again and add the cream stirring all the time. Season to taste and serve hot.

Hand-made Mayonnaise

To the astonishment of friends, I always make my mayonnaise by hand. It never takes very long, and so far it has never curdled! But for those who feel happier with a machine taking the strain, here are two variations. For hand-made mayonnaise two tips might be worth remembering: the ingredients are best at room temperature, and very fresh eggs do not work as well as older ones (I wish that could be said of women).

Makes about ½pt/300ml

2 egg yolks
½ teaspoon Dijon mustard
½pt/300ml good olive or sunflower oil

1-2 tablespoons vinegar or lemon juice
pinch of salt and ground white pepper

Put the egg yolks and mustard into a small bowl and mix well together. Hold the bowl and start adding the oil, very slowly, drop by drop, stirring all the time to make sure each drop is well amalgamated. Once about a third of the oil has been incorporated like this, you can speed up, adding it in a continuous trickle and beating all the time to make sure that it is all properly combined. As you do this it will get thicker and thicker. If at any point it curdles, break another egg yolk into another bowl and start incorporating the above mixture drop by drop, stirring all the time and you will regain another good mayonnaise. Add the lemon juice or vinegar at the end, plus the seasoning to taste. You will find that this will thin the mixture a bit.

Blender Mayonnaise

Makes about ½pt/300ml

As above, except that you can use either 2 egg yolks or 2 whole eggs

Put the eggs, mustard and vinegar into the blender and whizz for 20 seconds. Keep the machine going and slowly add the oil in a very fine stream and continue whizzing until the consistency is thick and creamy. Then add the rest of the vinegar and season to taste, adding more vinegar if necessary. Whizz for another 20 seconds and if you want to make the sauce lighter you can add a tablespoon of hot water.

Fresh Horseradish Sauce

Horseradish grows like a weed in the garden, and it makes such a good sauce fresh that it's worth the trouble needed to grate the fresh root. A good food processor makes the job very easy – but have a Kleenex nearby for the tears.

2 tablespoons horseradish
1 teaspoon English mustard
1 dessertspoon vinegar
squeeze of lemon juice

¼pt/150ml double cream
sugar to taste
salt and white pepper

Peel the horseradish, cut it into small chunks and whizz in the food processor till it is finely shredded. Whip the cream till it stands in peaks. In a bowl mix the grated horseradish, mustard, vinegar, lemon juice, sugar, salt and pepper. Fold in the cream. Taste and adjust any of the seasonings, adding more horseradish according to taste. Serve with venison, wild boar or smoked fish.

Traditional Danish Cream Sauce for Game Birds

Spread a layer of butter or margarine over your game, sprinkle with salt and pepper, and roast. Remove the birds from the pan. If there isn't any residue add a little more butter or margarine to the pan. Then add ¼-½pt (150-300ml) single cream (depending on the size of the bird), a teaspoonful or two of redcurrant jelly, and stir over the heat till it is all well amalgamated. It is in the end!

Shellfish Sauce

A good accompaniment to either *quenelles de brochet* (page 159) or *quenelles de saumon* (page 144).

3oz/75g crayfish or prawns
1½oz/40g butter
pinch cayenne
touch of tomato purée for colouring
pinch of sugar
pinch of salt

For the Béchamel
1oz/25g butter
1oz/25g flour
½pt/300ml milk
salt and white pepper
single cream to taste

First make the *Béchamel* by melting the butter in a small non-stick saucepan and then stirring in the flour till it is completely absorbed. Very slowly add the milk bit by bit, stirring all the time to ensure no lumps form. When it is all poured in, continue stirring till the sauce reaches the boil. Season to taste and add a dash of cream to thin as required. Set to one side and peel the prawns or crayfish and then pound in a mortar with pestle or whizz in a food processor with the butter, and cayenne. Add this to the warm *Béchamel,* stir and add a touch of tomato purée to make a soft pink colour, and a pinch of sugar and salt to taste.

Sauce á la Catalane

This goes very well with wild boar, venison or hare and makes a pleasing change from the more traditionally used Cumberland Sauce in Britain.

Makes 1¹/₄ pints/³/₄ litre

1 onion, finely sliced and chopped
4 tablespoons olive oil
10 cloves of garlic
16fl oz/450ml tomato purée
finely grated rind and squeezed juice of 2
*   oranges*

finely grated rind and squeezed juice of 1 lemon
2 tablespoons finely chopped fresh oregano
2 tablespoons finely chopped fresh mint
pinch of cayenne pepper
dash of mustard
5 tablespoons Madeira

Warm the oil in a saucepan over a gentle heat and cook the onions and garlic till they are translucent and golden. Add the tomato purée, the rind and juice of the lemon and oranges, the cayenne, oregano, mint, mustard and Madeira. Mix well together till they are all well amalgamated and serve hot. It can also be served cold with terrines, pâtés etc.

Salsa Samfaina

This is another classic Catalan sauce, normally served hot with meat or fish. It is a glorious colour. I sometimes add some chilli for a bit of bite, but this is not traditionally in the recipes that abound.

Makes 1 pint/600ml

1 large onion, chopped
2 tablespoons olive oil
3 yellow and/or red peppers
1 ripe aubergine, cut into cubes and salted and
*   drained for ¹/₂hour*

3 large ripe tomatoes, skinned, seeded and
*   chopped*
salt, pepper and chilli powder (optional)

Warm the oil in a large non-stick pan and fry the onions gently till translucent. Add the peppers and cook for between five and 10 minutes till soft. Add the aubergine and cook for another 5 minutes. Finally add the tomatoes and cook all together, gently, adding seasoning to taste. Cook for five minutes, remove from the heat and whizz in the blender for 30 seconds or until roughly puréed. Return to the pan and heat up once more adjusting the seasoning to taste. Serve hot with game (wild boar, venison, hare etc) or cold with game terrines.

Tomato Butter

This is a delicious light sauce that goes very well with fish, or even lightly, cleanly cooked or chargrilled breasts of pheasant or guinea fowl. An invaluable stand-by.

Serves 6

3 medium sized tomatoes
6oz/175g salted butter

any mixture of fresh aromatic herbs (basil,
*   coriander, parsley, rosemary, chives, marigold*
*   petals, thyme)*
salt and pepper to taste

Liquidise tomatoes, sieve well making sure no pips or skin pop through. Transfer the purée to a saucepan and bring to the boil. Remove to one side and keep warm. Add the butter and allow to dissolve. Mix well together till they emulsify (it will not curdle as the tomato has been boiled), add chopped mixed fresh herbs to taste and season with salt and pepper. Serve warm.

Apple and Madeira Sauce

This is as good cold with cold game as it is hot with hot game or meat (roast guinea fowl, wild duck, goose, quail, pork etc).
Makes approx 1½ pints/½ litre

9 cooking apples, peeled, cored and sliced
sugar to taste
knob of butter to taste
water to cover

½pt/300ml Madeira
grated rind and squeezed juice of 2 oranges
juice of 1 lemon

Place the sliced, peeled apples in a saucepan, just cover with water and cook gently until they disintegrate into a soft pulp. Add sugar to taste, and stir in a good knob of butter till it is melted. Remove to one side. In a separate saucepan combine the grated orange rind and Madeira and boil gently until the liquid is reduced by half. Add the apple purée and stir in over the heat, continue to cook until it has reduced to the consistency required. Leave it to cool and then stir in the orange and lemon juice. Serve hot or cold as required.

French Dressing to go with Pulse Salads

This is my back-to-front vinaigrette! By adding the mustard last instead of first the dressing doesn't emulsify and therefore gives a lighter texture – with the tiniest drops of mustard swirling around in it. It has absolutely no sugar and therefore goes much better with savoury salad mixes, such as the pulse and woodcock (see page 112).
Enough for one largish bowl of pulse salad.

¼pt/150ml vegetable oil
2 tablespoons vinegar
1 teaspoon salt

1 teaspoon ready-made Dijon mustard
plenty of freshly ground mixed black and white
*   peppercorns*

Pour oil into a bowl, add the vinegar and mix well together. Add salt and pepper and stir in well, and then finally add the mustard stirring in well till it breaks up into tiny droplets throughout.

Sauce Tartare

I use this with my pheasant goujons (page 82), which are also very good cold, on a picnic or for a summer lunch. Equally good is the Tomato Sauce Provençale (page 180) as a fresh antidote to the fried breadcrumbs.

½pt/300ml mayonnaise (see page 176)
1 teaspoon very finely chopped pickled gherkins
2 hardboiled eggs very finely chopped
1 tablespoon very finely chopped capers
1 tablespoon very finely chopped parsley
1 tablespoon very finely chopped chervil

1 tablespoon very finely chopped chives or
*   spring onions*
1 tablespoon grated onion
1 teaspoon Dijon mustard
1 teaspoon sugar (optional)
1 teaspoon lemon juice (optional)
freshly ground white pepper

Fold all the chopped herbs and pickles, hard-boiled eggs and mustard into the mayonnaise. Add lemon juice and sugar to taste – some people like a touch of sweetness, many prefer the sharpness derived from the pickles, mustard and extra squeeze of lemon juice.

If you can't get all the herbs and pickles for the sauce, don't worry, just use a combination of whatever is available, as long as you still include the gherkins and capers.

Tomato Sauce Provençale

A wonderful accompaniment to the goujons of pheasant (page 82) in particular.

³/₄lb/350g onions
2lb/1kg ripe tomatoes
3 tablespoons good olive oil
sprig of thyme
sprig of rosemary

1 bay leaf
1 bouquet garni
salt and freshly ground black pepper
1 dessertspoon caster sugar
2 cloves garlic

Warm the olive oil in a large saucepan and place in it the roughly chopped onions, skinned tomatoes and garlic and cook till soft but not brown. Add the sugar, salt, pepper and herbs, bring to the boil, then cover the pan, reduce the heat and simmer for 1 hour until a thick purée has formed. Remove the herbs and then work the purée through a sieve. I quite often just put it all through a liquidiser as I personally rather like the texture of the seeds and I also think they make the sauce look 'real'. If it is too thick add a drop or two more oil, and then adjust the seasoning to taste.

Spinach and Sorrel Sauce

To serve with fish. This can of course be made just with spinach if sorrel is not available.
Makes about ³/₄pt/450ml

¹/₄pt/150ml fish stock or chicken stock
5 tablespoons dry white wine
3 tablespoons dry vermouth
1 medium onion, finely chopped
¹/₂pt/300ml single cream
4oz/100g sorrel leaves, stalks removed, finely chopped

2oz/50g spinach leaves, stalks removed, finely chopped
or 6oz/175g either sorrel or spinach
1oz/25g butter
squeeze of lemon juice
salt and pepper

Put the stock, wine and vermouth in a saucepan with the chopped onion, bring to the boil and cook rapidly till the liquid is reduced to about a tablespoon. Add the cream and simmer, stirring all the time, until the sauce thickens. Add the chopped leaves and cook for another half minute, adding the butter in bits. Season with lemon juice and salt and pepper and serve, or whizz in a liquidiser for a finer texture. Reheat carefully and serve.

Saffron Sauce

This sauce needs careful handling. Excellent with both sea trout and salmon, and most white fish.
Makes ¹/₂pt/300ml

1 small onion or 2 shallots, chopped very fine
¹/₄pt/150ml dry white wine
¹/₄pt/150ml double cream or fish stock OR

2¹/₂fl oz/75ml double cream and 2¹/₂fl oz/75ml fish stock
pinch saffron powder or threads

Put onion or shallots into a saucepan with the wine and boil rapidly till it is reduced to two tablespoons. Drain and pour the wine into another saucepan. Add the cream or fish stock (or both) and warm. Add the pinch of saffron. If you are using saffron stems, put them into a bowl. Pour a generous tablespoon of boiling water over them and let them steep. Press through a very fine nylon sieve and add to the sauce.

Game Stock

This can be made with any game carcases you have, or with a combination of chicken and game carcases. It makes 1¹/₂-1³/₄ litres/2¹/₂-3 pints. If you are keeping stock to use later, never add salt. The seasoning is added when it comes to cooking.

4lb/2kg approx bones, offal, hearts etc
3³/₄ pints/2¹/₂ litres water
3 carrots, halved
3 small onions with 2 cloves stuck into each

2 celery stalks, halved
1 leek, halved lengthways
bouquet garni
8 peppercorns

Remove the tough skin from the necks, slice any meat, cut the neck into pieces and divide the heart. If only using bones make sure any fat is removed from the carcase as it tends to taint the taste of the stock – especially pheasant fat. Place all in a big pan, cover with water and add vegetables, herbs and peppercorns. Bring to the boil, remove the foam, and allow to simmer for 2-12 hours, skimming the foam when necessary. Remove and strain through a sieve and cool. Once cooled, skim off fat again. If you want a stronger taste boil to reduce.

Sos z Jalowca

This juniper sauce is a traditional accompaniment to game in Poland where the juniper berry is a staple ingredient in the kitchen.
Serves 8

1 small carrot
1 medium onion
2 slices bacon
2oz/50g butter
1pt/600ml game stock

¹/₂pt/300ml dry white wine
2¹/₂ tablespoons juniper berries
1 tablespoon double cream (optional)
salt and pepper

Peel and dice the onion, chop the carrot and bacon and place in a heavy bottomed pan with the melted butter. Add the bacon and juniper berries and cook, stirring, until the bacon and onion are lightly browned. Add the stock and simmer, uncovered, for about an hour, stirring every so often. Strain the vegetables and bacon, pour the sauce back into a saucepan, add the wine and double cream and boil for five minutes. Adjust seasoning and then pour into a sauceboat.

Salsa Verde/Sauce Verte

This is a strong and piquant vinaigrette popular in Italy and France and along the Mediterranean litoral. It is made with anchovy, parsley, garlic and mustard and is particularly good with simple fish (see salmon kebabs, page 148) or cold pheasant, or game or fish kebabs.
Makes just over ¹/₂pt/350ml

1 small tin anchovy fillets
1 hard boiled egg
1 green pepper, seeded
4oz/100g parsley
1oz/25g basil

1oz/25g chives
juice of 1 lemon, strained
¹/₄pt/150ml olive oil
1 teaspoon strong mustard (optional)

Whizz all the ingredients together in a food processor to form a fine sauce, then leave to rest for several hours before serving.

Sos z Dzikiej Rózy

This is a rosehip sauce from Poland, another favourite accompaniment to game. Make it when
the rosehips are ripe and freeze for another time.
Makes about 1½ pints/750ml

½pt/300ml rosehips (picked after the first frost)
1oz/30g butter
1 heaped tablespoon plain flour
½pt/300ml game stock
¼pt/150ml red wine

4 juniper berries
1 bay leaf
2 whole cloves
sugar to taste
salt and pepper

Wash the rosehips, and remove the stalks and calyces. Put in a pan and just cover with water and bring to
the boil. Simmer until tender and then liquidise. Melt the butter, stir in the flour, cook for a few minutes and
gradually add the stock, the wine, the puréed rosehips and the seasonings. Cook gently for 30 minutes and
then strain and serve.

Rouille

This is the wonderful rich Mediterranean sauce that can bring even the thinnest fish soup alive
with its fiery taste. It is usually spread thickly on baked croûtons or sliced French bread (dried
in the oven till golden and crunchy) which are then floated in the soup. I usually have a pot of it
in the fridge as a stand-by. Some French recipes call just for the use of the fish liver (of
whichever fish is being used in the soup) combined with the mayonnaise-type base; others
include the use of red chilli peppers, which I prefer. I also sometimes add tomato purée.
Here is a base to take off from...
Makes about ¼pt/150ml

1 fish liver (according to the main fish in the
  recipe)
2-3 fat cloves of garlic
2 red chilli peppers
1 slice white bread, crust removed
2 egg yolks

1 teaspoon cayenne pepper
1 tablespoon fish stock or water
3 tablespoons olive oil
pinch salt
1 teaspoon tomato purée (optional)

Pound the garlic cloves in a mortar with the salt, add the egg yolks, fish liver, chopped peppers and bread,
squeezed out in fish stock or water, and pound all together into a paste. Add salt and tomato purée according
to taste, and pound again. Now, slowly, drop by drop, as if making mayonnaise, add the oil till you have a
thick creamy red sauce, brilliant in colour and full of fire.

Salsa all'aglio

This is probably better known under its Provençale name of Aioli, but since it goes so well
with the *Frittura di pesci misti del pescatore* on page 140 I have plumped for it under its
lesser known Italian guise. In Spain it is called Alioli. The method is the same in both,
achieving really rich but terribly strong results (so best eaten, perhaps amongst good friends!)
Did you know that one antidote to a strong dose of garlic is to eat a handful of parsley? Despite
the after-effects, this sauce is a brilliant accompaniment to so many things – game terrines, as
well as the more obvious fish and vegetables.
Makes ¼pt/450ml

3 egg yolks
6 garlic cloves
pinch of salt

12fl oz/350ml olive oil
2 tablespoons lemon juice or vinegar
1 tablespoon hot water

Some purists only make this with lemon juice, but I like the option of using vinegar. Lemon juice makes a
lighter coloured sauce than vinegar, and it is tarter. Try and make this at room temperature. If the oil and eggs
are cold, they won't emulsify; but if they are too warm it is difficult to tell if they are thickening properly. It is
also worth making this in a mortar and pestle, and not crushing garlic to add to an already-made mayonnaise –
though shortcuts can be life-savers at times. Crush the garlic cloves in a mortar until they are pounded into a
paste, add the egg yolks and a pinch of salt and mix all together well. Then continue as for mayonnaise,
adding the oil drop by drop and stirring constantly to emulsify. Once you have added a third of the oil, you
can add the rest by pouring it in a steady thin stream and stirring all the time. From time to time add a few
drops of lemon juice or vinegar. By the time you have added all the oil the sauce should be very thick and
glossy. Now add the hot water to prevent any separation and stir all very well together. If by any chance the
mixture should curdle or separate, do not panic. The remedy is easy. Break a yolk into another clean bowl,
whisk it with a fork, then very slowly, spoon by spoon, add the errant sauce to it, stirring all the time. It *will*
come right again.

White Stock

This is the base for many things, including the invaluable velouté sauce (see page 184) and,
depending on what it goes with, can be made with veal bone, chicken, or fish bones. It is always
worth having some at hand in the freezer for a base for many a sauce.

2½lb/1.2kg veal knuckle or bones (or chicken or
*   fish bones)*
½pt/300ml white wine
1 large onion, sliced
2 large carrots, peeled and sliced
1 celery stalk, sliced

1 bouquet garni
1 teaspoon salt
a few white peppercorns
1-2 teaspoons lemon juice
abut 3 quarts cold water

Place the bones in a large pan, and just to start cover them with water (not the three quarts in the
ingredients). Bring to the boil and remove the scum which rises to the surface. Drain and rinse. Replace the
bones in the pan and add the white wine. Bring to the boil and reduce to about 2 tablespoons. Now add all the
other ingredients, cover with the 3 quarts of water and simmer for 2-3 hours. Drain and allow to cool,
removing the surface fat once it has set so that the stock is completely fat free for use in any subsequent sauce.

Velouté Sauce

This is the basis for a host of other divine sauces – *suprème, duxelles, chivry* and so on. But on its own, it is a brilliant and adaptable accompaniment to white meat, and fish, smooth, light and creamy. Its success depends on the stock. My husband gets fed up with pans of stock constantly on the simmer in the house, but stock is as important in a good kitchen as disregard of grumbles is in a good marriage!

1 tablespoon butter
1 scant tablespoon flour
1½ pints/900ml white stock (veal, chicken or
*   fish)*

salt and white pepper to taste
a few drops of lemon juice to taste

In a non-stick saucepan, melt the butter and stir in the flour over a gentle heat to make a roux. When they are completely amalgamated slowly add the stock, stirring all the time to avoid lumps. Season with salt, pepper and lemon juice to taste and continue to cook until the sauce thickens and looks semi-clear. At this point you can add any liaison you want – egg or cream, or egg and cream – to make the smooth finish that makes this sauce so delectable.

French Dressing

The traditional accompaniment for all salads, but also good for tossing any leftovers of game for a cold game salad. The ingredients can all be varied; herbs can be added, honey substituted for sugar, and differently flavoured oils and vinegars, not abundant everywhere, can ring the changes. The ingredients below are the classic ones.

1 small teaspoon Dijon mustard
1 teaspoon wine or cider vinegar
2 teaspoons caster sugar

twist of black pepper
6fl oz/200ml olive or other oil
1 teaspoon salt

Into the bottom of a small glass jar, put the teaspoon of mustard. Mix into it the sugar, salt, pepper and vinegar. Add the oil and mix all together.

Tomato Coulis

A lighter version of the Tomato Provençale on page 180. As with almost anything in cooking you can vary the seasoning and herbs according to taste. If you are using very sweet ripe tomatoes, you can leave out the sugar. If you can't get good fresh tomatoes, use tinned ones and add a bit more seasoning.
Makes about ½pt/300ml

1½lb/750g very ripe tomatoes, peeled and
*   seeded*
1 onion, finely chopped
2 cloves garlic, finely chopped
1 tablespoon olive oil

1 teaspoon dried thyme (or parsley, oregano,
*   basil, marjoram etc)*
1-2 teaspoons caster sugar
salt and freshly ground black and white
*   peppercorns*

Pour the oil into a large heavy-bottomed pan, and in it cook the onions and garlic till they are softened. Add all the other ingredients and simmer very gently, uncovered, for about half an hour stirring occasionally. After half an hour the mixture will have reduced and thickened. Either pass through a sieve or whizz in the blender till smooth. Then return to the pan and cook gently for another 30 minutes. Adjust seasoning and serve either hot or cold. Excellent with fishcakes (see page 146).

Beurre Rouge

Recently this has taken over in popularity from *beurre blanc* and it certainly has a good rich colour. But *beurre rouge* can be served with red meat as well as white, and it also goes well with fish. It is made in exactly the same way as *beurre blanc* but needs red wine (good red wine!) instead of white.

10fl oz/300ml good red wine
1-2 tablespoons finely chopped shallots

½pt/300ml finely diced butter, kept very chilled
freshly ground salt and pepper

Put the finely chopped shallots into a saucepan, add the wine and bring to the boil until the liquid has reduced to about two tablespoons. Remove from the heat, add some seasoning and allow to cook for a few minutes. Then whisk in two or three cubes of butter till they are completely absorbed. Return the pan to a very low heat and slowly, one by one, add each cube of butter whisking all the time. Do not add the next cube until the preceeding one has been absorbed. The sauce will slowly thicken to the consistency of pouring cream. Remove from the heat and add any further seasoning to taste.

Beurre Noir

This is traditionally served with wings of skate or ray which have a sweetish flesh, but I also like it with any of the game fish, and it makes a refreshing change from the richer eggier accompaniments like Sauce Hollandaise. It is not actually black but allowed to bubble till brown.
Makes about 4fl oz/120ml

6 tablespoons slightly melted butter
1 tablespoon parsley, very finely chopped

1 tablespoon pickled capers, drained
1 tablespoon vinegar

Heat the butter in a small, preferably non-stick, saucepan and allow to bubble till well browned. Quickly stir in the parsley and capers, remove from the heat and add the vinegar. Pour over the fish while it is still frothing and very hot.

Beurre Blanc

This is a classic sauce, the staple of the French cuisine for ever, and revived again during the craze for *Nouvelle Cuisine*. It goes with practically anything – any sort of fish and any sort of white meat (try it with the hot pheasant sausage on page 84). It is excellent with *quenelles* (see pages 159 and 144) and Hot Smoked Salmon (see page 149) and also most vegetables. Light and creamy, if you can't think of anything else, *beurre blanc* will never let you down.
Makes about 6fl oz/175ml

½pt/300ml white wine (with lemon juice or vinegar added according to taste
1-2 tablespoons finely chopped shallots

½pt/300ml finely diced butter, kept very chilled
freshly ground salt and pepper to taste

Put the finely chopped shallots into a saucepan, add the wine and bring to the boil until the liquid has reduced to about two tablespoons. Remove from the heat, add some seasoning and allow to cool for a few minutes. Then whisk in two or three cubes of butter till they are completely absorbed. Return the pan to a very low heat and slowly, one by one, add each cube of butter whisking all the time. Do not add the next cube until the preceeding one has been absorbed. The sauce will slowly thicken to the consistency of pouring cream. Remove from the heat and add any further seasoning to taste. Add cream too, if desired.

Basic Marinade for Game

Marinating is a process used to tenderise meat you might suspect to be tough, to improve the flavour, to help moisturise any meat that tends to dryness, and to provide a base for any accompanying sauce or gravy. Acidity, in the form of wine or vinegar, helps preserve the flesh; oil adds lubrication for roasting and general cooking. The combinations for any marinade are almost limitless; to a basic liquid mix of oil and wine/vinegar you can add any number of herbs, spices and seasonings that you feel will complement that particular meat. I like being very *ad hoc* about marinades, chucking in anything that is around or that I'm in the mood for on that particular occasion. However, the following gives an outline for a basic marinade, for just about any type of game, which you can vary to will or whim.

Liquids	*2-3 tablespoons oil (I prefer vegetable to olive)*	**Vegetables**	*1 carrot, chopped*
	3-4 glasses wine (red or white)		*1 celery stick, chopped*
	½-1 glass vinegar		*1 onion, chopped*
Options	*orange juice*		*2 or more cloves garlic, according to taste*
	brandy	**Herbs**	*bouquet garni*
	lemon juice	**Spices**	*cloves*
	Pernod, cassis, ginger wine, or other spirits like gin		*black peppercorns*
			baies rose (pink) peppercorns
			juniper berries
			any fresh herbs – parsley, thyme, oregano, rosemary, etc.
			orange zest
			lemon zest
			coriander, cinnamon, nutmeg, etc.

Never ever use a metal container for marinating – always use glass or crockery. You only need enough marinade to just cover the meat, as long as you make sure that it is turned often. A marinade can be either cooked, or 'neat'. If it is cooked and poured straight off the heat on the meat it will sink into the flesh more quickly than an uncooked marinade, and will work more quickly. A neat marinade can be left to work longer and more gently into the meat, as long as the temperature doesn't get too hot. If you are at all worried, you can always cook it up, let it cool off again and replace the meat. Sometimes you can add saltpetre (see Spiced Wild Boar, page 130) which is nitrate of potash for pickling, and this you can leave for 10 days or so. To use a cooked marinade, combine all the ingredients in a saucepan and simmer for about half an hour. Pour over the game either hot or cold. For 'neat marinade' combine all the ingredients in a bowl and immerse the meat in the mixture, turning till it is completely coated. When you come to cook the meat, remove it from the marinade with a slotted spoon, drain the marinade off and wipe off any clinging herbs or spices with kitchen paper. Strain the marinade and combine with stock to reduce to a rich sauce.

ACCOMPANIMENTS

Shortcrust Pastry

Good for game pies, pasties etc, but also for tartlets filled with cold game to take on picnics. If I'm in a hurry, I use Saxby's ready-made shortcrust pastry which is brilliant, but if it isn't around, it's back to good old home-baking. The secret with pastry is to keep everything as cool as possible, and if time try to chill the pastry after making it for a short time. Always try and use butter, or butter and lard if possible and always make more than you think you'll need. You can use the extra for decoration, or freeze it for the next time.

¹/₂lb/225g plain flour
4oz/100g butter - or equal amounts of butter and lard, diced

pinch of salt
2-2¹/₂ tablespoons ice cold water

Sift together the flour and salt. Rub the diced fat in with the fingertips lifting the mixture constantly to aerate as much as possible. Once it looks like breadcrumbs add the water, stirring with a spoon till it forms a stiff paste. Roll into a ball with your hands, then chill in the fridge for at least 20 minutes. Roll out on a floured board and with a floured rolling pin and use as required.

Flaky Pastry

This is sometimes used instead of shortcrust for pies and pasties. If you can take the trouble to make it at home rather than buy the ready-made it really is a different world.

1lb/450g plain flour (brown is also excellent)
10oz/275g butter or butter and lard already mixed together

ice cold water to mix (about 8-10 tablespoons)
pinch of salt

Sift the flour and salt into a large bowl. Divide the fat into four and lightly rub one quarter into the flour. Add enough water to mix to a soft dough. Roll this out into an oblong strip about 5 inches (10cm) wide and keep all corners as square as possible. Take the next quarter of fat, neatly diced, place it evenly over two thirds of the pastry and lightly dredge with flour. Fold the uncovered third over the middle of the oblong and fold the other third over that neatly pressing all the edges together with a rolling pin to prevent the air from escaping. Allow to chill for 15 minutes, then take out and place on a floured board with the folded edges to the right and left of you. Use the rolling pin to press ridges into the pastry to distribute the air evenly. Then roll out as before and repeat the whole process again twice with the other two quarters of fat. Chill again before use. When ready for cooking, place in a very hot oven (230C/450F/Gas Mark 8) until it is set, and then reduce the heat to fairly hot (180C/375F/Gas Mark 5).

Easy Redcurrant Tartlets

Pretty and colourful, these are also dead easy to make, and go well and look well with most game, in particular pheasant and venison.

Serves 6

6 vol-au-vent cases
redcurrant jelly

fresh redcurrants (optional)

Bake the vol-au-vent cases following instructions until they are puffy and golden. Leave to cool slightly, but while they are still warm, fill with redcurrant jelly, and top with fresh redcurrants. Serve immediately.

Puy Lentils

These are from France and available in good delicatessens and groceries. They make an
excellent accompaniment to game and, unlike the better known orange or brown lentils, don't
need soaking overnight before cooking.

Serves 4-6

½lb/225g Puy lentils
2-3 tablespoons vegetable oil
4 cloves garlic, finely chopped

1 knob root ginger, finely chopped
2 balls stem ginger, finely chopped (optional)
½ red pepper, very finely chopped (optional)

Heat the oil in a non-stick saucepan, and cook the garlic, pepper and ginger till they are softened. Add the
lentils and cook gently for 20 minutes adding enough water to stop them from drying but not to make any
extra liquid. You can cook them longer if you prefer them softer, but they should all be intact and just a bit
softer than *al dente*.

Parsnip Chips

If people haven't had these before, they can never quite work out what they are. They are the
most moreish crispy, crunchy, nibbly vegetable ever. Even my husband and two small sons who
simply can't stand parsnips normally will eat these. I always make extra and have any that are
uneaten (if there are any) as nibbles with drinks. Otherwise serve them warm with roast
grouse, or any other roast game. You can make them hours or days in advance as they
keep their crispiness very well.

Serves 6

7 medium parsnips
large saucepan vegetable oil

salt

Peel the parsnips with a potato peeler and then slice finely in a food processor. Bring the oil to smoking
point over a highish heat, and deep fry the parsnip chips in batches till they are golden brown. Drain and keep
warm on kitchen paper in a shallow ovenproof dish till they are all cooked. Sprinkle light with fine salt and
serve.

Bitter Winter Salad

All the bitter winter salads – endive, chicory, radiccio, rocket, oak lettuce – go as well as the
more classic watercress with game. They all mix very well together too, so that you can make
any combination you want, depending on availability. In more remote areas they are one item
that is not often available on the greengrocery shelves in the large supermarkets, but they do
grow very easily in the garden and are worth making the effort for.

Serves 4-6

Any combination of bitter winter salads – endive,
  chicory,
radiccio, rocket, oak lettuce etc

a handful of fresh white croûtons
French dressing (see page 184)

Carefully wash and trim the salad and throw loosely into a wide bowl. Add French dressing to taste and toss.
Sprinkle with crunchy fresh croûtons.

Sweet and Sour Cucumber

This is a very popular salad throughout Eastern Europe, particularly in Austria and Hungary where it is inevitably to be found at a cold table. There you will find it garnished with dill or poppy seeds, but maybe chopped mint is more to the British taste in summer.

Serves 4-6

2 smallish cucumbers
10fl oz/300ml white wine or cider vinegar
2 tablespoons caster sugar

1-2 dessertspoons salt
freshly chopped mint

Wash and peel the cucumbers and slice very thinly. Lay the slices in a wide, flat bowl sprinkling each layer with a bit of salt to extract the water. Cover with clingfilm and refrigerate for half an hour. Meanwhile mix the sugar and vinegar adding a little freshly ground black pepper if desired. Drain off any excess liquid from the cucumbers and cover with the sugar and vinegar mixture. Leave to stand for a further half hour or more, then drain off excess liquid before serving. Sprinkle with finely chopped fresh mint for garnish.

Sweet and Sour Courgette Salad

This is a traditional Austrian recipe for cucumbers (see above) which I have adapted for courgettes. Both make a very refreshing accompaniment to cold salmon.

Serves 4-6

4 medium courgettes
10fl oz/300ml white wine or cider vinegar
2 tablespoons caster sugar

1 tablespoon salt
freshly snipped dill

Wash the courgettes and cut each lengthways, scoring out any seed down the centre. Slice the courgettes very thinly and lay the slices in a wide flat bowl, sprinkling each layer with a bit of salt to extract the water. Cover with clingfilm and refrigerate for half an hour. Meanwhile mix the sugar and vinegar and add some black pepper to taste. Drain off any excess liquid from the courgettes and cover with the sugar and vinegar mixture. Leave to stand for a further half hour or more, then drain off excess liquid before serving. Sprinkle with finely snipped fresh dill for garnish.

Courgette Salad

Courgettes or zucchini are now available all the year round in nearly all supermarkets. The following salad recipe not only rings the changes but also makes a very good accompaniment to cold salmon, for example, at a buffet.

Serves 4

1lb/500g courgettes, finely sliced
4 tablespoons olive oil
4 spring onions
1 teaspoon paprika
¼ teaspoon sugar

1 teaspoon dill seeds or finely chopped fresh dill
2 tablespoons vinegar
salt and freshly ground black pepper
juliennes of orange, blanched

Heat the oil in a large, heavy-bottomed frying pan and toss the spring onions in it. Add the courgettes and toss until tender but still crisp – about 2 minutes. Add all the other ingredients and toss for about another minute. Remove from the heat, cool and then refrigerate. Serve chilled, and add more fresh dill to garnish. Scatter the blanched juliennes or orange over for extra zest and colour.

Orange and Watercress Salad

The contrast between the vibrant green and orange colours in this salad make it a
brilliant accompaniment to almost any dish, but the sharpness of the taste particularly offset
richer game like duck or hare.

Serves 4-6

4 bunches watercress
2 medium oranges

French dressing (see page 184)

Wash and trim the watercress, removing any very long stalks. Drain. Taking a very sharp knife peel the oranges, removing the skin in a long coil and taking the pith with it. This leaves a naked orange with the outside of each segment exposed. Remove each segment by cutting into the skin either side and releasing it. Squeeze the juice from the leftover membranes and, if desired, add to the dressing for a change of flavour. Scatter the segments among the watercress, add the dressing, toss and serve immediately.

Rösti Celeriac

The idea for this comes from those scrummy rösti potatoes you get in Switzerland. I substitute
them for potatoes with game and they are always a hit.

Serves 4-6

1 large celeriac
knob of butter

Peel the celeriac and grate on the largest holes in your grater. Arrange into small piles, depending on the number you are feeding. Drop a knob of butter into a large pan, but only enough to 'paint' the surface. Place the piles of celeriac in the pan, flatten them and allow the pan to get hot enough to sear and slightly blacken each little cake. At this point turn each 'cake' over with a fish slice and repeat. Arrange each little 'cake' around your game on a large serving platter, or to accompany a portion on individual plates.

Buttered Salsify

Root vegetables are amongst the best with game, and particularly good to my mind
are salsify with their nutty flavour and texture. They are now available
from most good large supermarkets.

1lb/450g salsify
2 lemons
sea salt

1oz/25g butter
1 tablespoon finely chopped fresh parsley

Wash the earth off the salsify and peel the skin off thinly with a potato peeler. Cut the long thin roots into two-inch lengths. Squeeze the juice from both lemons and add to two-three tablespoons water in the pan (salsify need to be well acidulated during cooking). Add a pinch of salt and bring to the boil and then simmer the salsify until tender for 20-40 minutes depending on the thickness of the root. Note: salsify blacken very quickly after peeling so put them in a bowl of cold water if you are not going to cook them immediately. To serve, arrange in a shallow dish, cover with melted butter and sprinkle with parsley.

Red Cabbage

The perfect vegetable with nearly all game, and such a beautiful colour.

2lb/900kg red cabbage
1 cooking apple, peeled and finely chopped
1 medium onion, peeled and finely chopped
1oz/25g butter

1oz/25g soft light brown sugar
3fl oz/75ml red wine vinegar (white will do)
3fl oz/75ml water
salt and freshly ground black pepper

Discard any tough outer leaves of the cabbage, remove any tough outer stalks and shred evenly and finely. Melt the butter in a saucepan and gently cook the onions till they are translucent. Add the cabbage to the pan along with the sugar, vinegar and water. Stir well and bring to the boil, then cover and simmer for about 40 minutes. Check the pan every ten minutes to turn all the cabbage over and add a drop more water if necessary. Season to taste. You can also make this in the oven, by starting on top with a flameproof casserole and transferring to a medium oven once it has come to the boil. I think it cooks more evenly this way, and you don't have to worry about the bottom getting burnt. For variety, I sometimes add raisins during the cooking.

Potato and Celeriac Purée

This is a delicious alternative to plain mashed potatoes, particularly good with salted or spiced game (see Christmas Spiced Wild Boar, page 130).
Serves 4-6

1lb/450g potatoes
1lb/450g celeriac, peeled and cubed
4oz/100g butter

a dash of milk
salt and freshly ground pepper

In separate pans of salted water boil the celeriac and potatoes till they are soft enough to mash (they will cook at different rates depending on the sizes you cut them into). Drain and return to one pan together. Add the butter, diced, and mash all together. Add some milk if you want a softer consistency and adjust the seasoning with a final pinch of salt and some ground pepper.

Knoedel

Dumplings are widely used right across Eastern Europe and in Austria (where they are called *knoedel*) and Germany (where they are called *kloesse*) as a traditional accompaniment to game, cabbagey dishes and most forms of casserole. They are made with a huge range of different carbohydrate bases: in Hungary they like to make them with potatoes or cornmeal or grated noodles; in Poland ground with mixed winter vegetables. The French word quenelle (as in *quenelles de brochet*, see page 159) derives from the German word *knoedel*. My own preference is for the Austrian *semmel* (meaning bun) *knoedel* which are much lighter than our own dumplings being made of day-old white buns rather than flour.

Makes 20

7fl oz/200ml milk
1 egg
½lb/225g day-old bread rolls (white)
1oz/25g self-raising flour
2oz/50g butter melted and used lukewarm/bacon
   fat is another

alternative
salt and pepper to taste
1 tablespoon fresh chopped mixed herbs or
   parsley (optional)
1 tablespoon finely chopped onion
1 dessertspoon butter

Crumble the breadrolls and mix all the dry ingredients together. Beat the milk and egg with a pinch of salt, pour over the mixture and leave to soak for at least an hour. Meanwhile soften the chopped onion in 1 dessertspoon butter until translucent and add to the breadcrumb mixture. Add the flour and melted fat, and mix all really well together, then knead together until the mixture is smooth. On a floured surface, break the mixture into equal sized balls and roll to about 1 inch in diameter (2.5cm). Make sure that the balls are compact or they may disintegrate during cooking. Leave to settle for 15 or so minutes. Bring a large pan of salted water to the boil, drop the dumplings in about five at a time and wait till they rise to the surface which is when they are cooked. Drain well and serve with game casserole or any game with a good rich sauce.

Potato 'Apple Slices'

I was taught this very simple but pretty way of doing boiled potatoes some 15 years or more ago by a brilliant professional cook, Amanda Downes. I have done them ever since as they are so light but have never yet come across anyone who has seen them done like this before!
Peel the potatoes and then cut them in half lengthways. Starting from one end cut thin slices across the width forming the shape of sliced apples. Boil for 5-10 minutes depending on the type of potato. Serve with some melted butter poured over, and a sprinkling of chopped parsley.

Saffron Potatoes

To make a change from roast potatoes, try these. They keep people guessing.

Serves 6

*3lb/1.3kg roasting potatoes (*Desirée, Maris
  Piper)
6fl oz/175ml chicken stock, salted
3fl oz/75ml white wine

1 packet powdered saffron or strands
4 tablespoons vegetable oil
2oz/50g butter
salt

Peel and shape the potatoes into neat even sizes, round or cubed. Remember if you cut them into smaller sizes, they cook more quickly. Pour the stock and wine into a pan, bring to the boil and add the saffron. Heat the oil and butter in a roasting pan on top of the cooker, add the potatoes, turn them so they are completely coated and then add the stock and wine mixture. Transfer to a preheated hot oven (210C/425F/Gas Mark 7) for 40-50 minutes. The potatoes will absorb the stock during cooking and become a crispy golden brown. Sprinkle with salt when ready to serve.

Redcurrant Jelly

any amount of redcurrants
1½lb/675g preserving sugar to each pint of juice

You can make redcurrant jelly without stripping the berries off the stems; in fact it is better with the stems, but wash and clean all stalks thoroughly. Put into the preserving pan and simmer gently for 30-40 minutes until the juices have broken through and the fruit is disintegrating. Strain through a jelly bag and leave to drip overnight. Measure the liquid and allow 1½lb sugar to each pint of juice. Add the sugar and gently let the sugar dissolve, stirring all the time. Bring to the boil and boil very fast for one or two minutes. Redcurrant jelly sets very fast and should be put into scalded jars immediately.

Mint Jelly

2lb/1kg green apples
a bunch of mint
water to cover

juice of half a lemon
1lb/450g preserving sugar to each pint of juice
muslin bag containing a bunch of chopped mint

Wash the apples, do not peel, and cut into quarters. Put into a pan with the water and lemon juice and a few sprigs of mint and simmer until soft and pulpy. Strain through a jelly bag and leave to drip into a bowl overnight. Measure the juice next day and to each pint weigh out 1lb/450g preserving sugar. Gently heat the juice up and add the sugar stirring all the time until it is dissolved. Then boil it all up rapidly for 5 minutes. Now add the muslin bag of mint and leave to boil in the syrup until setting point is reached. Remove, and pour jelly into scalded jam jars.

Crab Apple Jelly

The sight of the bright red crab apples on the trees towards the middle of September always heralds the advent of autumn and another season of game. Crab apple jelly is my favourite. I love its clear amber colour and it seems to go with just about any type of game.
Makes about 6-7lb (3kg)

8lb/3.6kg crab apples, quartered
the juice of 4 lemons

1lb/450g of preserving sugar to every 1
pint/600ml juice

Cover the apples with water and cook till they are mushy. Strain through a jelly bag and leave to drip into a bowl overnight. Next day add the strained juice of the 4 lemons, measure out the amount of juice and add 1lb/450g sugar to every pint/600ml liquid. Bring the juice slowly to the boil adding the sugar bit by bit and stirring till it is completely dissolved. Boil rapidly for 5 minutes, but just test a drop on a saucer to see if it will set before taking it off the heat. If it doesn't, boil a little longer until it does. Pour into scalded jam jars.

Apple or Quince Jelly

9lb/4kg cooking apples or ripe quinces
the juice of one lemon

1½lb/675g preserving sugar to each 1½pt/1 litre
juice
1oz/25g vanilla sugar or ¼pt/150ml white wine

Wash and clean apples or quinces (or both, if you want to make a mixture). Quarter, leaving the core and skin, place in a pan, cover with water and simmer for about 30 minutes or until mushy. Leave to stand overnight. Next day pour into a jelly bag and leave to drip all day – even 24 hours. Next, measure the juice, and add 1½lb/675g preserving sugar to each 1½pt/1 litre juice. Bring to the boil and boil rapidly until it reaches setting point when it will turn amber in colour. Add the lemon juice and vanilla sugar or wine, and pour into scalded jam jars. Makes about 9lb/4kg.

Rowanberry Jelly or Wild Fruit Jelly

Although it is a classic accompaniment to game – in particular venison – I personally find rowan jelly just too bitter in taste. If you are like me, then this recipe is ideal – you can have some rowan for the flavour, but dilute with any other berries from the hedges. On the other hand, if you are a great fan of rowan jelly (and people either are or aren't) then you can still use this recipe, but stick to rowan berries alone. Otherwise it's a standby for any wild fruit – elderberries, sloes, bilberries, blackberries, wild raspberries etc.

2lb/1kg rowanberries (or any mixture of any wild
* berries)*
2lb/1kg cooking or crab apples

the juice of one lemon
1lb/450g preserving sugar to every 1 pint/600ml
* juice*

Wash and roughly chop the apples, leaving the core and the skin, and put with the other fruit (also washed) into a pan. Just cover the fruit with water, add the lemon juice and bring to the boil. Simmer for about 40 minutes until the fruit is soft and pulpy. Strain into a jelly bag and allow to drip into a bowl overnight. Measure the juice and weigh 1lb/500g preserving sugar to every pint/600ml juice. Warm the sugar in a heatproof bowl in a warm oven (110C/225F/Gas Mark ¼) for 10 to 15 minutes. This reduces the cooking time of the jelly, giving a fresher flavour. Heat the juice and as it nears simmering point add the warmed sugar, stirring until it is dissolved. Boil rapidly till it reaches setting point – about 10-12 minutes. Pour into scalded jam jars. Makes about 6-7lb (3kg).

Buttered Crumbs

I have a suspicion that some people like having game just as an excuse to eat the fried breadcrumbs that traditionally accompany it! Have you ever observed the amounts that even the most modest eaters take in proportion to the meat on their plate! Crispy and crunchy, they are indeed delectable. The usual way is just to have plain fried breadcrumbs, as below, but you can add crispy crumbled bacon as well for a change, or even some dry chopped parsley.

4oz/100g fresh white breadcrumbs　　　　　　　　*1 tablespoon light vegetable oil*
4oz/100g butter

Melt the butter and oil in a heavy-bottomed frying pan, and add the breadcrumbs. Stir constantly to make sure they are browned all over, and cook till golden. If you have cooked too much it doesn't matter at all, as they keep very well in the fridge for weeks (unless a family nibbler gets at them).

STUFFINGS

The variety of stuffings is infinite and allows for as much imagination, ingenuity and creativity that you're in the mood for. Fruit, vegetables, nuts, herbs, spices, any sort of liver or sausage meat, chopped ham, and leftovers of practically anything can be popped in; nothing is sacrosanct. The traditional stuffings always remain popular – sage and onion, lemon and herb, chestnut, sausage meat, walnut and celery and so on. Prunes and apricots are nearly always infallibly good additions – especially with game (see Wild Goose with Prune, Apple and Celery Stuffing, page 64). The bindings are usually breadcrumbs, or rice, or forcemeat (from the French *farcer* to stuff) based on sausage meat or minced veal. But nowadays many stuffings are made without such heavy bindings – see the Boned Stuffed Pheasant on page 91, filled simply with cream cheese and spinach. In the words of the immortal song – 'anything goes'!

Traditional stuffings

Sage and Onion Stuffing

Good with duck, goose and pheasant.

4oz/100g onion, very finely chopped
4 sage leaves finely chopped, or ¹/₂ teaspoon
*   powdered sage*
1oz/25g butter

2oz/50g breadcrumbs
freshly ground salt and pepper
¹/₂ egg (beaten)

Melt the butter in a non-stick saucepan and in it soften the onion and sage. Remove from the heat and combine with the breadcrumbs, egg and salt and pepper to make a firm ball. Use to stuff.

Lemon and Herb Stuffing

Good with all the white-fleshed game, as well as fish.

4oz/100g onion, very finely chopped
2-3 teaspoons mixed herbs
grated rind ¹/₂ lemon
2oz/50g breadcrumbs

1oz/25g butter
freshly ground salt and pepper
¹/₂ egg, beaten (optional)

Melt the butter in a non-stick saucepan and in it soften the onion till it is translucent. Combine with the breadcrumbs, herbs, grated lemon rind, seasoning and egg till it forms a firm ball. Use to stuff.

Rice Stuffing

You can vary the additions to the rice – pine nuts instead of almonds; chopped celery or peppers instead of the herbs and so on. It is particularly good with the lighter game birds like quail and partridge.

2oz/50g rice
1 chicken or other game bird liver
2oz/50g raisins
2oz/50g chopped almonds
2 tablespoons chopped parsley

2 dessertspoon chopped chives or spring onions
1oz/25g butter
pinch of dried herbs (thyme, marjoram, oregano
- one or any of them)
1 egg, beaten (optional)

Boil the rice till it is *al dente*. Drain and rinse with cold water. Melt the butter in a small non-stick pan and soften the chopped onion till it is translucent, adding the chopped liver just before the end to cook a little but still remain pink. Remove from the heat and then add the rice and all the other ingredients, mixing well together till they form a cohesive ball. Use to stuff.

Chestnut Stuffing

Good with the heavier, dark meated wild fowl.

2lb/900g chestnuts
¹/₂pt/300ml chicken stock
2oz/50g butter

pinch of cinnamon
¹/₂ teaspoon sugar
salt and pepper

Using a very sharp pointed knife, slit the chestnuts and bake or boil for about 20 minutes until the outer and inner skins are ready to peel off (use rubber gloves to protect you from the heat). When the chestnuts are all completely peeled replace them in a saucepan and just cover with stock. Simmer them for another 20 minutes or so, until tender (test with a fork) and drain. Press through a strong but fine metal sieve and then add the butter, sugar, cinnamon and salt and pepper and enough stock to help mould it into a firm ball. Use to stuff.

Forcemeat Stuffing

Good with rabbit as well as pheasant.

1oz/300g minced pork or sausagemeat
5-6oz/150g bacon or raw ham
³/₄oz/100g veal
a handful of white breadcrumbs, soaked in milk
3 garlic cloves, crushed

1 teaspoon mixed dried parsley and thyme
salt and pepper
4 tablespoons brandy
1 egg, beaten

Dice the bacon or ham and veal very, very finely and combine with the minced pork or sausagemeat. Add all the rest of the ingredients, binding with the beaten egg to form a well-mixed, firm ball. Use to stuff.

Apple, Celery and Walnut Stuffing

This, of course, is one of the classics with the good old Christmas turkey, though
I find the addition of some chopped dried apricots helps to pep it up somewhat.
Prunes also mix in very well, but you could also try dates or raisins or candied peel just as well.
Good with duck and goose and pheasant.

1 large sour apple
4 tablespoons chopped celery
2 tablespoons chopped walnuts
2oz/50g pork sausagemeat
1 large onion, finely chopped
2oz/50g breadcrumbs

½ teaspoon dried mixed herbs
grated rind of ½ lemon
1 tablespoon chopped parsley
1 egg, beaten
extra milk to bind, if necessary
1 tablespoon butter

Melt the butter in a non-stick pan and gently cook the chopped onion and celery till softened. Peel, core and chop the apple, and taking one big bowl combine all the ingredients, mixing well together and using the egg to bind. Add a dash of milk if the mixture seems too stiff and then use to stuff.

HANGING GAME

Game is not necessarily synonymous with "gameyness", and by no means all game meats and fleshes are dark, pungent or especially strong in taste. However, certain game species *are* like this, either because of the natural characteristics of the flesh itself, or because it is brought about by a period of hanging and the deliberate "ripening" of the flesh and the flavour. Most gamey flesh is a combination of both, as with grouse or hare or venison, all of which tend to be comparatively dark-coloured meats with a fairly pronounced intrinsic flavour. This can be altered (and is usually heightened and emphasised) by hanging the bird or animal for a period of some days before it is gutted and skinned or plucked to be made ready for the oven.

Hanging affects more than flavour alone, and allows the natural processes of post mortem breakdown and the beginnings of decay to act upon both the texture and flavour of the meat. All this may seem a little grisly, but it is important to grasp the principles if game is to be prepared and cooked in prime condition. Certain types of furred game (e.g. hares), and most gamebirds, are not eviscerated until after hanging, and for these types of game the fermentation of the gut and its contents also contribute to the general process of maturing. To hang game is therefore to take advantage of some of the positive contributions which the natural processes of decay can bring to the flesh of the game bird or mammal you wish to prepare and eat.

But there is a world of difference between game which is well hung, pleasantly gamey or even a big "high", and the meat which has been left to hang to the point where it has begun to go rotten. The art of hanging meat and poultry lies in knowing when to stop the hanging, and thus to halt the processes of decay at the optimum point, when they have made a positive contribution to the texture and flavour of the flesh, but have not yet begun to cause the corruption which progressively makes meat foul and inedible – and probably downright poisonous, too.

Hanging is not some arcane or near-barbarous procedure confined only to game. Almost all types of meat benefit by being hung, and both lamb and beef improve very considerably in taste and texture if the gutted carcase is allowed to hang in a cool and sanitary place. Much of the scorn for the allegedly flavourless character of so much of today's lamb and beef can be traced directly to the processors' desire to get the meat from the abbatoir to the consumer as quickly as possible, allowing insufficient time for hanging. Unfortunately the average consumer of beef or lamb knows little – and is usually happy to know as little as possible – of what goes on in abbatoirs and butchers' shops, and therefore is seldom aware of the fact that his delicious steak or leg of lamb or rib roast has only achieved its peak of texture and flavour as a result of the butcher's careful judgement of the hanging time and temperature conditions necessary to bring the meat to that state of culinary perfection in which we enjoy it most. The sportsman who brings home game he has shot or caught owes it to himself, his family and friends – and to the quarry – to learn how to deal with it correctly and to present it for cooking in optimum condition.

The dressing of a carcase in the field – for example the paunching of a rabbit, or the gralloching of a deer – is a sporting skill, though not an especially difficult one, and it lies outside the scope of a book on game cookery. Every novice sportsman sees it done, and is best taught the arts of gutting and gralloching on the spot by more experienced friends. But once the game is brought home for the larder it comes within the cook's domain, and therefore within the wider framework of how to begin preparing game for the table. Although there is no mystery about hanging game, when well done it can contribute greatly to the success of the meal, while game that has hung too long or not long enough may be disappointing – or much worse!

The hanging of game is, quite literally, a matter of taste – and *"de gustibus non est disputandum"!* If you eat game regularly – and most sporting households get plenty of opportunity to do so in due season – you will soon find out what is best suited to your personal taste. Some people like their game really well hung, to a point where it is within a whisker of slipping over the fine line that distinguishes the ripe from the rotten, in which case it is fairest on everyone if you do your own gutting and plucking before the cook tackles the rest of the job. Others prefer game lightly hung, or even not at all; and some of the most delicious red grouse I have ever tasted were young birds cooked the very same day as they were bagged – actually in late July, and a full fortnight before they were strictly legal! It had been a day of baking heat when we were doing a pre-season count of grouse on a moor, and an over-zealous spaniel belonging to one of the keepers had grabbed several well-grown youngsters as they lay tight in the heather. It would have been a terrible shame to waste them, and they were mouthwateringly delicious at supper that evening – but very different from grouse given just a couple of days' hanging in a cool place before plucking and cleaning. An old grouse will need more hanging than a young bird of the year, and a mature stag should hang longer than a plump yearling deer. Certain elderly specimens gain still further tenderness from marinating after a period of hanging, and there are many hints on the use of marinades in the individual recipes here. Some other species, notably woodcock and plover, seem neither to benefit nor deteriorate with long hanging, while wildfowl (duck and geese) are probably best not hung at all. If in doubt, and especially if you plan to serve game to guests who may not be accustomed to it, it is always best to err on the under-hung side.

Temperature is critical when hanging game or meat of any kind; and just one day's hanging in a hot and stuffy garage in August may push a grouse over the top, compared with several days in a cool pantry or larder. By the same token, in mid-winter game may hang safely for a couple of weeks or more in an outbuilding where the temperature may only be slightly above freezing for weeks on end. As a general guide, it is best to hang game in similar conditions to those in which you would keep cold cuts of meat, and a steady temperature of 50-55°F is ideal for game (and for storing wine, too – so if space is at a premium, wine and hanging game can share a cool corner). Provided the temperature is reasonably constant, you can soon get the measure of your chosen game larder and will know almost automatically when individual birds and beast are right for the kitchen.

A vital word of caution about bugs and other pests. It is absolutely essential that a game larder should be quite impenetrable to insects, mice, and reprobate dogs and cats. Ventilators and windows are best covered with a thin sheet of perforated zinc or some equally fine-meshed barrier, and doors and windows should fit well in their frames. Fly-blown meat is useless, rodents are a vile health hazard – and many a beloved and otherwise well-behaved dog or cat has been lured from the path of righteousness by the irresistible scent of hanging game, to try and grab it off the hook. No-one wishes to see a prime grouse or pheasant borne off in the jaws of a dog, probably to be buried in a flower bed until it is really fruity enough for *his* taste!

All gamebirds should be hung by the neck, but hares by the heels, and neither is normally skinned or plucked or eviscerated until hanging is completed. For a semi-permanent game larder the excellent V-shaped brass "Glenmuick" game hooks are excellent, and cost about 60 pence each. As advertised, they will hang anything from a snipe to a goose, with no need for any string or other securing. Hooks of all kinds are best mounted on a projecting batten or wooden strap that sits out two or three inches from the wall of the room, so that the game hangs well clear of the wall, with air circulating freely all around it; and a row of round-headed 4-inch or 6-inch nails will do in lieu of hooks, with each item hung by a separate loop of cord or baler twine.

Deer, and other large game such as wild boar, are fully gralloched before they go to hang in the larder. Liver, kidneys, lights, tongue and sweetbreads should be removed to the kitchen or the fridge at this stage, as they definitely do *not* improve by being left. Each beast's chest cavity should be sawn or split along the full length of the breast-bone and the ribs wedged apart to allow the free circulation of air. The hind section of the pelvis should be sawn away so that the two haunches can be fully spread.

Many enthusiasts prefer to hang deer and boar carcases in the skin until they are ready for jointing for the kitchen or the freezer, and argue that this may help to prevent moisture loss by evaporation. However, skinning is a much easier task if it is done before the carcase goes cold; and a skinned carcase should not deteriorate through drying if it is hung in a cool larder at average humidity. All ragged and bloodshot pieces of meat should be trimmed off, paying particular attention to the areas around the bullet entrance and exit holes, and the head and lower legs should also be removed. The carcase is best hung from a gambrel or spreader bar approximately 20-30 inches long, with a slot or hook at each end to grip between the bone and the sinew at the hock joint of each hind leg, and a simple pulley system is best for all but the smallest carcases of roe and chamois. As with all game, the hanging carcase should not be in contact with the wall, but should be suspended freely.

To summarise, these are suggested hanging times for game in a larder at a steady temperature of 50-55°F:

Young gamebirds:	5-7 days
Old gamebirds:	7-10 days
Duck & geese:	nil
Venison, boar, etc:	7-14 days
Woodcock, snipe & plover:	optional

KEEPING AND SERVING WINE

There is nothing complicated or demanding about keeping bottles of wine in good conditions, and in preparing them for serving at their best. It is largely common sense, and chiefly involves making sure that the temperature is suitable, just as cooks use fridges, cool pantries and warm kitchens as different temperature environments for keeping foodstuffs in good order. Wines keep best when stored away from bright light, vibration, a dryish atmosphere, and strong smells. They fare best in darkness or sombre lighting, with a minimum of handling or shaking, and a humid or damp atmosphere is a bonus. The best storage temperature is around 53-58°F, without too much fluctuation in winter and summer. A high cellar temperature tends to make wines age more quickly, while a very cold cellar does the reverse. The presence of strong-smelling liquids or gasses can gradually intrude upon the bottled wine, attacking and destroying its natural aroma and taste.

Until it is removed from storage and prepared for serving, bottled wine should be stored on its side, preferably in racks of some kind, so that an individual bottle can be removed without disturbing the others. Bottles kept on their sides in racks or wine-bins are stable and, most importantly, the cork is kept doused in the wine and remains soft and moist, maintaining a good seal against the inside of the bottle's neck. Wine stored with the bottles upright will suffer gradual drying out of the cork, which breaks the airtight seal and allows the contents to react with the air, turning it sour and undrinkable. If upright bottles are kept in a warm, dry atmosphere this process can happen quite quickly. Few houses, especially those built this century, have a proper purpose-built cellar. (My own substantial stone-built house in southern Scotland, dating from the seventeenth century, lacks a proper cellar, partly because it is sited directly on top of a rocky outcrop, which would have necessitated explosives to excavate a basement cellar; but mainly because it was built as a Church of Scotland manse, and the elders of the Kirk were most unlikely to encourage their ministers to indulge a taste for the Demon Drink! In contrast, many old Church of England rectories and vicarages just a few miles south across the border have splendid wine cellars, testimonies to the more liberal lifestyles of the Anglican clergy.)

If your house does have a cellar, or if you can arrange to store your wine in a friend's cellar, you are very fortunate and should make the most of it. But it is perfectly possible to create good storage facilities for wine in a small modern house or flat. Favourite places for a mini-cellar in a modern house are under the stairs, or in a roof-space, or in the garage, or in a garden shed. All these can be fine, provided you avoid placing your wine racks close to hot water pipes, smelly cans of lawnmower fuel, or vibrating central heating boilers.

The first stage in preparing and presenting wines at the table is when you choose your bottles and remove them from their resting places on their sides in their storage racks or crates. Let the bottles stand upright for at least an hour or two, and much longer – a day or so – in the case of old ports, older red wines and some whites, which develop a crust or sediment in the bottles. The act of disturbing these bottles will have broken and stirred up the sediment, and this needs to be given time to settle. As a general principle red wines, including port, should be served at a temperature not much below that of your dining room, while most white wines, including sherries and rosé wine, are best served much cooler.

But beware of warming or chilling wine too fast. Wine dislikes sudden shocks, and changes of temperature should be brought about gradually. An unopened bottle of red wine will gently warm up to a good temperature for drinking if it is placed for a few hours in your dining room, and a white wine can be gently chilled in a normal household fridge. Avoid trying to warm a bottle of red wine by immersing it in hot water, or chilling white wine fast by putting it into your deep-freeze. Too cold a wine is usually unpleasant astringent and devoid of any depth of flavour, while overheated red wine is like lukewarm soup, disgustingly bland and flat and flabby, and almost tasteless.

The drawing of the cork is a simple operation, requiring only a little care and the correct implement. Two main types of corkscrew can be recommended, and the more straightforward involves only a simple crosspiece handle above a spiral of strong steel wire. This should enter the cork with the point almost centred, and must be driven in until the point almost breaks through the base of the cork. If it does pierce the base it may push off a few fragments of cork which will fall and float on the top of the wine, but this is unimportant, provided the wine is decanted and filtered before serving, or the cork dust and chips is at least skimmed off. Cork dust floating on top of a glass of wine is not a sign that the wine is "corked" – this technical term refers to an unpleasant smell and taste caused when the wine has had a chemical reaction with the cork, rendering the wine foul and undrinkable.

The second type of screwpull is a simple wire corkscrew within a 3-4 inch wooden or metal barrel, and shrouded within a contra-rotating sleeve. When the wire spiral has been twisted fully home, a steady turning of the other handle presses down against the neck of the bottle and gradually pulls the cork upwards and out. This double-action type of corkscrew is particularly useful for the gentle, disturbance-free extraction of corks from bottle of old wines which have formed a heavy crust in the bottle. Vintage ports, old rhones and burgundies, and fine old clarets are obviously candidates for this careful treatment. The steadiest method involves placing the bottle in a semi-recumbent position in a wicker bottle cradle, which will hold it at a comfortable angle for uncorking and gentle pouring. But never, ever use such a cradle for serving wine at the table – its place is strictly in the kitchen or the cellar only.

Traditionally, fine red wine is decanted before serving. But this can be both unnecessarily complicated and even a bit pretentious, except when the wine is old and has thrown a heavy crust or sediment. Wine in a decanter deprives your guests of the simple pleasure of seeing and reading the wine label, and even when a very old and noble wine is decanted before serving, it is a good idea to place one of the empty bottles on the side- or serving table, so its label and cork can be seen. Vintage port is always decanted, but the bottles are seldom lavishly labelled and have little of interest to reveal, so they can be left in the kitchen or consigned straight to the rubbish bin. It is both practical and perfectly acceptable to serve young or non-crusted red wines direct from the bottle, and most rosé and white wines require no decanting. Where any sediment is present it is usually clearly visible in the clear or lightly tinted bottles used for most whites and roses, and you can decant or pour with especial care, as appropriate. Decanting calls for nothing more than a steady hand, a sharp eye, and a suitable decanter. Plain, clear glass is best for table wines, which are thereby revealed in their true colours, and heavily cut glass decanters are best reserved for port, madiera and sherry. Tinted blue, green and rose-pink glass decanters were popular for white and rosé wines in Victorian times, but are now chiefly collectors' items, and look better in a display cabinet than on a table.

To decant from bottle to decanter, grasp the bottle firmly in one hand and the neck of the decanter in the other, and position yourself in front of a light-coloured surface or a source of reasonably bright light, so that you can clearly see the wine in the shoulder and near the neck of the bottle as you pour. The traditionalist will use a lighted candle placed just behind the bottle. Tilt the decanter so that it is inclined towards the bottle, and then tip the bottle gently so that the rim of the neck rests inside that of the decanter. Pour the wine gently with a steady raising of your arm, maintaining a slow rate of pouring. On no account allow the wine to come out in abrupt slurps and glugs, which is both messy and likely to stir up any sediment by causing the wine in the bottle to slop to and fro. Similarly, let the cascade of wine slide gently down the inside of the decanter, as when pouring a bottle of beer, and do not let it splash straight in like water from a tap. In this way the freshly uncorked wine adjusts gradually to the new atmosphere to which it is being exposed.

As soon as any wine is uncorked it begins to oxydise — to react with the air — and the ageing processes which have been proceeding at a snail's pace in the corked confines of the bottle now race ahead. An old and fragile wine may be unable to take more than a few minutes exposure to the air before it should be served, while massive and complex wines like Hermitage and some burgundies only taste their best after breathing for several hours. In decanting, or in pouring straight from the bottle, the breathing process which releases the full scents and flavours of a wine can be considerably accelerated by pouring the wine fast and splashily, so that it mixes with the air very rapidly. In the professional wine world the most exaggerated example of this is when sherry is drawn from a barrel in the cup of a long-handled metal *venezia* ladle, and the *capataz*'s dexterity causes it to flow from ladle to *copita* glass in a long, golden parabola, which lets wine and air mingle swiftly for a full appreciation of flavour and bouquet.

Wines served cool or really cold can quickly rise to an unpleasantly high temperature in a warm dining room or kitchen, and are best kept cool with the help of an ice-bucket, which can either be set on the table or on a side table. (Many restaurants have rather twee little portable stands to hold their ice-buckets.) The bucket should contain a mixture of ice-cubes and cold water, which provides a very chilling medium in which to immerse a bottle, and the bucket should be about two-thirds full. An ice-and-water mixture is far more effective than just ice-cubes alone, and only requires that the bottle, when removed from the bucket for pouring, should be wrapped in a fresh absorbent napkin to soak up the chilled water which will otherwise drip messily off the bottom of the bottle. An effective alternative, especially if a wine is to be served cool rather than cold, is the modern style of double-skinned plastic bottle holder, which provides good short-term insulation and takes up little space on a table top, although its appearance is functional rather than elegant, and you may not care to use it on more formal occasions.

PREPARATION OF GAME
Plucking, drawing, boning, trussing, jointing

Plucking

We always do this at home over a large wheelie bin or rubbish bin, but you can pluck straight into bin liners, plastic bags or just onto sheets of newspapers spread over the floor to catch wayward feathers. Try and make sure there is as little draught as possible to prevent the feathers from flying all over the place. Use your thumb for leverage and always work by pulling the feathers upwards and away from the way they naturally lie in. Lay the bird on its back and start with the wings, extending them right out, pulling the under feathers and leaving the feathers at the tips. Do this with each wing, then turn over and remove the others. Now move to the neck and work down the whole bird towards the tail. Pluck the breast last and hold the skin and keep it taught. This helps against tearing. Finally remove the tail feathers and teak out the quill ends either with tweezers or between your thumb and the blade of a small knife. Now cut the wing tips at the joint and either trim or cut the feet according to bird and preference (small birds like snipe and woodcock very often have them left on — I personally find them rather creepy on a plate). Next cut off the head, about a third down the neck. Get rid of any final left over hairs *et al* by singeing. You can either do this with a taper or long match, or by lighting methlayted spirits in a small dish and passing the bird over the flame.

Lay the bird on its back, and start with the wings.

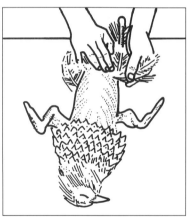

Work down the whole bird.

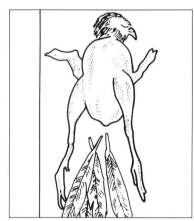

Remove tail feathers.

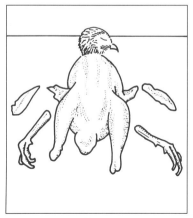

Trim wing tips and feet.

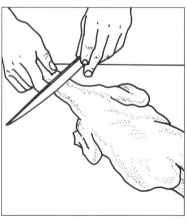

Cut off the head about a third down the neck.

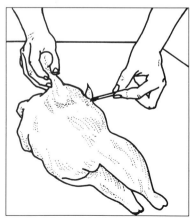

Singe the bird all over to remove leftover hair.

Drawing

It is vital to have a small, very sharp knife for this operation. Start by slitting the skin on the underside of the neck along to the body. Pull the skin up towards the body and cut the neck away as close to the body as possible (scissors might help) leaving a good flap of skin to fold over. You can put the neck to one side, with the giblets that you take our later, for stock. Now pull out the windpipe and crop, putting your hand, palm down, into the neck cavity and using a damp cloth if necessary to get a good grip. The crop is often still full of food — corn, heather, whatever. Keeping your hand high up inside the bird, gently loosen the entrails (use a finger or two if it's a small bird). Now turn the bird over onto its back and cut a slit to enlargen the vent at the tail end. Hold the bird firmly in one hand, and work the other, using two fingers only if necessary, carefully inside to draw out the entrails. Be very careful not to break the gall bladder attached to the liver as it has a very bitter taste. Everything (gizzard, intestines, heart, liver, gall bladder) *should* come away in one go, but don't worry if you can't totally extract all of the lungs from the ribs as it won't affect the final flavour. Rinse all through with cold water and keep to make stock. Wash or wipe the inside of the bird with more cold water or a damp cloth. Finally, snap the legs at the base of each drum stock to expose the tendons. Use a tweezer or skewer to pull out each tendon, but take care not to tear the flesh. To finish, bend the joint backwards, twist and snap the bone, and then cut through the skin.

Boning

If you can master this technique, it is an incredibly useful way of transforming a mundance roast into something out of the way (see Boned Pheasant with Lemon Cream Cheese and Spinach Filling, page 91). The most important thing is to have a very sharp, small pointed vegetable knife to work with. I also find a pair of scissors or pliers very handy for dealing with unrelenting sinews and tendons where a knife might just slip. It is sometime easier for boning to work on an undrawn bird, but this isn't essential. There are two methods of boning — total (mostly for galantines) and partial, leaving the bones in the lower legs and wings (for stuffing and reshaping). The latter is certainly easier to do and the bird tends to keep its shape better. After boning the carcase can be kept for stock.

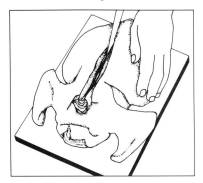

Lay the bird on its breast, and cut along the back from neck to tail.

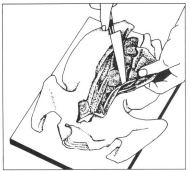

Work the flesh away in short clean cuts to the leg.

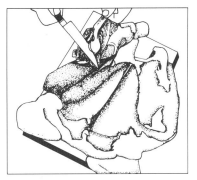

Scrape away the meat that surrounds the thighbone, and cut through.

Continue to work flesh off the carcase until you reach the ridge of the breastbone. Repeat the process on the other side.

Lift the ribcage and cut along the ridge, to free it. The carcase can now be removed completely.

Total boning (for galantines). Place the bird breast-down on the table and make a clean cut along its back from the neck to the tail. Keeping the knife right up against the bone, work the flesh away in short, clean cuts as far as the leg. Now slit the skin around the lower joint, snap the joint and pull off the feet bringing the sinews with them. Work round the bone very carefully, probably from the bottom and the top, scraping the flesh off and being very careful not to pierce into the skin. Push the bones through the slit, turning all the time, and working the flesh free with the tip of the knife. Continue working the flesh off the carcase until you reach the centre breast-bone. Repeat the whole process on the other side of the bird starting from the centre back. When you reach the breast-bone for the second time carefully release the skin attached all along it, but watch out as it is very thin and tears very easily.

Partial boning (for stuffing). Proceed as above, but leave the bones in the drumsticks and wings. Work all around the bird, turning the flesh and skin inside out. When it is off the breast bone, wipe it clean, turn it back again and fill with a delicious stuffing. Then reshape and fold the legs and wings neatly into the sides. The stuffing will help the bird keep its shape, but you may need to use toothpicks for skewering.

Trussing

Eye appeal is half the secret of successful cooking, and a nicely trussed bird looks so much more appetising that one with its limbs all over the place in a sort of hot *rigor mortis*. Start by placing the bird on its breast and covering the neck by folding the loose skin over the back. Fold back the wings and hold them in place either using a skewer passing right through and pinning the flap of skin to the body, or with a trussing needle and fine string. To do this, pass the neck through one wing joint, across the inside of the body, out at the top of the far leg, back through the other wing joint and out at the other leg again. Tie the ends firmly together. Then turn the bird over onto its back. Make a horizontal slit in the skin above the tail vent and push the parson's nose through it. Now pull in the thighs close to the body which will make a nice plump shape and cross the legs over the tail end. Secure either with a skewer passing right through both drumsticks, or by simply looping some string around the legs and the parson's nose and tying firmly. Nowadays few people bother with securing the wings and rely solely on making the legs firm enough to help the bird keep its shape.

Paunching and skinning rabbit or hare

Rabbit is usually paunched before it is skinned, preferably as soon as possible after being killed. Hare is the opposite; it is hung and skinned before being drawn. You can skin them both in the same way, but obviously you have to be careful not to slit open the belly of the hare as you work up its front. For the best results work with a very sharp pointed knife and a pair of kitchen scissors.

Paunching. Game birds and fish are gutted, venison is gralloched, hare and rabbit are paunched! Rabbit has white flesh and is usually quite clean of blood, but the blood from the dark fleshed hare is kept for the famous Jugged Hare. Some drops can be collected in a bowl while the hare is hanging, the rest has to be caught deftly during paunching. Add a drop of vinegar or two to stop coagulation. Place the animal on its back and slit along its belly from top to bottom but without cutting into the intestines. Working carefully put your hand into the slit (you may want to us rubber gloves — I do) and loosen the intestines and pull gently out. The kidneys ought to come out in one piece later, and so should the liver which is further up. This can be rinsed off immediately and used in mousses, pâtes or stuffings.

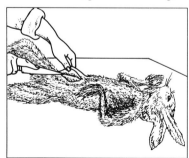

Place the animal on its back, and slit along its belly from top to bottom, without cutting into intestines.

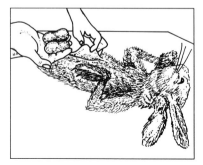

Put your hand into slit and pull gently out. Finally remove kidneys and liver.

Skinning. Place the animal on its back, make a slit inside each hind leg and then carefully pull the skin down the leg so that it is hanging towards the back of the animal. Then, following the incisions down the legs, cut along the centre of the stomach from the back to the head. Ease the skin away off the body, towards the spine and holding up the hind legs, down over the behind and along the back, until it peels off the body. Next, cut the skin round the front legs just above the paws, make an incision along the inside and peel off pulling downwards toward the head. When you reach the neck, cut the whole skin off with a pair of scissors and then chop off the head. (Traditionally, roast hare or rabbit was served with the head on, but this fashion seems to be dying. Anyway, it is quite difficult to peel the skin over the head leaving the furry ears, and you might be better off asking the butcher to do it!).

Place the animal on its back. Make a slit inside each hind leg and pull the skin down the leg.

Cut along the centre of the stomach from the back to the head.

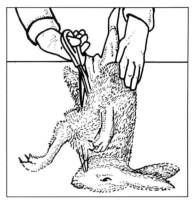

Ease the skin away from the body, towards the spine until it peels off.

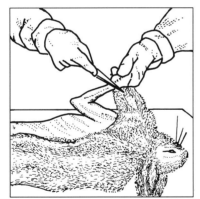

Cut the skin round the front legs and peel off downwards towards the head.

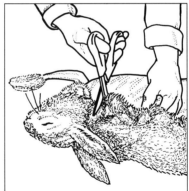

Cut the skin off with a pair of scissors, and chop off head.

Gutting game fish

The principle is the same as that for paunching rabbit and hare. If you have a Tweeny, the ideal way to gut fish is under a running cold tap, allowing the innards to wash away down the Tweeny and get gobbled up. The roe of some fish can be kept as a tasty addition to sauces. Rubber gloves and a pair of sharp scissors make this a really easy job. Just insert the tip of the scissors into the vent and cut along the stomach to me head. Scoop out the contents and snip away the membranes near the head to release them completely. Then using your fingernail or the tail end of a teaspoon, *remove the blood completely* along the backbone, rinse well and pat dry. If you like (we do), you can sprinkle salt along the backbone. This clears the taint of any blood as well as adding flavour. Finally remove the gills if you are going to cook the fish whole as they can leave an unpleasant taste.

Boning game fish

Boning fish is a bit of a fiddle, but you can make such wonderful dishes — with delicious stuffings — that is worth the effort. There are two ways of doing it — through the stomach and through the back.

To bone through the stomach. Gut and trim the fish as above, and extend the incision along the belly to reach from head to tail. Using a very fine and sharp knife work along the length of the fish cutting each rib free and extricating it with your fingers or tweezers. Repeat along the other side. Run the knife along each side of the spine making sure each cut-off rib is free and not sticking into the flesh. Then with a pair of scissors cut through the backbone at the head, lift it up from the flesh and pull up and away the length of the body. Cut it free at the tail. You can secure the fish together again after stuffing by skewering with toothpicks (trout) or skewers (salmon).

To bone through the back. Practice makes perfect! After a couple of goes, you'll be able to do this in a jiffy. The gutting is done after the boning. First trim the fins, then taking a very sharp pointed knife stand the fish on its stomach and cut in behind the head and along the backbone to the tail. Keeping the knife upright, cut down along either side of the rib cage, easing the bones away from the flesh. Next, with a pair of kitchen scissors, snip the backbone at the tail and pull it out along the body to the head. Snip it out at the head and remove completely. Stand the fish on its stomach, fill its body with a delicious stuffing, and bake.

Jointing game

It is usually fairly obvious as to how to joint the piece of game before you; its natural contours tend to set the guidelines. Since barbecuing has become such a universal form of cooking, most people know how a chicken gets jointed and the same principles apply to game birds. You can halve them by simply cutting — with a strong pair of scissors or game shears — along the backbone and breastbone. For quarters, cut these two sections in half again, keeping the wing and breast as one piece and the thigh and the drumstick as the other. Spatchcocking is a popular way of dealing with small game birds when it comes to grilling or barbecueing: simply cut along the backbone and then open the bird right out flat, helped if necessary with skewers to keep them flat. These same joints are as suitable for casseroles, or light roasting with rich accompanying sauces, as for grilling and barbecueing. Rabbit and hare are divided similarly, though as the hare is so much larger it is usually cut up into more pieces. The hind legs are cut in half at the joint (except when the rabbit is very small) and the front legs kept whole; the saddle can either be kept as a whole (and carved from for roasts) or cut up into even pieces, usually about 4-5 for a rabbit and 6-8 for a hare. As far as venison is concerned, a small roe deer cod be butchered and joined quite easily at home on the same lines as a hare; but the large red deer and wild boar really need a proper butcher or gamekeeping to make the most of their carcases — spare ribs, stewing meat, liver, loin, fillet, shoulders and legs for roasting.

GLOSSARY OF COOKING TERMS

Acidulated water
Water to which white wine vinegar or lemon juice is added. It is usually for immersing vegetables that brown easily (celeriac, globe artichokes, salsify etc) to prevent discolouration, but also used to describe the basis for a marinade (water plus vinegar and/or wine).

A la lyonnaise
Usually used to describe a dish of potatoes sliced with onion and cooked in cream and stock. Otherwise refers to the addition of onions as a garnish.

A la provençale
Recipes made with tomatoes and garlic.

Al dente
In Italian it means "to the tooth". Used to describe pasta and vegetables which have been properly cooked but are still firm or crunchy to the bite.

Aspic
A clear savoury jelly, sometimes set with meat or vegetables, and served with salad; or used as a glaze over meat, fish and terrines, sometimes with various decorations arranged to show through the glaze.

Au blanc
Usually of a white sauce or velouté, meaning to cooking without colouring.

Au bleu
Usually used of trout, but also applies to other fish, freshly caught and poached immediately, without scaling, in a court bouillon so that the skin gets a blueish look.

Au gratin
Dishes (fish or vegetables, usually) precooked in a white sauce and which is then sprinkled with breadcrumbs and/or grated cheese and reheated under a high heat to give a crunchy golden brown topping.

Bain marie
French for water bath. Any vessel or baking tin half filled with hot water either for keeping delicate sauces warm without further cooking, or for terrines, steamed soufflés, custards which need to cook in the oven without drying out. Very useful.

Bake blind
To precook a pastry case before adding the filling, thereby avoiding a soggy bottom.

Bard
Thin layers of pork fat or bacon which are wrapped or tied round lead meat — to keep it moist while roasting. They can be removed just before the end of cooking to allow last minute browning.

Baste
To spoon the pan juices over the food to prevent drying out.

Baurre manié
Kneaded butter: equal quantities of butter and flour worked together to form a paste and then dropped into casseroles, soups, sauces and gravies and stirred in to form a thickening agent.

Béchamel
A white sauce made with roux and milk.

Blanch
To pass very quickly (usually a minute or two) through boiling water for various reasons: to make firm before cooking (as in scallops or sweetbreads); to whiten or reduce strong flavour; to make less salty (as in diced bacon, before frying); to partially cook vegetables before using in salads or other dishes.

Bouillon
Stock or consommé, of poultry, veal or beef.

Bouquet garni
No kitchen should be without! A small muslin bag filled with dried herbs (normally parsley, bayleaf, thyme), used in the cooking of stock, soups and casseroles and can be easily removed before serving.

Brine
Salt water solution used for preserving meat, fish, vegetables and seasonings (green peppercorns, capers).

Chaudfroid
Game, chicken or other meats cooked and then coated in a brown and white chaudfroid sauce, decorated and glazed with aspic jelly.

Civet
A stew, usually made with some vinegar and thickened with blood, and usually of furred game (hare, rabbit, venison, wild boar).

Clarify
To free fats, particularly butter, of any impurities by melting and then straining through kitchen paper in a sieve.

Cocotte
Also known as ramekin. Small ovenproof dish for cooking individual moulds, eggs, soufflés, mousses in. Very useful!

Compôte
Fruit slowly cooked in syrup, sometimes seasoned with spices. Usually eaten as a pudding, but also served with various meats, especially ham and game.

Confits

Fruits and vegetables preserved in sugar, but also meat preserved in its own fat, especially duck and goose as in *confit de canard* and *confit d'oie*.

Court bouillon

Water with vinegar or white wine, peppercorns, carrot, onion and bouquet garnish used for poaching fish.

Croquettes

Minced or chopped meat, fish, eggs or vegetables, sometimes mixed with white sauce, rolled into balls or lozenges, dipped in egg and breadcrumbs and deep fried.

Deglaze

Vitally important for good sauces and gravies! To add hot liquid — water, wine, brandy etc. — to the browned and solidified juices and scrappings at the bottom of a roasting or frying pan, stir and dissolve for the basis of the sauce or gravy.

Demi-glace

A semi-clear brown sauce, syrupy in consistency, and usually made with Medeira or sherry.

Devil

To season food with spicy, hot ingredients (mustard, paprika, cayenne, Worcester sauce).

Draw

To remove the internal organs and blood from the inside of a fish.

Dress

To prepare poultry or game birds for cooking by plucking, cleaning and trussing. To add the sauce or vinaigrette or "dressing" to a salad.

Duxelles

Finely chopped mushrooms, sautéed with very finely chopped onions or shallots, and added to stuffings or used as a garnish, particularly with game birds.

En croûte

Any food, but particularly pâtés and terrines, cooked in a pastry case.

En papillote

Food cooked and served in paper cases to retain moisture.

Escabeche

From Spain and Portugal, a way of pickling fish, game and poultry. It is first cooked, then steeped in a marinade of vinegate.

Farce

Savoury stuffing for meat and poultry and game.

Fécule

Potato flour, cornflour or arrowroot.

Frappé

Stuffing made of minced meat, vegetables or breadcrumbs, or a combination of any.

Friture or fritura

French or Italian for something fried.

Fumet

A reduced stock, usually of fish, but can be of game or meat, giving richness of flavour to a sauce.

Galantine

Usually of poultry, but also of game and meat, which has been boned and stuffed, and often glazed in aspic. Served cold.

Game chips

Paper-thin rounds of potatoes, deep fried until very crisp.

Game straws

Very fine matchsticks of potatoes, deep fried until very crisp.

Gibelotte

A fricasee made with white wine.

Glacer or glaze

To make a shiny coating for food in a variety of ways: with reduced gravy or sauce poured over a dish and exposed to high heat to become smooth and shiny; with very hot syrup which fruit is dipped into; with beaten egg or milk on pastry which is then cooked. Glacer also means to freeze.

Gut

To remove the internal organs and blood from the inside of a fish.

Julienne

Very, very thin strips of vegetable or peel used for decoration — or even just cooked lightly as a vegetable. Can also be used of meat.

Lardons or lardoons

Little strips of fat inserted into meat, very often with a special needle, to moisturise during cooking.

Liaison

A thickening agent for soups and sauces such as egg, cornflour, *baurre mainé*, cream, arrowroot etc.

Marinate (mariner, marinade)

To steep raw meat or game, less often fish and vegetables, in liquid which contains wine or vinegar and/or spirits, herbs, spices and seasonings for anything from 24 hours to 2 weeks to tenderise and enhance the flavour.

Poach/pocher

In this case not to pinch game, but to cook very slowly in simmering liquid.

Purée

Any type of food, but usually cooked fruit and vegetable, that gets passed through a sieve or liquidiser to form a thick, smooth paste or liquid.

Quenelles

Very fine light purée of flesh, sometimes poultry or meat, mixed with cream and egg whites and poached in small oval shapes to form little dumplings.

Rafraîchir/refresh

To pour very cold, preferably iced, water over vegetables, fruit or meat after they have been blanched.

Ragoût or ragu

French or Italian for stew.

Reduire/Reduce

To concentrate the flavour of a liquid by boiling rapidly until it is reduced by half or a third, depending on the recipe.

Render

To melt any hard animal fat to a liquid and then strain to remove impurities.

Saddle

The back of some animals (in game, hare and venison) between the base of the ribs and the leg.

Scald

Usually used of milk, and meaning to bring to just under boiling point when bubbles form around the edge of the pan.

Score

To cut into meat with a sharp knife, often in a diagonal or criss-cross pattern, to tenderise by cutting through the tissues. Also to cut into external layers of fat (as in the crackling of park) to let extra fat run out.

Seviche

Originating from Latin America, a method of "curing" raw fish by marinating in lemon or lime juice, usually accompanied by some raw vegetables and/or herbs.

Simmer

To keep a liquid cooking at just below boiling point so that it is moving but not bubbling.

Spatchoock

The method of splitting a small bird down the back, opening out without dividing and then flatening for grilling, spit-roasting, barbecuing and frying. Known as *á la crapaudine* in French.

Steam

To cook food in steam, usually fish or vegetables, in a perforated container supported above a pan of boiling water.

Sweat

To cook, extremely gently and slowly, any vegetables, but in particular onions, till they become soft enough to release their juices.

Timbale

Small domed-shaped mould of metal or earthenware, and the dish made inside it which can be a light moussey mixture of meat, fish or vegetables, hot or cold, or a helping of rice or pasta.

Truss

To fix the wings and legs of a bird in place with string or with a skewer so that it is presentable for the table.

Velouté

One of the finest basic sauces made from a roux combined with the appropriate stock for the dish — fish, poultry or meat.

Zest

The oily outer layer of the skin of the lemon or orange (or any citrus fruit), pared very thinly from the fruit without the pith, and sued for flavouring, or cut into *juliennes* and blanched or glazed for decoration.

INDEX